Contemporary Culture and Everyday Life

Edited by Elizabeth B. Silva and Tony Bennett

Published by:
sociologypress
[c/o British Sociological Association,
Units 3F/G, Mountjoy Research Centre, Stockton Road, Durham, DH1 3UR
Or http://www.britsoc.org.uk/sociologypress]

sociologypress is supported by the British Sociological Association. It furthers
the Association's aim of promoting the discipline of sociology and disseminating
sociological knowledge.

British Library Cataloguing in Publication Data
A CIP catalogue record for this book is available from the British Library

ISBN 1-903457-09-2

Printed and bound by York Publishing Services, 64 Hallfield Road, Layerthorpe, York
YO31 7ZQ

Contents

Notes on Contributors

Gaynor Bagnall – Lecturer in Sociology at Liverpool John Moores University

Tony Bennett – Professor of Sociology at the Open University

Andrew Blaikie – Professor of Historical Sociology at the University of Aberdeen

Gill Dunne – Senior Lecturer in Sociology at the University of Plymouth

Jane Juffer – Assistant Professor of English and Women's Studies at Penn State University, USA

Gail Lewis – Senior Lecturer in Social Policy at the Open University

Brian Longhurst – Professor of Sociology at Salford University

Angela McRobbie – Professor of Communications at Goldsmiths College, University of London

David Morgan – Emeritus Professor of Sociology at Manchester University

Ann Phoenix – Professor of Psychology at the Open University

Mike Savage – Professor of Sociology at Manchester University

Elizabeth B. Silva – Senior Lecturer in Sociology at the Open University

Chapter 1

Everyday life in contemporary culture

Tony Bennett and Elizabeth B. Silva

At the start of a new century, certain features of the everyday have acquired fresh significance. Western values are being challenged by a more diverse culture of relationships and social arrangements. Social guidelines have been in unprecedented flux, and societies have to find ways of living with difference (Beck, 1992; Giddens, 1991, 1994). In the industrialised western world most people have been affected by a prevailing movement away from traditional assumptions about gender roles, power dynamics, sexualities, styles of work, personal relationships and life trajectories. The circumstances in which individuals find themselves regarding their location in homes, communities and work are also being transformed through the development of increasingly flexible arrangements, personal wants, and ways of talking about these. The boundaries of 'right' and 'wrong' have been debated in new experiments of daily living, while a unique degree of choice is exercised when deciding between these. In many situations today, there is no choice but to make a choice. Yet, collectively, western individuals living under these conditions, are not masters of their destiny. Our futures, individual and collective, appear unpredictable, sometimes threatening, making the notion of risk, and its opposite, trust, central to contemporary culture (Giddens, 1994). The apparently contradictory movements towards choices and risks are most obvious in the everyday, where our engagement with normal daily routines masks the complexity which gives everyday life its shape.

Partly because of this, the category of everyday life is enjoying something of a renaissance in contemporary social thought. This is also due to recent developments in the social sciences which, dismissing the idea of institutions and structures as timeless and fixed entities, emphasise instead the active processes of human creation through ordinary interaction. (Examples include Morgan (1996) regarding families, Weeks *et al.* (2001) on sexuality, and Lewis, in Chapter 7 of this book, about 'race'.) The everyday is also a subject which meshes well with the focus on the micro-physical aspects of power, and the typically unnoticed routine mechanisms of its operations, that characterises much of contemporary social theory. And the everyday provides a useful 'contact zone' between the concerns of feminism, sociology and cultural studies, albeit that its meaning has varied as it has been shaped, and re-shaped, by the varied histories of its use within and across these fields of study.

Drawing on these different strands of inquiry, our concerns in this book focus on the changing practices and meanings of daily living, particularly with a view to understanding how the current fluidity of everyday life practices relates to how we perform gender, sexuality, caring, 'racialising', ageing, and other significant axes of everyday situations. The following chapters consider these issues in the context of the intermeshing of technologies with daily life, the unstable and globalising nature of work, and the shifting meanings of identity and place. Are there new 'everyday cultures' emerging? Social theory has talked about a new culture of intimacy, of caring, or of gender. What has been meant by these various cultures and what is 'contemporary culture'?

A discussion of these questions means that the concept of culture will need to occupy our attention just as much as that of everyday life. The notion of 'culture' implies that there are distinctive ways of doing things and that these distinctions are usually imbued with moral predicaments. Culture helps individuals to make sense of the variety of social life, providing a type of explanation that is, at the same time, a mode of action. Culture as, in this sense, a way of life (Williams, 1958) can be seen as a corollary to the everyday, and we discuss this in detail later on in this chapter. For now, though, it is the pluralisation of cultures that needs to be noted if analysis is to deal effectively with the increasingly diverse relations between culture, as a varied repertoire of resources for practical action (Swindler, 1986; Wuthnow, 1988), and everyday practices.

To engage with these issues, this chapter addresses four main themes. Firstly, we discuss the approaches to the everyday that emerge from 'classic' conceptualisations, placing special emphasis on the concept of defamiliarisation and its association with the critique of everyday life. Secondly, we consider some of the more influential ways in which the everyday has been resituated as an object of both study and politics in the context of more recent tendencies in social and cultural theory. Thirdly, we consider particular aspects of contemporary culture and the ways in which these are addressed by the contributors to this book. Finally, we outline some methodological approaches to studies of the everyday exemplified in the contributions assembled in the book, and conclude by reflecting on the theoretical coordinates and analytical practices relating to the changed, and changing, place of everyday life in contemporary culture.

Classic approaches to the everyday: critique and defamiliarisation

The concepts of the everyday and of everyday life are far from trouble-free terms. Both concepts are loaded with the freight of their own difficult and divided histories as the meanings invested in them have proved to be both varied and contested. At the same time, the categories themselves have become a bone of contention in the different interpretations that have been placed upon them in current theoretical debates.

Within the most long-standing tradition of analysis, everyday life is constituted as an object of critique that is to be taken to task for the denial of authenticity that is said to inhere in the routines which define it. While the roots of this tradition go back to the early twentieth century – to George Simmel and Georg Lukács, with echoes of their concerns in the work of Theodor Adorno and Walter Benjamin – Henri Lefebvre (1971) and Michel de Certeau (1984) were its most important representatives in its 'second phase' sparked off by the radical movements of the 1960s. However, their negative assessments of the everyday have been countered by more recent approaches in social theory which validate the routine aspects of the everyday for their role in creating a sense of ontological security for the conduct of social life (Giddens, 1991; Silverstone, 1994). A similar concern to bring down the threshold of what is at stake in the everyday, and in its analysis, is evident in current feminist revisions of the concept. Rita Felski (1999–2000) has thus recently excoriated Lefebvre for his uncritical validation of male-centred and modernist understandings of time. For in preferring a linear and ruptural understanding of time – of a time that advances through epochal shifts which shatter the smooth and repetitive time of the everyday – such accounts depend on a bipolar construction of masculine and feminine time in which women are associated with, and condemned to, the cyclical time of the everyday, marked by the eternal recurrence of the same, while male time and the public historical time of progress are equated (see also Davies, 1990; Odih, 1999).

Steven Crook (1998) offers a more thoroughgoing criticism, encompassing the sociology of everyday life as a whole. While conceding differences between its various branches, he contends that all of the major traditions within this literature – the critique of everyday life, the approaches of Agnes Heller and Alfred Schutz, and Jürgen Habermas's contrapuntal construction of the relations between system and lifeworld – share key structural features which reproduce aspects of modernist social theory. 'In its heyday', he argues, '"everyday life" served as a rubric through which to assert the sociological significance of the structures and practices of micro-social settings from streets to lounge rooms and bars to backyards' (Crook, 1993: 539). The difficulty, he suggests, is that it has often proved difficult to engage with these concerns empirically, owing to the degree to which the field of analysis has been over-determined by the theoretical and mythological freight that the currency of the 'everyday' has carried with it. Crook argues that the most debilitating aspect of this freight has consisted in the assumption that the everyday somehow indexes a 'plane' of pure sociality, a realm of society which, since it is not yet affected by the impurities of system, bureaucracy, capitalism, and the state, can serve as the well-springs of authentic social action and, thereby, as the source of resistance and social renewal.

Much of the current literature on everyday life continues to labour under the weight of this legacy. Indeed, for writers like Michael Gardiner (2000) and Robert Shields (1999), the essential task is to reassemble and renew its components as a means of renovating the practice of critique. Faced with this prospect, Crook proposes that it might be better to jettison the concept of the everyday altogether:

> *The best service we can render to the spirit of the earlier sociology of the everyday is to continue to study the local production of social (or socio-technical) solidarities and orders, but to do so under a self-denying ordinance that excludes 'the everyday' and 'everyday life' as rubrics for inquiry.*
> (Crook, 1998: 539)

While sympathising with the analysis which prompts this conclusion, we would not go quite so far. To the contrary, the categories of the everyday and everyday life remain valuable and valid in their references to the ordinary and mundane, but only provided that these categories are emptied out of much of their earlier theoretical and political content. This requires, among other things, a reappraisal of the role that the concept of defamiliarisation has played in association with the critique of everyday life.

Both 'critique' and 'defamiliarisation' have generalised meanings and more specific ones which need to be distinguished. In its more general usage, 'critique' serves as a synonym for critical analysis in which the prevailing pattern of social relations or cultural dispositions is examined from the point of view of a stated set of ethical and political norms. Similarly, in its more general usage, 'defamiliarisation' refers to intellectual procedures which disrupt the familiarity of prevailing social relationships or cultural practices in order that their historical specificity might be made more clearly perceptible. The study of everyday life has typically furnished a privileged site for the pairing of these senses of critique and defamiliarisation. Owing to the degree to which the everyday is defined by its taken-for-grantedness, its analysis provides a particularly telling means of demonstrating how critical analysis both requires and enables a disruption of what Schutz (1967: 208–9) called the 'natural attitude' governing our spontaneous immersion in everyday social and cultural practices. This is a commonplace rationale for the pedagogic value of everyday life as a topic within sociology curricula as well as for its broader political purchase as a field of study. This is, indeed, one of the reasons why, in contrast to Crook, we think that everyday life remains a valid rubric for inquiry.

Yet the two terms also have more specific meanings which, when brought together in relation to the study of everyday life, increase the threshold of what is at stake in its critique and defamiliarisation. The sense of critique we have in mind here is still best summarised by Reinhart Koselleck's account of the relationship between critique and the distinctive temporality of modern societies. Koselleck argues that the emergence, in the Enlightenment, of a self-authorising standpoint of critique located outside the political structures of absolutism transformed 'the future into a maelstrom that sucked out the present from under the feet of the critic', with the result that 'there was nothing left for the critic but to see progress as the temporal structure appropriate to his (sic) way of life' (Koselleck, 1988: 109). As a consequence, critique was written *into* that temporal structure as an integral component of the mechanisms of progress. It supplied the means through which the present, in being constantly negated by critique, is constantly 'sucked into an open and unknown future' (Koselleck, 1988: 3) that will come to rest only when the antinomies posited by critique (politics and morality; freedom and necessity; subject and object; being and authenticity) have been reconciled.

This sense of critique gets tangled up with accounts of everyday life from their origins in early twentieth-century social theory. Georg Simmel is important here in view of his influence on Georg Lukács who first introduced the concept of *Alltäglichkeit* (variously translated as ordinariness or everydayness) into European thought in his 1910 text *Soul and Form*. Lukács, comments Shields (1999), also took from Simmel a concern with the relationships between forms of life and social structure, and translated this into a critique of existing forms of life from the point of view of more authentic ones through which a path to the future might be opened up, thereby unfreezing the stasis of everyday life and re-introducing mobility into history. This concern is most evident in the opposition between the dull, meaningless and contingent nature of ordinary life and the authentic form of existence represented by the tragic hero or heroine, which governs the essay 'The metaphysics of tragedy'. Of ordinary life, Lukács has this to say:

> Our life ordinarily has no real necessity, but only the necessity of being empirically present, of being entangled by a thousand threads in a thousand accidental bonds and relationships. But the basis of the whole network of relationships is accidental and meaningless; everything that is, could just as well be otherwise, and the only thing that seems really necessary is the past, simply because nothing more can be done to change it.
> (Lukács, 1974: 157)

The defining moment of tragedy is one in which, when faced with impossible choices, the tragic hero or heroine shuns the compromises of empirical life in the name of ethical absolutes which embody the demands of authenticity. Poised on the cusp between the everyday and its transcendence, it is a moment beyond time in which everyday time is suspended and negated. As such, however, it suggests how ordinary life and history can be opened up to new possibilities as the demands of and for authentic existence are pitted against the force of empirical causality. Tragedy is, in this sense, engaged in a 'fight for history' which is 'a great war of conquest against life, an attempt to find the meaning of history (which is immeasurably far from ordinary life) in life, to extract the meaning of history from life as the true, concealed sense of life' (Lukács, 1974: 167). And as such, it is a bid to re-animate history by rescuing it from the dull force of compulsion arising out of everyday empirical causality.

This is the conceptual space into which there is subsequently grafted the critique of everyday life developed by Lefebvre and continued through into the work of de Certeau. The key mediating figure here is Martin Heidegger whose *Being and Time* translated Lukács's opposition between ordinary and authentic life into a more formally elaborated contrast between two modes of existence: the dull, mechanical repetition of the everyday with the timeless time of the authentic life or 'Being' (Heidegger, 1962). While this division is carried over into Lefebvre's work, it is, at the same time, re-politicised as, like Lukács in his later Marxist phase, Lefebvre struggled to identify a social force that would be able to free itself from the repetitive structure of the everyday and, in embodying a more authentic life through revolutionary social action, bring about a transformed set of social relations in which the demands of authenticity could be realised in and through the everyday. Here, as in Lukács's *Soul and Form*, the everyday must be analysed for the sources of self-transcendence that it contains within itself, but to which it is ordinarily blind.

It is this dual quality of the everyday, secreting a potential which its apparent humdrum ordinaries belies, that governs the meaning and function of defamiliarisation within the critique of everyday life. More than a disruption of the natural attitude affording a critical insight into the historical particularity of current social arrangements, defamiliarisation is, in this tradition, a moment of revelation. It is a moment of pure seeing when, cleared of the habitual dross which clouds everyday vision, things can be seen clearly for what they are, and for the potentialities that lie hidden and repressed within them. It is, in short, a moment of epiphany, a moment marking the transition from the degraded ordinariness of the everyday to a more authentic form of existence and political vocation, when everyday time is placed in suspension. The influence of early twentieth-century forms of vanguard aesthetic modernism has also been important here. While Lukács notoriously had little time for these, Lefebvre was strongly influenced by them, especially by Dadaism and surrealism whose critiques he sought to emulate through the development of forms of social analysis that would seek to identify 'moments of presence' within the everyday. These moments, as Shields defines them, are ones that 'break through the dulling monotony of the "taken for granted"'; moments that 'outflank the pretensions of wordy theories, rules and laws, and challenge the limits of everyday thinking' (Shields, 1999: 58). Such moments are sudden flashes of insight, revealing the latent possibilities that lie hidden within the everyday. And they are moments upon which the world is, ideally, to be made to turn. For they are flashes through which the tiniest little things, the most ordinary and seemingly insignificant aspects of everyday life, are read as the symptoms of a deeper malaise affecting the social totality which – if the demands of authenticity are to be realised – stand in need of a ruptural transformation.

It would, of course, be churlish to deny the power and resonance of Lefebvre's analysis of the changing conditions of everyday life in post-war France. His discussion of the new economic tendencies associated with what he called 'the society of bureaucratically controlled consumption' remains of value, as Celia Lury (2002) notes, for its perception of the ways in which everyday life is increasingly transformed into a resource for, and colonised by, capitalist economic imperatives. It is rather the political imaginary within which Lefebvre's analyses are set that is in question here. Crook is, we believe, right to suggest that these are now increasingly problematic. A political topography within which the worlds of system, bureaucracy, capitalism and the state are granted an increasing pervasiveness over everyday social life, but which then generates the demand that agents of social change must be located in some realm or moment of pure sociality that is unaffected by those forces, has little to recommend it.

However, the proper response to this is not to abandon the everyday as a field of study and political engagement but, rather, to retrieve its analysis from the search for the exceptional and ruptural possibilities that has characterised the critique of everyday life. And this means, as Tony Bennett argues in Chapter 2, being concerned with how social changes comes about in and through the ways in which political issues are worked through in the context of the mundane dynamics of everyday life rather than seeking a generalised transcendence of the everyday, seen as a one-dimensional realm of social stasis and repetition, to be effected by some singular and exceptional social force. This requires a resituation of the intellectual contexts in which the everyday is engaged with.

Resituating the everyday

There are a number of intellectual traditions that can be drawn on for this purpose. The resonances of Raymond Williams's contention that 'culture is ordinary' (Williams, 1958) have been important in enabling cultural practices to be studied as a part of the everyday rather than – as in aesthetic definitions of culture – in contrast or even in opposition to it. Yet culture, in Williams's hands, always turns out to be anything but ordinary as it too, like the Lefebvrian concept of the everyday, contains within itself the seeds of self-transcendence. In Williams's case, however, this is not a matter of the ruptural transformations that might flow from moments of presence (as in the Lefebvrian sense); rather, it concerns the longer and more gradual unfolding of community out of the slower dynamics of the relations between culture and ordinary life. That said, the emphasis on culture as a way of life that is most associated with Williams's work does establish a useful set of connections between the study of cultural practices as a part of everyday routines and social relations and earlier, as well as contemporary, traditions of work developed at the interfaces of anthropology and sociology. The currently burgeoning areas of work in consumption and material culture studies are examples.

Another insight into the interfaces of sociology and anthropology is evident in Pierre Bourdieu's notion of habitus. This often loses much of its critical force in, so to speak, its everyday sociological interpretation. Here is how the concept is glossed in the *Penguin Dictionary of Sociology*:

> Habitus ... refers to the ensemble of dispositions by which actions and attitudes in the everyday world are habituated and as a result the everyday world is taken for granted. It becomes thoughtless, because it is embodied.
> (Abercrombie et al., 2000: 3?)

We doubt that Bourdieu would have recognised himself in that last sentence. In his own retrospective gloss on the concept, Bourdieu stressed that, to the contrary, he wished to stress the creative, active, and inventive capacity of social actors while avoiding any notion of a transcendental subject. Hence, he argues:

> The notion of habitus as a system of acquired dispositions functioning on the practical level as categories of perception and assessment or as classificatory principles as well as being the organising principles of action meant constituting the social agent in his (sic) true role as the practical operator of the construction of objects.
> (Bourdieu, 1990: 13)

As such, the concept does not form a part of any generalised account of social stasis resulting from a singular structure of repetition characterising the everyday. Indeed, the intelligibility of such a contention is disputed as the everyday inevitably becomes pluralised in being dispersed across different habituses.

Characterising a second phase of concern with the everyday in social theory, the work of Lefebvre, de Certeau and Bourdieu suggests that critical engagements with everyday life was re-energised by the radical interventions of the 1960s.

Historically connected, and central to the 1960s radicalism, the feminist critique has, however, diverged from androcentric thinking about the everyday, repeatedly demonstrating that the ideas and even vocabulary of culture are rooted in men's experiences. It has been argued that the pervasive lack of fit between women's experiences and the forms of thought available to understand these experiences is a general problem in social theory. Dorothy Smith (1987) has referred to this gap in social knowledge as a 'line of fault'. This is part of how the category of the everyday, as formulated through men's concerns, has been alien to the concerns of women. Combining materialist and ethnomethodological approaches, Smith (1987) builds 'a sociology for women', where what happens in people's everyday lives is as important as the processes of interpretation that give meaning to their everyday lives. The approach calls for analyses that can explain how everyday lives shape, and are shaped by, larger social relations.

Employing Smith's approach, Marjorie DeVault (1991) remarks in her study on *Feeding the Family* how an analysis based on the fundamentally organised character of social life can show the ordering of women's everyday activities by social relations which extend beyond the immediate, local setting. This is a feminist project because of its political engagement with explaining to women (as Marx and Engels did to the working class) that although their social relations are the relations of their real life-process, these social relations assume an independent existence acting against them (Smith, 1987: 104). This is typical, for instance, of the combination of family and school settings, where formal education is organised in coordination with a discourse of 'mothering' that teaches women how to supervise and support their children's performance at school, without which the educational system would succumb (Smith, 1987: ch. 4, 5).

As we noted earlier, analyses of contemporary social change have consistently referred to a trend towards the diminution of the constraints and controls that structure ordinary life. Yet, routine and repetition are considered to have an important role in creating a sense of ontological security for the conduct of current social life. But, in contemporary life, many different everydays are possible and, indeed, required. In a context of 'do-it-yourself' biographies (Beck and Beck-Gernsheim, 1995) new opportunities of choosing ways of being transform allegiances to the structured everyday. This breakdown of traditional assumptions about life trajectories and the social places of subjects places a vital emphasis on creativity in the everyday. In the contemporary everyday individuals cannot do without being creative. The stress has changed from earlier concerns with locating a social force that would transcend the everyday to one that points to the routines of everyday life acting as a substratum for the necessarily demanded creativity of social life (Silva, 2003).

At the beginning of the twenty-first century, everyday life has been somewhat transformed in relation to the everyday that figured in most of the twentieth-century literature. Yet, it is not just that the everyday itself has changed: the ways of apprehending the everyday are also different. In this book we trace some of the ways in which new relations between contemporary culture and everyday life challenge the frameworks available for the study of the everyday.

Key aspects of contemporary culture

This book focuses on three areas of contemporary culture. These represent a core set of changes and challenges to everyday life, although they do not exhaust the field. Our discussion of these themes does not correspond precisely to the manner in which they are presented in the chapters that follow, but it speaks to common concerns. The themes are: (1) home, family and community; (2) sexuality, 'race' and age; and (3) technology and everyday practices.

Home, family and community

In a recent study of 'families of choice' Jeffrey Weeks, Brian Heaphy and Catherine Donovan (2001) have argued that home and community provide non-heterosexuals with the social capital to help negotiate the hazards of everyday life and of one's sexuality. They place this analysis in the context of emerging new historical forms of the 'family', where freedom in relationships has grown, challenging outmoded and often oppressive patterns of life (Beck-Gernsheim, 1998). This process was called by Giddens (1992) 'the transformation of intimacy', an argument that generated a great deal of controversy (see Jamieson, 1998, 1999). A lot of creative energy goes into making relationships work and into life experiments that do not conform to social norms. Fixed norms no longer support individual needs of how to live. Gender role arrangements, mothering needs, the financial resourcing of households and so on do not follow traditional guidelines, and home and local communities need to support a diversity of choices. Obviously this trend also involves heterosexual home arrangements where the model of homemaker and provider has long broken up. The home contemporary individual adults grew up in is where to start from, and this may well have been quite traditional. But the home created as adults is the most significant, and this is the home that is currently changing.

David Morgan (Chapter 3) considers everyday life events and how family practices construct these events. The discussion follows from his earlier argument that '"Family" represents a constructed quality of human interaction or an active process rather than a thing-like object of social investigation' (Morgan, 1999: 16). This formulation moves away from the idea of the family as a fixed and timeless entity to which one either belongs, or from which one is excluded. Family is instead a series of practical, everyday activities, which we live and engage with regularly. Family practices are not confined to the home, but they are involved in leisure, work activities and in a sense of the self. As Weeks *et al.* (2001) put it, home is about bonds. It is more than a private place, it is often about broader communities and a wider set of belongings.

The chapters by Elizabeth Silva, Gill Dunne and Jane Juffer contribute to this understanding of family and home as embedded in wider social contexts, with attention paid to how intimate relationships in homes shape the social. They are concerned with the translation of feminist practices into new forms of everyday living which challenge traditional family life, including everyday concerns with gender, the sexual and the domestic. Silva (Chapter 4) and Dunne (Chapter 6) consider how egalitarian relationships are worked through in heterosexual and non-heterosexual partnerships, and how differences persist, exploring stories of negotiations in everyday life about care, love and chores regarding the changing meaning of intimacy. Juffer (Chapter 5) focuses on the regulation of homes and the normalisation of the erotic in domestic spaces through a study of women's access to porn and domestic sexual technologies.

In Chapter 3 Morgan distinguishes three overlapping meanings of everyday life that have connections to family practices. The first are the 'talk-about-ables' events that shape one's everyday through the life course. These are linked to what Sarah Nettleton and Jonathan Watson (1998) see as a fundamental aspect of everyday life: the body, as the anchor of human experiences. This taken for granted, the body, reflects the trajectories of one's life through the lifecourse, as discussed by Andrew Blaikie (Chapter 9), and the personal-public interface of the everyday. The second meaning of everyday life is the not-worth-talking-about boring routines. This refers to matters that Silva (2002) has described as central to the ways contemporary British families organise their daily lives: the activities of childcare, cleaning, cooking, and the general household chores that resource homes, and the creative arrangements they require from individuals sharing a home. To understand everyday life as 'boring routines' alone, however, proves fragile, Morgan argues, since the arrangements in which routines are based have become easily disrupted and challenged. The third meaning of everyday life equates it with the 'normal', organising particular and often discriminatory forms of belonging by distinguishing between those who are, and those who are not, classified as being 'like us'.

The study by Mike Savage, Gaynor Bagnall and Brian Longhurst (Chapter 10) addresses this third meaning of everyday life and the fluidity of identifications of belonging which, in an increasingly mobile world, contribute to the blurring of boundaries of place while still stressing local identities and differences of class. They observe that cultural fields which depend on class identifications that depend on relations to fixed places, such as housing and residence, remain of fundamental significance for contemporary processes of cultural distinction. An illustration is the resounding importance of post codes. The study identifies in the everyday act of belonging to a place of class and locality a movement towards compensation for a sense of ontological security threatened by the implications of globalisation and time-space distanciation (Giddens, 1990). This is an instrumental attachment, however, insofar as location provides access to social capital. The argument by Weeks et al. (2001) about why people congregate around particular communities finds an echo here. The non-heterosexual community and the northern middle-class community are radically different as far as their insertion in 'normal' social living is concerned. But they are both significant communities of attachment and individuals belong to them because they find these communities anchor their own biographies, whilst permitting access to resources that they need. Traditional community studies do not offer a place for belongings of these sorts. Emerging arrangements for living require new questions from research. This is also the case as far as age, sexuality and 'race' are concerned.

Sexuality, 'race' and age

Over a third of births in England and Wales in 1996 were outside marriage, more than four times the proportion in 1971. Around four fifths of these births were jointly registered by both parents, while one fifth were registered to lone mothers. This trend has persisted into the new century (Office for National Statistics, 1997, 2001). The trend reflects changes in sexuality norms, with increasing social and moral indifference towards traditional conventions prescribing heterosexuality and limiting it to married couples (Silva, 1996). Certainly the boundaries of normality have been enlarged, even though some families are still portrayed as more deserving than others (Fink, 2001).

When the household economy shifts to accommodate gender roles and sexual practices not predicated on sex as procreative, or even partnered, and on the role of the mother as exclusive caretaker, the chances increase that domesticity will not be antithetical to sexual pleasure. Domestic technologies will then include the vibrator, the porn video, the computer and a volume of literary erotica. In this organisation of the household, sexual conduct becomes a matter of self-management, regulated by work and childcare routines. While acknowledging that debates on pornography in the USA and Britain have been influential in shaping conceptions of gender and sexual identity, Juffer (Chapter 5) argues that these debates have often extracted porn from the spaces in which it is produced, circulated, and consumed in order to represent political positions that have little to do with porn's mundane uses. She focuses on women's access to porn, indicating that the domestic sphere has become increasingly friendly to technologies of sexual pleasure for women within the routines of everyday life.

However, although there is for some women less stigma associated with consuming porn, economic issues shape women's access to porn. Moral and economic issues weigh especially heavily on women targeted by various state policies; the sexualities of women receiving welfare and those of immigrant women (the 'less deserving' ones), for example, continue to be policed by the state. Access to sexually explicit texts is still seen as problematic for those who lack the economic self-sufficiency that translates into the ability to use them without harm 'good morals'. If these conditions change, the consumption of erotica/porn is more likely to become a 'choice' women make in the interest of healthier and fuller personhood.

The expansion of normality of sexual mores has also been reflected in recently published work on non-heterosexual family relationships, of which Dunne (1998a, 1999) and Weeks et al. (1999, 2001) are examples. However, as with women's sexuality, this broadened horizon of 'normality' is uneven and predicated on the acceptance of difference. Dunne (Chapter 6) argues that at a time when mainstream cultural certainties about standard heterosexual frameworks of intimacy are being eroded, some creative solutions have emerged within the lesbian and gay communities. These are groups that have always experienced their lives in contexts of uncertainty and risk. This ordinariness is what makes the experiences of these groups extraordinary. Non-heterosexual ways of living have challenged taken-for-granted ways of being based on heterosexual assumptions of partnership, gender roles, and power hierarchies.

Yet, the individuals involved in these practices do not see themselves as extraordinary. Like heterosexuals, they are equally preoccupied by ordinary virtues and vices in their everyday experiments, although their particular social location has an impact on the material world and on how difference is imagined. As with the general use of the concept of 'defamiliarisation', to which we referred earlier, Dunne argues that significant insights emerge when we confront the other as familiar and we learn about the experiences of people living differently.

There are still other ways of referring to the tension of finding the ordinary in the alternative, and vice versa. There is an established method of literary and aesthetic styles of perception which can claim a long tradition of techniques for defamiliarising the apprehension of the everyday. Toni Morrison (1993: 15) remarks that the greatest achievement of a writer lies in an ability 'to familiarise the strange and mystify the familiar'. From her early position as a reader of American literature she assumed that black people signified little or nothing in the imagination of American writers. Shifting her position from reading as a reader to reading as a writer she saw that American literature could not help being shaped by its encounter with black people. It was complicit in the fabrication of racism but it also exploded and undermined it.

> The fabrication of an Africanist persona is reflexive; an extraordinary meditation on the self; a powerful exploration of the fears and desires that reside in the writerly conscious. It is an astonishing revelation of longing, of terror, of perplexity, of shame, of magnanimity. It requires hard work not to see this.
> (Morrison, 1993: 17)

Gail Lewis (Chapter 7) could be seen as building on Morrison's assertion that it is hard not to see racialisation, because it is so ordinary. She builds on Williams' (1961) account of the repetitive character of culture and the inclusion of everyone, everywhere, in the production of culture. But she draws on critiques (Kruger, 1993) that alternative modes of being are not included in this notion of culture. The complexities and anxieties of 'race' are ordinary, and we are all implicated in racialisation because it is relational. Belonging to gender or 'race' categories is not prescribed by the body in any automatic sense. But how the materiality of our bodies links up with our subjectivities is a consequence of a particular ordering of everyday practices. Schools are sites of prime importance where gendered and racialised cultures are produced and reproduced. Ann Phoenix (Chapter 8) studies the everyday schooling practices that construct masculinity, in personal and canonical narratives, to find that these practices are predicated on diverse axes of difference, with 'race' appearing as a key aspect. Masculinity appeared racialised through differential treatment, for example, by teachers, and through the attribution to black boys of particular characteristics of hegemonic masculinity like hardness, sporting prowess and resistance to teachers. In these constructions 'whiteness' is implicitly racialised as 'normal'.

The everyday cultures of secondary schools constrain the repertoire available to boys for the construction of their masculinity, as they grow up. As we grow old, argues Andrew Blaikie (Chapter 9), we face similar constraints from a traditionally limited repertoire of a 'culture of ageing'. Age has been neglected as an issue of social diversity in cultural studies. He remarks that today most people can expect to spend several decades in a post-work environment, whereas a century ago only 5 per cent of the British population was over 65. In the current culture of ageing there is a disharmony between the aspirations of our upbringing and the measures of inequality we are likely to face as we move up through the generations. Old age remains one of the 'others', our own future selves, that has not been properly included in researchers' concerns with contemporary social change, despite the ordinariness of ageing.

Technology and everyday practices

Social life is increasingly perceived as being thoroughly penetrated and reordered by technology. This is a key argument that Silva (Chapter 4) makes in her analysis of everyday home life in contemporary Britain. Technologies do not *structure* daily life in households because they are fully embedded in the ways home relationships and spaces are produced. Yet, common research questions about the roles or effects of technology in various areas of life often imply a disconnection between the two. Are we, as a recent TV advertisement proposes, to believe that it is thanks to T-Mobile – rather than their wealth and lavishly sponsored mobility – that Steffi Graff and Andre Agassi sustain a relationship while living in Germany and the USA? Mobile telephony might help, yet technology does not secure the maintenance of relationships.

It would be unwise, though, not to consider the role that new technologies have played in the enormous changes in contemporary ideas of time and space. For instance, we have accepted that the locations of family, home, community, work, and personal relationships can now stretch across indefinite distances of time and space (Giddens, 1994). In this context, different senses of belonging demand an active creation by individuals. Belonging is not given and taken for granted indefinitely. A relationship can be kept going even though people spend much of their time thousands of miles away from one another, like Agassi and Graff. Likewise, relationships may not survive even if they have the institutional blessing of traditions, like marriage and legitimate progeny.

There may be problems about interpreting gender practices and relations if researchers sustain visions of the ideal home, division of labour and roles traditionally viewed as masculine and feminine, when so much change has occurred in technological innovation and in social life. How ordinary people use technologies, artefacts and discourses to negotiate their environments relates to both private and public contexts. Contemporary morals can be said to be quite 'messy', since a lot is decided in particular contexts of relationships, as Silva shows in Chapter 4. Yet, connections exist between personal moralities and global interventions. Consider the case of pornography. Its imbrication with family sites is intimately connected to its integration in the global economy. Juffer (Chapter 5) shows that AT&T, Time Warner, and many other 'reputable' companies are now bigger players in the porn industry than *Hustler* and *Playboy*. The proliferation of porn across multiple technologies accompanied by fewer legal restrictions and greater acceptance of alternative family structures increases the likelihood that domestic technologies for women will include some things more intimate than the washing machine, microwave, and dishwasher.

These are significant changes in everyday life, but the interpretation and representation of the everyday is at the core of the management of cultural change. This relates to technology in the home, and to the world of work, as discussed by Angela McRobbie (Chapter 11). She considers how the new selves of workers are being produced in the everyday world of the flexible economy. Instability is the order of the day, unlike the prevailing pattern during early modernity. Highmore (2002), analysing the literature on everyday life, stresses that in western modernity the rational organisation of the world of work created a regimentation of the everyday. Intensified mechanisation appeared in nearly every form of everyday life, forcing individuals to conform to the rhythms of machines. Yet, technology alone was not sufficient for the development of capitalism (Weber, 1991), as it is not sufficient to account for the peculiar characteristics of the everyday in modernity. In contemporary working conditions, as McRobbie notes, self-monitoring workers must have access to information, analysis and personal resources to perform reflexively, following increasingly individualised careers. This may have many shortcomings if policies do not nourish creativity in individuals' pursuit of their paths.

Methodologies, theoretical coordinates and analytical practices

It is folk wisdom within the profession of sociology that the job of the scholar is to take ordinary events and make them extraordinary and to demonstrate how the extraordinary is routine.
(Glassner and Hertz, 1999: x)

Barry Glassner and Rosanna Hertz (1999) have addressed the problem of how sociologists can understand the everyday by turning the issue the other way around. They asked a group of recognised US scholars: 'How do you draw on your sociological knowledge as a tool for everyday life?' How does being a sociologist inform our living? Of course, we are a diverse group and our interests bring different lenses to what we study and how we view what we study. The 26 essays in Glassner and Hertz's edited collection show that the vicissitudes of everyday life shape sociologists' research agendas and that their interests became the material of sociological thought. As they argue, this is not surprising since it is because we need to make sense of the world that we seek to understand our experiences within broader contexts and not simply as isolated events. And it is not only because we are sociologists that we do this. All humans do this when immersed in processes of reflexivity.

Glassner and Hertz (1999) may be correct about this process of 'defamiliarisation' within sociology, but the question of how to understand everyday life remains. How can the sociologist know the everyday and apprehend 'new' realities? We have already referred to the approaches to these issues of Simmel, Lefebvre, de Certeau, and Smith, among others, and to recent syntheses of these and other approaches by Highmore (2002) and Gardiner (2000). We do not propose to replicate or summarise these rich analyses here, but to highlight certain elements of earlier approaches and to consider in more detail the approaches adopted by the contributors to this volume.

Everyday life seems difficult to represent and hard to grasp because it either appears irrational and disorderly, or, its opposite: too orderly because of its routine and repetitive nature. The methods of apprehending the everyday vary in these two opposing views. However, the two contrasting views are often combined within a single approach because order begets creativity, while the enormous diversity of life stimulates patterns of order.

In situations where everyday life is conceived of as 'orderly', more conventional ways of investigating the social appear to have predominated. Social science, as traditionally practised, has produced knowledge congruent with the rationalised requirements of modernity, and has preferred this to non-official knowledges. Practices have been isolated from their everyday, inter-subjective context, to be treated as 'facts' or 'data'. Positivist science is typical of these procedures, unlike the more recent emphasis on qualitative methodologies.

But other sociological work has treated everyday life by emphasising the varied and 'unpredictable'. This includes phenomenology (Garfinkel, 1967; Sudnow, 1972; Turner, 1974; and Schutz, introduced to English language by Berger and Luckmann, 1967), ethnomethodology (Goffman, 1971, 1974), and social interactionism (Glassner and Hertz, 1999; Truzzi, 1968). These approaches cover a wide variety of work, and have contributed a great deal to our understanding of everyday life. Yet, their emphasis on the practical aspects of mundane experience has not fully accommodated the significance of institutionalised practices or of discourses in framing meanings (see Chaney, 2002: ch. 3).

How do the contributors to this book approach the sociology of everyday life? All share a concern with showing alternatives to 'normality' as a constitutive part of contemporary culture. Being aware that the ordinariness of the everyday brackets the boundaries of the normal is a way of challenging normalised social practices: in the kitchen, in the family, in processes of racialisation, gendering and ageing, in sexuality, in the ways of using technologies, working and having home lives.

This book features a variety of innovative theoretical approaches and is clearly very distinct from the 'classic' sociology of everyday life, although these earlier approaches provide a critical point of departure for several authors whose work is closely related to cultural studies (Bennett, Blaikie and McRobbie). Many of the contributors draw on the work of Zygmunt Bauman (2000), Anthony Giddens (1990, 1991, 1992, 1994), Manuel Castells (1996) and Ulrick Beck (1992, 1995), and feminist theories are deployed for analyses of sexuality, moralities and gender identity (Morgan, Silva, Juffer, Dunne and Phoenix). Approaches to the social construction of gender, 'race', class and cultural identities are important concerns of the researchers (Phoenix, Lewis, Savage *et al.*, Blaikie), and theories of governance constitute a fourth important area of development in the studies presented here (McRobbie, Juffer, Bennett). Researchers usually draw from a combination of theoretical approaches. In place of projects to create a unified 'sociology of everyday life' the contributions represent multiple projects of sociology **about** contemporary everyday life.

The methods employed in this book involve direct investigations of current social practices, and research on secondary materials. Direct investigations include diverse styles of interviewing, focus groups, work-life histories, and ethnographic methods. While the ethnographies were overtly employed as a mode of reflexive consciousness using the cultural as an analytic resource, in the fashion proposed by Clifford (1986), Atkinson (1990) and Denzin (1997), the other methodologies also emphasised the role of cultural forces in the process of investigation. Often diverse methods were employed. The secondary material used includes texts of various sorts: government policies, sociological and socio-cultural analyses, literature, personal accounts, and media advertisements. Discourse and narrative analyses were employed when using texts and first-hand collected materials.There has been a clear preference for the use of qualitative methodologies, but the study of everyday life does not exclude quantification. Quantitative surveys are commonly used in the media to account for changes in lifestyles and ordinary opinions. Academic work has also employed quantification to account for the everyday (Bourdieu, 1984; Bennett *et al.*, 1999) and, in this book, Savage and colleagues employ quantitative methods.

In this book, the attention to research on everyday life identifies a range of small changes and implies that these can have significant cumulative effects. Something qualitatively new is being produced in social life. Researchers can only account for this by changing the categories data is gathered about and shifting the focus of attention away from traditional conceptualisations. Maffesoli (1989) has argued that the everyday needs an innovative analytic stance. For the contributors to this book, just such a shift in perspective to make the everyday visible in new ways is clearly underway. This is, however, not just a matter of methodological stance. The more self-reflexive individuals become in the contemporary condition of having to choose, the more the concern with the everyday as a lived experience is not just a matter for critical thinking but of existential, personal politics concerned with changing the conditions of social life.

References

Abercrombie, N., Hill, S. and Turner, B.S. (2000) *The Penguin Dictionary of Sociology.* London: Penguin Books

Atkinson, P. (1990) *The Ethnographic Imagination: Textual Constructions of Reality.* London: Routledge

Bauman, Z. (2000) *Liquid Modernity.* Cambridge: Polity Press

Beck, U. (1992) *The Risk Society: Towards a New Modernity.* London: Sage

Beck, U. and Beck-Gernsheim, E. (1995) *The Normal Chaos of Love.* Cambridge: Polity Press

Beck-Gernsheim, E. (1998) 'On the way to a post-familial family. From a community of need to elective affinities'. *Theory, Culture and Society*, Vol. 15, No. 3–4, pp. 53–70

Bennett, T., Emmison, M. and Frow, J. (1999) *Accounting for Tastes. Australian Everyday Cultures.* Cambridge: Cambridge University Press

Berger, P.L. and Luckman, T. (1967) *The Social Construction of Reality: Everything that Passes for Knowledge in Society.* London: Allen Lane

Bourdieu, P. (1984) [orig. 1979] *Distinction. A Social Critique of the Judgement of Taste.* London: Routledge and Kegan Paul

Bourdieu, P. (1990) *In Other Words: Essays Towards a Reflexive Sociology.* Cambridge: Polity Press

Castells, M. (1996) *The Information Age: Economy, Society and Culture: Volume I, II and III.* Oxford: Blackwell

Chaney, D. (2002) *Cultural Change and Everyday Life.* Basingstoke: Palgrave

Clifford, J. (1986) 'Introduction: Partial truths', in J. Clifford and G.E. Marcus (eds) *Writing Culture. The Poetics and Politics of Ethnography.* Berkeley: University of California Press

Crook, S. (1998) 'Minotaurs and other monsters: "everyday life" in recent social theory', *Sociology*, Vol. 32, No. 3, pp. 523–40

Davies, K. (1990) *Women and Time: The Weaving of the Strands of Everyday Life.* Aldershot: Avebury

De Certeau, M. (1984) *The Practice of Everyday Life..* Berkeley and Los Angeles: University of California Press

Denzin, N. (1997) *Interpretive Ethnography: Ethnographic Practices for the 21st Century.* Thousand Oaks, CA: Sage

DeVault, M. (1991) *Feeding the Family. The Social Organization of Caring as Gendered Work.* Chicago: The University of Chicago Press

Dunne, G. (1998a) '"Pioneers behind our own front doors": new models for the organization of work in partnerships', *Work Employment and Society*, Vol. 12, No. 2, pp. 273–95

Dunne, G. (1998b) '"A passion for "sameness": sexuality and gender accountability', in E.B. Silva and C. Smart (eds) *The 'New' Family?* London: Sage

Felski, R. (1999–2000) 'The invention of everyday life', *New Formations*, No. 39, pp. 13–31

Fink, J. (2001) 'Silence, absence and elision in analyses of "the family" in European social policy', in J. Fink, G. Lewis and J. Clarke (eds) *Rethinking European Welfare: Transformations of Europe and Social Policy.* Sage/Open University

Freud, S. (1975) *The Psychopathology of Everyday Life* (1901), trans. J. Strachey, Harmondsworth: Penguin

Gardiner, M. (2000) *Critiques of Everyday Life.* London and New York: Routledge

Garfinkel, H. (1967) *Studies in Ethnomethodology.* Englewood Cliffs, NJ: Prentice Hall

Giddens, A. (1990) *The Consequences of Modernity.* Cambridge: Polity Press

Giddens, A. (1991) *Modernity and Self Identity: Self and Society in the Late Modern Age.* Cambridge: Polity Press

Giddens, A. (1992) *The Transformation of Intimacy: Sexuality, Love and Eroticism in Modern Societies.* Cambridge: Polity Press

Giddens, A. (1994) 'Living in a post-traditional society', in U. Beck, A. Giddens, and S. Lash (eds) *Reflexive Modernization: Politics, Tradition and Aesthetics in the Modern Social Order.* Cambridge: Polity Press

Glassner, B. and Hertz, R (eds) (1999) *Qualitative Sociology as Everyday Life.* Thousand Oaks, CA: Sage

Goffman, E. (1971) *Relations in Public: Microstudies of the Public Order.* New York: Basic Books

Goffman, E. (1974) *Frame Analysis: An Essay on the Organization of Experience.* New York: Harper and Row

Heidegger, M. (1962) *Being and Time.* New York: SCM Press

Heller, A. (1984) *Everyday Life.* London: Routledge & Kegan Paul

Highmore, B. (2002) *Everyday Life and Cultural Theory. An Introduction.* London: Routledge

Jamieson, L. (1998) *Intimacy. Personal Relationships in Modern Societies.* Cambridge: Polity Press

Jamieson, L. (1999) 'Intimacy transformed? A critical look at the "pure relationship"', *Sociology*, Vol. 33, No. 3, pp. 477—94

Koselleck, R. (1988) *Critique and Crisis: Enlightenment and the Pathogenesis of Modern Society.* Oxford: Berg

Kruger, L. (1993) 'Placing the occasion: Raymond Williams and performing culture' in D. Dworkins and L.G. Roman (eds) *Views from Beyond the Border Country.* New York and London: Routledge

Lefebvre, H. (1971) *Everyday Life in the Modern World.* London: Allen Lane/ The Penguin Press.

Lukács, G. (1963) 'Probleme der widerspiegelung in alltagslebben', in *Ästhetik Teil 1: Die Eigenart des Ästhetischen, 1. Halbband*, Neuweid: Luchterhand, pp. 33–138.

Lukács, G. (1974) *Soul and Form.* London: Merlin Press

Lury, C. (2002) 'Everyday life and the economy', in T. Bennett and D. Watson (eds) *Understanding Everyday Life.* Oxford: Blackwell in association with The Open University

Maffesoli, M. (1989) 'The sociology of everyday life (epistemological elements)', *Current Sociology*. Vol. 37, No. 1, pp. 1–16

Morgan, D. (1996) *Family Connections. An Introduction to Family Studies.* Cambridge: Polity Press

Morgan, D. (1999) 'Risk and family practices: accounting for change and fluidity in family life', in E.B. Silva and C. Smart (eds) *The 'New' Family?* London: Sage

Morrison, T. (1993) *Playing in the Dark. Whiteness in the Literary Imagination.* Basingstoke: Picador (first edition 1992, Harvard University Press)

Nettleton, S. and Watson, J. (eds) (1998) *The Body in Everyday Life.* London: Routledge

Odih, P. (1999) 'Gendered time in the age of deconstruction', *Time and Society*, Vol. 8, No. 1, pp. 9–38

Schutz, A. (1967) *Collected Papers, Vol. 1: The Problem of Social Reality.* The Hague: Martinus Nijhoff

Shields, R. (1999) *Lefebvre, Love and Struggle: Spatial Dialectics.* London and New York: Routledge

Silva, E.B. (1996) (ed.) *Good Enough Mothering? Feminist Perspectives on Lone Motherhood.* London: Sage

Silva, E.B. (2002) 'Routine matters: everyday life in families', in G. Crow and S. Heath (eds) *Social Conceptions of Time: Structure and Process in Work and Everyday Life.* Basingstoke: Palgrave

Silva, E.B. (2003) 'Everyday invented and revisited', *New Formations*, no. 49, pp. 165–9

Silverstone, R. (1994) *Television and Everyday Life.* London: Routledge

Smith, D. (1987) *The Everyday World as Problematic: A Feminist Sociology.*, Milton Keynes: Open University Press

Office for National Statistics (1997) *Social Focus on Families.* London: Office for National Statistics

Office for National Statistics (2001) *Social Focus on Men.* London: Office for National Statistics

Sudnow, D. (ed.) (1972) *Studies in Social Interaction.* New York: Free Press

Swindler, A. (1986) 'Culture in action: symbols and strategies', *American Sociological Review*, Vol. 51, pp. 273–86

Truzzi, M. (ed.) (1968) *Sociology and Everyday Life.* Englewood Cliffs, NJ: Prentice Hall

Turner, R. (ed.) (1974) *Ethnomethodology.* Harmonsdsworth: Penguin

Weber, M. (1991) *The Protestant Ethic and the Spirit of Capitalism* (1904–5). London: Harper Collins

Weeks, J., Donovan, C. and Heaphy, B. (1999) 'Everyday Experiments: Narratives of Non-Heterosexual Relationships'in E.B. Silva and C. Smart (eds) *The 'new' family?* London: Sage

Weeks, J., Heaphy, B. and Donovan, C. (2001) *Same Sex Intimacies. Families of Choice and Other Life Experiments*. London: Routledge

Whuthnow, R. (1988) *Meaning and Moral Order: Explorations in Cultural Analysis*. Berkeley: University of California Press

Williams, R. (1958) 'Culture is ordinary', in N. Mackenzie (ed.) *Conviction*. London: MacGibbon and Kee, pp. 74–92

Williams, R. (1961) *The Long Revolution*. London: Chatto and Windus

Chapter 2

The invention of the modern cultural fact: towards a critique of the critique of everyday life

Tony Bennett

It sometimes happens, when reading in different fields, that the same phrases crop up, prompting unexpected insights in the light that their different uses throw on one another. It was with something of a jolt of this kind that I learned that Henri Lefebvre had used the term 'connective tissue' to describe how everyday life provided a largely taken-for-granted, yet also clandestine – in some way obscure and hidden – set of assumptions underpinning all human thought and activity (Gardiner, 2000: 2, 16). For the phrase called to mind the work of Walter Bagehot, the nineteenth-century constitutional theorist, who, in his *Physics and Politics* (1873), referred to the 'connective tissue of civilisation' as a quasi-physical mechanism – lodged in the body's nervous system – through which the lessons learned in one generation were passed on to the next as a cultural inheritance that had been inscribed in the body.[1] In doing so, it foregrounded an aspect of the critique of everyday life associated with writers like Henre Lefebvre and Michel de Certeau that I have always found deeply disturbing.

This is not to suggest that either Lefebvre or de Certeau was acquainted with Bagehot's work, although both would have been familiar with the Lamarckian concept of use inheritance on which Bagehot drew. More to the point, both were heirs to the broader tradition of what John Frow (1997) calls organicist conceptions of memory in which memory is said to be transmitted organically from the past to the present – through popular tradition, Durkheimian accounts of collective memory, or the Freudian unconscious – rather than being organised socially and materially, in the present, through the operation of storage and retrieval systems such as libraries, archives and museums.[2] We can see the legacy of these conceptions, and parallels with Bagehot, in the organicist mnemonics that both Lefebvre and de Certeau subscribed to in attributing the sources of resistance to subterranean forces that they sometimes described as being rooted in quasi-evolutionary tendencies grounded in the body. This is evident, for example, in de Certeau's (in)famous contention that the tactics of resistance might have their roots in 'the age-old ruses of fishes and insects that disguise or transform themselves in order to survive' (de Certeau, 1984: xi).[3]

All of this is disturbing enough. But it is the collateral issues that are worked through in association with these understandings of memory that pose greater cause for concern. In Bagehot's work, the concept of the 'connective tissue of civilisation' formed part of a broader political vocabulary in which some people were qualified for, and others disqualified from, full membership of the political community depending on the extent to which the lessons of the past had been stored up and passed on within their bodily inheritances. Those who had a thinly organised bodily inheritance – that is, those who were regarded as still belonging to the early stages of civilisation and who were therefore judged to lack the complexly structured and multi-levelled selves associated with those who had a more deeply-layered inheritance – were judged to be incapable of the kinds of self-reflexivity required for political discussion. They were, accordingly, excluded from Bagehot's definition of political community (see Bagehot, 1963: 62–3). There is no parallel to this argument in favour of a mainly male and middle-class suffrage in the literature that critiques everyday life. However, this literature does exhibit similar properties in the distinction it draws between two different modes of relation to the everyday which depend on similarly differentiated architectures of the self. On the one hand, there are those who are said to live spontaneously at the level of everyday life, reproducing its habitual routines through forms of consciousness and behaviour that remain resolutely single-levelled – the bearers of Marcuse's 'one dimensional consciousness', for example (Marcuse, 1964). On the other hand, the critique of everyday life is also concerned to identify those whose social position, in vouchsafing them an ability to acquire a double-levelled consciousness, enables them to pierce the flat surface of the everyday by introducing another dimension (the extraordinary in the ordinary) which, by warding off the prospect of endless repetition, re-animates the movement of history.

To explain more fully why I think this aspect of the critique of everyday life is a worrying one, I look first at its relationship to what I call 'the modern cultural fact'. I then look at how such arguments orchestrate the relationships between different times and the architecture of the self in ways which reproduce politically questionable aspects of modernist discourse.

The modern cultural fact

I can best explain what I mean by 'the modern cultural fact' by elaborating more fully the allusion it makes to the account Mary Poovey's offers, in *A History of the Modern Fact,* of the relationship between the emergence of subjectivity, as a conceptual problem, and its emergence as a practical problem of governance. Conceptualising subjectivity, she argues, 'did not seem politically important until the demise of the sovereign mode of government, for only when individuals were allowed to govern themselves did it seem necessary to theorise how they did so' (Poovey, 1998: 114). Her argument here forms part of a broader thesis concerning the transition from the role that political arithmetic had played, in the projects of the Restoration, in fashioning abstract numerical calculations into instruments of absolutist rule to the later development of liberal forms of self-government. In place of earlier strategies aimed at rendering the population knowable through abstract and impersonal forms of calculation monopolised by the sovereign authority, the emerging forms of social relationship associated with eighteenth-century markets and civil society depended increasingly on new forms of self-rule that operated through the subjectivities of those whom they enlisted. This need, Poovey argues, was initially met by the new discourses of aesthetics which provided a means for knowing, cultivating, developing, and acting on the self through what we would now call specific practices of cultural consumption. But these were, of course, elite practices restricted, in the eighteenth-century culture of civic humanism, to the male members of the landed and mercantile classes, and, in the nineteenth century, to the middle classes (see Barrell, 1986).

It is not here, then, that we should look for the origins of the 'modern cultural fact' – by which I mean the representation, in either statistical or ethnographic form, of the everyday cultural practices of subordinate social groups. Its roots lie rather in the relations of knowledge and governance that were generated *outside* these newly emerging aesthetic practices of self-governance, in contexts where the capacity for the complex, multi-layered selves that such practices required was denied. Poovey casts light on these contexts in an earlier study where she traces the emergence of a split, along class lines, in nineteenth-century strategies of liberal government. She relates this to the influence of Adam Smith's 1853 text *The Theory of Moral Sentiments*. This argued that the cultivation of virtue depended on the mechanisms of a specular morality in which individuals learned how to govern themselves by internalising the moralising gaze of middle-class standards of propriety and respectability and adjusting their behaviour accordingly. In Smith's analysis, however, the distribution of this double-levelled self was restricted, by and large, to the gentry and middle classes. The ability to lift one's self out of the immediacy of everyday behaviour and habit and to view that behaviour reflexively in the light of internalised moral standards so as to cultivate a self-developing moral capacity was, Poovey argues, denied to the new urban working classes. New forms of residential segregation also meant that the working classes, sunk in the obscurity and darkness of the urban slums, were placed beyond the reach of the moralising gaze of the middle-classes. The working poor had therefore to be treated differently: because they could not govern themselves, they had to be governed from above. And this, in turn, required the acquisition of new ways of knowing the poor in order that their ways of life might be so represented as to make it possible for them to be acted on – by the state or by benevolent associations – to bring about those reforms of belief and behaviour that the poor could not be counted on to develop for themselves.

It is, then, the flurry of new knowledges of the working poor, generated mainly in the second part of the nineteenth century, that I have in mind by 'the invention of the modern cultural fact'. As such, it was an invention prompted by the new and distinctive problems of liberal government associated with the difficulties of extending the reach of newly-emerging forms of cultural self-governance across the divide which separated those deemed to posses the forms of self-reflexiveness associated with a multi-levelled self from those deemed to lack any such complex architecture of the self. This flurry of new knowledges was as evident in the literature of social observation produced by middle-class 'social explorers' who visited the urban poor to produce ethnographic accounts of ways of life on the other side of the class divide as it was in the new ways of statistically mapping the distribution of working class neighbourhoods that were evident in new cartographies of the city, or in the elementary cultural statistics that emerged from surveys of the reading habits of the poor. Nor was the perception of a radical otherness that denied the capacity for full self-reflexive subjectivity to whole groups of people limited to the sphere of class relations. By the end of the century, the influence of evolutionary thought meant that women, of whatever class, were often viewed as more likely to be ensnared in the pre-reflective immediacy of their natural roles than were men (see Richards, 1989). The same was true – indeed, more so – of the other context in which 'the modern cultural fact' had its origins: that of the administration of colonised peoples who, in being viewed as 'primitive', came increasingly to be regarded as unable to free themselves from outmoded ways of life in order to embark on a course of economic, moral or cultural self-development. Here, again, any momentum for self-reform and self-development could only be introduced from outside, through the activities of missionaries or liberal reformers. The ways of knowing colonised peoples associated with early colonial statistics, ethnography and ethnographic film were designed to facilitate precisely such interventions into primitive ways of life – either that or, where the case was judged hopeless, to record their customs and mores before, withering under the onslaught of western civilisation, they became extinct (Edwards, 1992).

The transference of meanings between these two contexts for the emergence of the 'modern cultural fact' is well documented in studies tracing how the languages of race, gender and class intersected in the mutually reinforcing metaphors of 'darkest Africa' and 'darkest England' (Marriott, 1999; McClintock, 1995). Its influence, moreover, has been enduring. It emerges again, in that distinctively English form of the 'modern cultural fact' that was fashioned in the rich mix of statistical, ethnographic and photographic observation developed, in the 1930s, by Mass-Observation. For although envisaged, in the words of Tom Harrisson, as an 'anthropology of ourselves' (Harrisson, cit. MacClancy, 2001: 7), Mass-Observation was most characteristically an anthropology of others.[4] Its preoccupation with the working classes of the industrial north thus resulted in a construction of the strange 'folk up there' as a race apart in a vocabulary of class and region that was to find its post-war echo in the writings of George Orwell.

Yet, in some aspects of its original formulation, Mass-Observation echoed the continental critique of everyday life whose emergence it paralleled. For it, too, was initially characterised by a search for potential sources of new social movement that might arise out of the psychic automatism of the 'collective unconscious' that was said to govern the inherited mental life of the masses. This reflected a broadly similar set of influences. In their 1937 letter announcing the establishment of Mass-Observation, Charles Madge, Humphrey Jennings and Tom Harrisson made clear their debt to the converging influences of the works of Darwin, Marx, Freud, Breuer, and Edward Tylor's anthropology of the 'primitive' in providing a basis for a scientific understanding of human behaviour. To which there was added the influence of surrealism. This was especially true of Madge. Drawing, on the one hand, on the stress that Darwin placed on the circumscribing effects of a genetic-cum-historical inheritance, and, on the other, on the emphasis that surrealism placed on the potential for a ruptural break with such an enchaining legacy – a legacy that was coded into the very ordinariness of everyday life – Madge constructed the mental life of the masses as a site for the potential emergence of a double-levelled consciousness.[5] This was, however, less true of Tom Harrisson's more conventional anthropological and scientific understanding of Mass-Observation and, as Harrisson's influence came to prevail over that of Madge, less true of Mass-Observation as a whole, especially when it was integrated into the government's war effort (see Robins and Webster, 1999: 22–4). As Madge protested at the time, this replaced Mass-Observation's earlier optimistic expectations of the masses with a *dirigiste* conception of the masses as bewildered and therefore in need of leadership and direction (see Hubble, 2001: 82–3).

Here too, then, we find concerns similar to those characterising the earlier invention of 'the modern cultural fact' which, borrowing from Johannes Fabian (1983), we might say is inherently anthropological in its denial of coevalness to others. For withholding from the observed the complex architecture of the self which the observer, as heir to a cumulative historical process of self formation, lays a claim to is the same, in both procedure and effect, as placing the observed in a different time from the observer. And it is across the spaces created by this denial of coevalness that the fault-lines of modern forms of cultural governance are to be found, split in their logic according to the historical depth or shallowness of the selves that they have to deal with. Where there is a layered structure to the self within which the self can act on itself so as to become self-regulating, liberal forms of indirect governance are possible. Where the self is denied an interior space within with such a reforming activity of self-on-self can be fashioned, more direct forms of rule are called for.

The everyday and its transcendence

The provenance of the concept of the everyday is a different and more varied one encompassing a range of contrasting meanings in its use across the fields of phenomenological sociology, critical theory (in its opposition between system and lifeworld), and – my particular concern here – the critique of everyday life associated with the tradition running from Georg Lukács, through Henri Lefebvre to Agnes Heller and Michel de Certeau. There are, nonetheless, significant similarities between these different accounts of the everyday. Stephen Crook suggests that they share three fundamental moves:

> First, they identify the everyday as the source and site of particularly valued aspects of social and cultural life. Secondly, they locate the everyday on one side of a distinction between two distinct modalities of order and practice (lifeworld and system for Habermas). Thirdly, they privilege the 'everyday' modality, aligning it with the most basic defining principle of social and cultural life as such.
> (Crook, 1998: 530–1).

There is a fourth move, too. This consists in the dualistic conception of everyday life which, to stay with Habermas's terms, results from the increasing invasion of the lifeworld by system. For it is this that allows everyday life to be figured as the source of a tension between, on the one hand, the oppressive stultification arising from the routinisation of everyday life that is dictated by the invasion of system, and, on the other, the sources of renewal – provided they can be identified and tapped into – derived from the residues of a pre-modern period in which everyday life was inherently authentic and whose traces have been carried organically from the past into the present. It is this fracture within everyday life that allows its analysis to serve as a privileged locus for engaging with the dynamics of modernity. Everyday life is figured, as Crook puts it, both as the victim of the loss of pre-modern forms of sociality and as the residual bearer of that lost unity. And it is in relation to this split structure of the everyday that the critique of everyday life seeks to recover the potential for the extraordinary that lies 'hidden, and typically repressed' (Gardiner, 2000: 6) beneath the ordinariness of the everyday.

Yet it is precisely here, in this conception of everyday life as simultaneously the plane of a flattened, single-dimensional social existence and the source of forces through which such an existence might be transcended, that the problems lie. For this commitment to deciphering the relations between the ordinary and the extraordinary within the everyday brings in its tow a form of reasoning similar to that associated with the genesis of the modern cultural fact. For this act of decipherment also entails a denial of the capacity for a full, self-reflexive subjectivity to whole groups of persons. At the same time, it adds a new aspect to this form of reasoning, annexing it to what purports to be a radical politics by granting the members of other social groups the capacity to free themselves from their immersion in the everyday to acquire a critical self-consciousness of the forces organising and structuring their lives and, thereby, through this possession of a multi-layered self, to become agents of progressive social change.

This is a particularly conspicuous aspect of the construction of the everyday in the work of Henri Lefebvre, the key figure, according to Robert Shields (1999), in mediating and connecting pre- and post-war debates about the everyday. The former took their lead from Lukács's account, in *History and Class Consciousness*, of the relations between commodity fetishism and the reification of everyday life (Lukács, 1977). This needed to be adjusted, in Lefebvre's view, to take account of the integration of everyday life into the new 'bureaucratic society of controlled consumption' of the post-war period (Lefebvre, 1971). For Lefebvre, the everyday is the site and scene of repetition, of mechanical actions bound into a cyclical recurrence of time in which habit is spontaneously reproduced. The everyday is, above all, not conscious of itself as such. Lacking that dualistic relation to itself that is produced by its construction – in critical discourse – as 'the quotidian', the everyday consciousness is characterised by precisely those forms of pre-reflective insertion into the repetitive structure of everyday routines that critical thought must break with in order to make 'the everyday' thinkable.

Nevertheless – and this by way of distinguishing his position from traditional philosophical approaches to the everyday – Lefebvre also approaches the everyday as the place where there might be glimpsed new meanings and creative energies that are capable of breaking the deadening cycle of routine and repetition. But this is a possibility that is available only to some and not to others. Women, in particular, come off badly here:

> *Everyday life weighs heaviest on women. ... Some are bogged down by its peculiar cloying substance, others escape into make-believe, close their eyes to their surroundings, to the bog into which they are sinking and simply ignore it; they have their substitutes and they are substitutes; they complain – about men, the human condition, life, God and the gods – but they are always beside the point; they are the subject of everyday life and its victims or objects and substitutes (beauty, femininity, fashion, etc.) and it is at their cost that substitutes thrive. ... Because of their ambiguous position in everyday life – which is specifically part of everyday life and modernity – they are incapable of understanding it.*
> (Lefebvre, 1971: 73)

Intellectuals – who, for Lefebvre, are not women – do not fare much better. Nor do the middle classes. It is only among the working classes, youth and students – ostensibly neutral subjects, but implicitly male – that a critical, dualistic relation to the everyday can be discerned. In the case of the working classes – and here the influence of Lukács's *History and Class Consciousness* is clear – a capacity to resist integration into the one-dimensional structure of the everyday and to pierce its reification is seen as essential to its historical mission as the proletariat. This mission, however, is one which, in Lefebvre's more chastened assessment, the proletariat is no longer capable of fulfilling the more it becomes integrated into the society of bureaucratic consumption. For this undermines its ability to pull off the dialectical conjuring trick, urged by Lukács, of introducing a double-levelled consciousness into history as – in being both the supreme object of commodity production and an emerging self-conscious political force portending history's completion – the proletariat becomes aware of itself as both the subject and object of history. In the case of youth and students and, reflecting the moment of the publication of *Everyday Life in the Modern World* in 1968, all those practices which revive the spirit of festival, it is the fact that these are not yet integrated into the regular rhythms of everyday life that allows them to serve as potential leverage points from which the glacial structures of the society of bureaucratic consumption might be nudged into movement.

These formulations are evidently different from those characterising the genesis of the 'modern cultural fact' in the nineteenth-century literature of social observation. Far from being motivated by a concern with the limits of the social reach of liberal forms of cultural self-governance and how to compensate for these, their concern is to identify mechanisms at work in the midst of everyday life that will produce self-activating agents of radical social change. But they are, in terms of the form of reasoning involved, uneasily similar in attributing to some groups a capacity to develop a critical, dualistic relation to the everyday that might serve as a source of change whilst simultaneously and axiomatically denying that capacity to other groups.[6] Nor would it be difficult to trace how this form of reasoning is echoed in the more recent literature on nomadism which seeks to open up chinks of movement in history by attributing to those whose lives are characterised by movement and mobility the kinds of capacity for critique that come from multiple-layered selves that are, in the very process of this gesture, denied to those less mobile selves doomed to be forever trapped in the everyday.[7]

How, then, are we to account for these similarities? It is with a view to answering this question that I now turn to probe more closely the relations between the critique of everyday life and discourses of modernity.

We are always becoming modern

The notion of modernity, Bruno Latour argues, indicates 'an acceleration, a rupture in time' and, as such, always produces, by contrast 'an archaic and stable past' (Latour, 1993: 10). He elaborates this argument more fully as follows:

> *The moderns have a peculiar propensity for understanding time that passes as if it were really abolishing the past behind it ... They do not feel that they are removed from the Middle Ages by a certain number of centuries, but that they are separated by Copernican revolutions, epistemological breaks, epistemic ruptures so radical that nothing of that past survives in them – nothing of that past ought to survive in them.*
> (Latour, 1993: 68)

And again:

> *Since everything that passes is eliminated for ever, the moderns indeed sense time as an irreversible arrow, as capitalisation, as progress ... They want to keep everything, date everything, because they think they have definitively broken with their past. The more they accumulate revolutions, the more they save; the more they capitalise, the more they put on display in museums.*
> (Latour, 1993: 69)

Insightful and provocative at the same time, there is, however, something not quite right about these formulations. For the discourse of modernity, in the very process of organising the radical distinctions between past and present which sustain it, also reinscribes the past in the present – and not simply as museum relics of a time past. To the contrary: the present, in modernist discourse, is constantly haunted by the archaic – by remnants of the past from which it ought to have, but has not, pulled free as, at some level of the social or in the colonial relations between societies, the past survives as a still active and potent force which threatens modernity's advance by virtue of its potentially degenerative retro-momentum. It is in this sense that the project of modernity is one that is never completed. For there is always a residue of the past in the present that has to be struggled against before we can be fully modern. If Latour is right to contend that we have never been modern, it is also true that we are, at the same time, always becoming modern in the sense that this is an ever-beckoning destiny that can never be finally achieved.

The critique of everyday life is perhaps best understood as the flip-side of this conception in aspiring to produce a continuing momentum within modernity – to guarantee it the potential to keep on becoming – by ascribing a split structure to the everyday in which it is the tension between the subterranean residues of earlier social formations and the repetitive structure of everyday life in the present that augurs the prospects for change. This is clearly expressed in the passage from Maurice Blanchot (1987) which Gardiner quotes in his introductory chapter. If, for Blanchot, the everyday is 'what lags and falls back, the residual life with which our trash cans and cemeteries are filled: scrap and refuse' (Blanchot, cit. Gardiner, 2000: 1), this is not a residue that is ripe for museumification. To the contrary, for Blanchot, it is precisely because this stagnant residue of past forms of life continues to exist as a spontaneous force in the midst of the bureaucratisation of modern life that it can be expected to introduce new movement and flow into the structures of the present. Within Mass-Observation, crises – like the 1936 Abdication Crisis that prompted its formation – were invested with similar expectations in view, as Kevin Robins and Frank Webster put it, of their 'ability to outwit the force of habit'. Quoting from Madge and Harrisson's 1937 report on the Abdication Crisis, they continue: 'Where usually there was a tendency "to perform all our actions through sheer habit, with as little consciousness of our surroundings as though we were walking in our sleep", the crisis subverted the automatic nature of social experience' (Robins and Webster, 1999: 25). Similar conceptions inform de Certeau's argument that sources of resistance are secreted in the subterranean history of the body, thus producing a split self that is not fully integrated into the prevailing social order. We see this also in Levebvre's claim that it is the body rather than 'some form of "knowledge" or other' that supplies 'one of the elements and foundations of subversion' (Lefebvre, cit. Gardiner, 2000: 16), which Gardiner – in another version of the 'connective tissue' argument – glosses as evidence that human embodiment 'retains the trace of a longing for communal solidarity'. This apparently gender-less invocation of 'the body' should not, however, blind us to the fact that, for Lefebvre, women are 'out of time' in a different way. They are, Rita Felski (1999–2000) argues, manifestations of the cyclical repetitions of natural time rather than archaic survivals of an earlier time. They are therefore irrelevant to the dynamics of modernity, exiles from the flow of historical time rather than a grit left over from an earlier time that might put some leverage back into the machineries of history.

It is, however, in Agnes Heller's work – in which the everyday is explicitly thematised as the ground of history's dialectic – that the forms of reasoning I am concerned with here are most evident. For Heller (1984), the everyday is both historically specific and universal: it is the ground for the development of the species life in all social and historical societies while also, in the specific historical form of capitalist society, existing in an alienated form in which everyday life, in being split off from high artistic and intellectual culture, comes to be regarded as dull and repetitive, of no significance. Yet, everyday life in capitalist society also contains the seed of its own transcendence. In harbouring residues of premodern forms of totality in which, so the story goes, everyday life was not objectified as such because it was not clearly separated off from a more rounded set of social relations and cultural practices, the everyday also constitutes a force within the present that can help generate movement within the otherwise solidifying structures of modernity. The role of this residue, moreover, is precisely that of leading the everyday beyond the depthless flatness of its existing forms – in which, in Heller's terms, the everyday exists more or less pre-reflectively as a form of 'objectivation-in-itself' – to a form of objectivation-for-and-in-itself characterised by increasingly reflexive forms of double-levelled consciousness in which the everyday becomes the site for the self-conscious development of humanity's species being.[8] Here Hegel and the everyday meet in a conception which translates the historical process of *Aufhebung* from the self-alienating activities of Spirit or, as in Marx, the unfolding of a dialectic grounded in the contradictory structure of relations of production, to a process that is enacted in, as Gardiner puts it, 'the terrain of everyday life' as that upon which 'flesh-and-blood men and women must pursue the unrestricted development and enrichment of species-specific or generic potentialities' (Gardiner, 2000: 138). Except that, once the everyday is translated into the ground for overcoming the dualisms generated by Hegelian philosophy, precious little flesh and blood remains as historically specific and actual relations are translated into the mere ground on which there takes place a more general historical process which always supercedes them.

The everyday in question

What value, then, if any, can be claimed for the concept of the everyday? My purpose has been to suggest that those understandings of the everyday which probe the mundane repetitions of everyday life in order to bring to light the hidden social forces which, in rupturing those repetitions, will enable the everyday to transcend itself into a more authentic mode of social life rest on deeply problematic conceptual and political foundations. Rita Felski, working with a broader canvass, takes a similar view in her assessment of everyday life as an 'invention' whose qualities are best understood as side-effects generated by modernist forms of social and cultural critique. Felski is particularly concerned to take issue with the tendency of the critique of everyday life to oscillate between, on the one hand, everyday life being 'rhapsodically affirmed and painted in glowing colours' where it is celebrated as the font of resistance, or, on the other, being 'excoriated as the realm of ultimate alienation and dehumanisation' (Felski, 1999–2000: 31). In taking issue with such critiques of the everyday, Felski foregrounds their negative assessments of repetition – which, for Felski, constitutes the distinctive temporality of everyday life – and habit, which she sees as 'the characteristic mode of experiencing the everyday' (ibid: 18). Nor is this true solely of the critique of everyday life. Indeed, one of the merits of Felski's discussion concerns the light she throws on this tradition by placing it in the broader perspective of modernist social and critical theory, literature and theatre where the repetitive and habitual have been subjected to remorseless criticism: 'the ballast that chains the dog to its vomit', Felski tells us, was Samuel Beckett's summary assessment of habit (ibid: 26). In arguing the need for an approach to the everyday that will take its ordinariness seriously without either 'idealising or demonising it' (ibid: 31), Felksi draws on both Dorothy Smith's feminist perspective on the gender dynamics at play in the everyday (Smith, 1987) and Alfred Schutz's phenomenological approach to the 'natural attitude' which governs our relations to everyday life (Schutz, 1967: 208–9) to urge the need for a more positive assessment of the routine aspects of everyday life. To 'see habit only as a straitjacket and constraint', is, she argues, 'to ignore the ways in which routines may strengthen, comfort and provide meaning' (Felski,

1999–2000: 28). Recommending instead the need 'to make peace with the ordinariness of everyday life', she endorses those perspectives – evident in Roger Silverstone's account of the role of the media in providing everyday life with an ontological security and grounding (Silverstone, 1994) – that can be traced, ultimately, to Heller's ontological validation of routine, habit and repetition as untranscendable aspects of human modes of being-in-the-world.

Yet, I am not sure that affirming, on the one hand, the necessity and even desirability of habit as a constitutive feature of everyday life while, on the other, arguing that there are circumstances in which habit or the routinisation of everyday practices 'may be personally constraining and socially detrimental' (Felski, 1999–2000: 28) entirely escapes the pull of the critique of everyday life. What is needed, I think, is a different angle of vision from which to approach the question of habit. Mariana Valverde (1996) provides the means for this in her account of the role of habit – conceived as a socially enforced form of learning via repetition – as a despotic mechanism that was inscribed at the heart of late-nineteenth-century programmes of liberal government. Its role here was as a means of compensating for the individual's capacity for autonomous self-regulation where (among the working classes and women, for example) that capacity could not be counted on either to be in place or to be functioning properly.[9] Habit, in other words, was to be invoked as a mechanism for automated forms of self-governance, in circumstances and among populations in which the forms of specular morality associated with the double-tiered architecture of the middle-class self were viewed as lacking or underdeveloped.

The influence of these concerns is evident in Walter Bagehot's understanding of 'the connective tissues of civilisation'. For it is through what he calls the social mechanism of drill – of learning through repetition – that, for Bagehot, competencies are acquired and deposited in the body for transmission from one generation to the next as 'stored virtue' (Bagehot, 1873: 6). However, while habit is thus presented as essential to the developmental dynamic of civilisation, it also emerges as an obstacle to that dynamic to the degree that the force of habit, or what Bagehot called the 'cake of custom' (ibid: 53), can accumulate to such an extent that any developmental momentum is lost as social life locks in on itself in a cycle of endless repetition. Stefan Collini (1991) places these concerns in a broader perspective in his discussion of the tensions that wracked late-nineteenth-century liberal thought as it sought to balance and reconcile the conflict between, on the one hand, the need for a population that had become habituated to new disciplinary forms of regulation, and, on the other, the need for the kinds of striving, self-reliant, reflexive and adaptable forms of behaviour that would produce an ongoing developmental social momentum. Although resolved in different ways, what this tension pointed to was the need for a circuit breaker, a mechanism which, much like those associated with the critique of everyday life, would ward off the threat of an endless, habitual repetition of the same.

My point here, then, is that we shall deal better with questions concerning the role of habit and repetition in everyday life if we view their negative assessment within the critique of everyday life as an inverted variant of the tensions generated within the history of liberal forms of self-governance considered in their relations to the developmental imperatives of modernist social theories. If this is so, the key issues at stake in developing new approaches to the study of everyday life might concern less the need for a positive, rather than a negative, evaluation of habit and repetition than the development of frameworks that will free the analysis of everyday life from two of the constraints that have characterised its critique. The first consists in the tendency to place *all* forms of habit and repetition on one side within bipolar constructions of the social (system versus lifeworld, for example) with the result that they have then *all* to be seen as operating in the same way with the same consequences in reinforcing monolithic power structures which function uniformly negatively and oppressively. For it is precisely this procedure that generates the expectation that the role of habit and repetition will give rise to generalised forms of social stasis which can only be pierced by locating a social force with the potential to effect some general kind of social transcendence. And the second consists in the annexation of this propensity to a system for the differential evaluation of persons which, depending on the degree to which their actions are governed by the force of habit, ranks them hierarchically in terms of the degree of depth or complexity which characterises their selves.

Once these two, reciprocally sustaining dualities which have characterised the critique of everyday life are questioned, there are no compellingly good reasons for thinking that the rhythms, routines, repetitions and habitual aspects of everyday life all work to the same effect in imposing a singular and seemingly unchangeable structure on the everyday. The diversity of the ways in which we are put to work in managing ourselves in the context of our everyday activities; the range and variety of the different and sometimes conflicting forms of social authority that are involved in the regulation of everyday social practices; and the contradictions which emerge from these – there is sufficient potential for dissonance and clash within the *multiplicity of powers* that are at play in the everyday to suggest that everyday life is more pertinently viewed as the source and site of incessantly transformative social mechanisms than of a seamless structure of habit and repetition that has to be transcended in some general way. And this, in turn, suggests that it is simply wrong to argue that those who live solely within the confines of everyday life are somehow the victims of a simple, flat organisation of the self which excludes a capacity for critical, self-reflexive awareness. More to the point, it suggests that everyday life cannot be homogenised in a way that makes it meaningful to speak of some people being entirely constituted within and by it. This is not to call into question the value that has customarily been placed on the study of everyday life as a means of defamiliarising everyday practices and experience with a view to opening up critical intellectual and cultural spaces in which alternatives to those practices might be glimpsed and debated. But these alternatives need to be conceived in the context of the complex shaping of everyday life by a multiplicity of forces rather than in the context of a simple bi-polar logic.

It is here that the 'technological turn' evident in recent approaches to the study of everyday life is so promising. The incorporation of the perspectives of science and technoscience into the study of everyday patterns of behaviour and interaction between humans and non-humans opens up too many questions to be pursued here. However, Mike Michael (2000) puts his finger on what is perhaps the most central issue from the point of view of the concerns aired in the foregoing discussion when he suggests the need to focus the study of everyday life on the role of 'mundane technologies' in both normalising and regulating the everyday while also initiating change within it. In defining mundane technologies – which he contrasts with 'exotic technologies', that is, new technologies which are said to mark and bring about 'epochal cultural shifts' – Michael construes these as technologies that have been 'black-boxed' in the Latourian sense that they have lost their novelty and 'now linger in the background, doing their "job"' (Michael, 2000: 3) largely unnoticed. The challenge, he goes on to suggest, is to examine the ways in which such mundane technologies do not simply order the everyday but are also implicated in its *disordering* and *reordering* because of their heterogeneity and the heterogeneity of the practices within which they are inscribed. When Michael says that he wants 'to explore how mundane technology … at once reinforces and undermines the typical arrangements and processes that comprise everyday life' (ibid: 4), one can both see the legacy of the concern, within the critique of everyday life, to identify the extraordinary within the ordinary as a means of locating epochal lurches of a modernist type, and glimpse an alternative to those concerns in the construction of everyday life as a scene for the ripple effects of more varied dynamics arising from the socio-technological relations in which it is constituted.

Acknowledgements

My thanks to John Frow and Elizabeth Silva for their insightful and helpful comments on an earlier version of this essay.

Notes

1   I have discussed this aspect of Bagehot's work more fully elsewhere: see Bennett (2001).

2   My discussion here also draws on Laura Otis's consideration of related organicist conceptions of memory in nineteenth-century literature, science and philosophy: see Otis (1994).

3   See Ahearn (1995) for a fuller discussion of this aspect of de Certeau's work.

4   The original slogan for Mass-Observation was 'Anthropology at Home' – the title of the letter calling for the establishment of a nation-wide network of observers of everyday customs and behaviours that Charles Madge, Humphrey Jennings and Tom Harrisson published in the *New Statesman and Nation* in 1937. This conception echoed Bronislaw Malinowski's concern that the methods of anthropology should be brought home and turned upon ourselves 'with the same mental attitude with which we approach exotic tribes' (Malinowski, cit. Mengham, 2001: 33).

5   I draw here on the discussions of Madge's work in Connor (2001) and Marcus (2001).

6   Crook (1998: 528) shows the incoherence of this procedure in noting the respects in which accounts of everyday life implicitly assume the reflexive capacities they deny if the ability of actors to move between the different frames or realities of everyday life (work, play, caring) is to be accounted for.

7   I draw here on David Morley's (2000) critical assessment of the epistemological privileging of nomadism that is evident in many versions of cosmopolitanism.

8   Charles Madge and Humphrey Jennings anticipated that Mass-Observation would have
      similar consequences for the empirical consciousness of those it recruited as observers.
      'The process of observing raises him [the "untrained observer"] from subjectivity to
      objectivity. What has become unnoticed through familiarity is raised into consciousness
      again' (cit. Marcus, 2001: 9).

9   I also draw here on the more general discussion of the place of habit in the history of
      social theory in Valverde (1998).

References

Ahearn, J. (1995) *Michel de Certeau: Interpretation and its Other.* Cambridge: Polity Press

Bagehot, W. (1873) *Physics and Politics: Or Thoughts on the Application of the Principles of 'Natural Selection' and 'Inheritance' to Political Society.* London: Henry S King & Co

Bagehot, W. (1963) *The English Constitution.* London: Collins/Fontana

Barrell, J. (1986) *The Political Theory of Painting from Reynolds to Hazlitt: 'The Body of the Public'.* New Haven and London: Yale University Press

Bennett, T. (1998) *Culture: A Reformer's Science.* Sydney: Allen and Unwin; London: Sage

Bennett, T. (2001) 'Pasts beyond memories: the evolutionary museum, liberal government and the politics of prehistory'. *Folk: Journal of the Danish Ethnographic Society.* No. 43, Autumn, pp. 49–75

Blanchot, M. (1987) 'Everyday speech'. *Yale French Studies*, Vol. 73, pp.12–20

Collini, S. (1991) *Public Moralists: Political Thought and Intellectual Life in Britain, 1850—1930,* Oxford: Clarendon Press

Connor, S. (2001) '"A door half open to surprise": Charles Madge's imminences', *New Formations*, No. 44, Autumn, pp. 52–62

Crook, S. (1998) 'Minotaurs and other monsters: "everyday life" in recent social theory'. *Sociology*, Vol. 32, No. 3, pp. 523–40

de Certeau, M. (1984) *The Practice of Everyday Life.* Berkeley: University of California Press

Edwards, E. (ed.) (1992) *Anthropology and Photography 1860–1920.* New Haven and London: Yale University Press in association with The Royal Anthropological Institute

Fabian, J. (1983) *Time and the Other, How Anthropology Makes Its Object.* New York: Colombia University Press

Felski, R. (1999–2000) 'The invention of everyday life', *New Formations*, No. 39, pp. 13–31

Frow, J. (1997) *Time and Commodity Culture: Essays in Cultural Theory and Postmodernity.* Oxford: Clarendon Press

Gardiner, M. (2000) *Critiques of Everyday Life.* London and New York: Routledge

Heller, A. (1984) *Everyday Life.* London: Routledge and Kegan Paul

Hubble, N. (2001) 'Charles Madge and Mass-Observation are at home: from anthropology to war, and after'. *New Formations,* No. 44, Autumn, pp. 76–89

Latour, B. (1993) *We Have Never Been Modern,* Cambridge, MA: Harvard University Press

Lefebvre, H. (1971) *Everyday Life in the Modern World.* London: Allen Lane, The Penguin Press

Lukács, G. (1977) *History and Class Consciousness.* London, Merlin Press

MacClancy, J. (2001) 'Mass-Observation, surrealism, social anthropology: a present-day assessment'. *New Formations,* No. 44, Autumn, pp. 90–9

McLintock, A. (1995) *Imperial Leather: Race, Gender and Sexuality in the Colonial Context.* New York and London: Routledge

Marcus, L. (2001) 'Introduction: the project of Mass-Observation', *New Formations,* No. 44, Autumn, pp. 5–20

Marcuse, H. (1964) *One Dimensionsal Man: The Ideology of Industrial Society.* London: Sphere Books

Marriott, J. (1999) 'In darkest England: the poor, the crowd and race in the nineteenth-century metropolis' in P. Cohen (ed.) *New Ethnicities, Old Racisms.* London and New York: Zed Books

Mengham, R. (2001) 'Bourgeois news: Humphrey Jennings and Charles Madge', *New Formations,* No. 44, Autumn, pp. 26–33

Michael, M. (2000) *Reconnecting Culture, Technology and Nature: From Society to Heterogeneity.* London and New York: Routledge

Morley, D. (2000) *Home Territories: Media, Mobility and Identity.* London and New York: Routledge

Otis, L. (1994) *Organic Memory: History and the Body in the Late Nineteenth and Early Twentieth Centuries.* Lincoln and London: University of Nebraska Press

Poovey, M. (1995) *Making a Social Body: British Cultural Formation, 1830–1864.* Chicago: University of Chicago Press

Poovey, M. (1998) *A History of the Modern Fact.* Chicago: University of Chicago Press

Richards E. (1989) 'Huxley and woman's place in science: the "woman question" and the control of Victorian anthropology', in J.R. Moore (ed.) *History, Humanity and Evolution.* Cambridge: Cambridge University Press

Robins, K. and Webster, F. (1999) *Times of the Technoculture: From the Information Society to the Virtual Life.* London and New York: Routledge

Schutz, A. (1967) *Collected Papers, Vol. 1: The Problem of Social Reality.* The Hague: Martinus Nijhoff

Shields, R. (1999) *Lefebvre, Love and Struggle: Spatial Dialectics.* London and New York: Routledge

Silverstone, R. (1994) *Television and Everyday Life.* London and New York: Routledge

Smith, D. (1987) *The Everyday World as Problematic: A Feminist Sociology.* Milton Keynes: Open University Press

Valverde, M. (1996) '"Despotism" and ethical liberal governance', *Economy and Society*, Vol. 23, No. 3, pp. 357–72

Valverde, M. (1998) 'Governing out of habit', *Studies in Law and Politics*, Vol. 18, pp. 217–42

Chapter 3
Everyday life and family practices

David Morgan

> *Everyday life consists of the little things one hardly notices in time and space. The more we reduce the focus of vision, the more likely we are to find ourselves in the environment of material life: the broad sweep usually corresponds to History with a capital letter ... If we reduce the length of the time observed, we either have the event or the everyday happening.*
> (Braudel, 1981: 29)

What is everyday life?

'Everyday life' is one of those ideas that is simultaneously so obvious and highly elusive. The word itself is a kind of rhetorical claim; of course 'we know' what everyday life is. The term is what it claims to be: nothing more or nothing less. Yet once probed, the idea becomes complex and slippery. What is everyday to most readers of this book will be very distant, for example, from the experiences of those living in what Castells describes as 'The Fourth World'. Castells considers some of the 'black holes of informational capitalism' and provides vivid accounts of what this means for many of the peoples of sub-Saharan Africa, the ghettos of the socially excluded in North America and children, in employment, as prostitutes or as soldiers throughout the world (Castells, 1998). Indeed it may be suggested that different understandings as to what is everyday or normal (although the terms are not exactly synonyms) are not only a fact of global life but play a major part in maintaining global divisions. A strong routine sense of what is everyday or normal further marginalises the experiences of those already at the margins.

To begin with we may identify at least three overlapping meanings:

1   In the first place, everyday life involves a sense of reference to those events or experiences that might be expected to happen to most people in the course of their lives. These events are often closely linked to our biology, however complex the links between biological processes and social meanings may be. We are talking about events linked to birth, to sexuality, to death and to sickness. These events may be described, rather clumsily, as 'talk-about-ables', in view of the role they occupy in everyday conversations.

2   Second, everyday life may refer to the regular, the repeated, the routine, the familiar, the quotidian, the banal, even the boring. Unlike the first set of experiences these events are frequently not seen as being worth talking about.

3   Third, the idea of the everyday sometimes shades over into the more
    normative idea of the normal. The everyday or normal here is attached to
    people like us, normal people. It is frequently linked to local, class or national
    identities.

All of these have distinct, although related, connections to family practices. By
family practices I am referring to those practices which are frequently associated
with ideas of family life or family relationships (Morgan, 1996, 1999). The
meaning of 'family' here arises out of the interplays between the perspectives of
the observers and the perspectives and reflexive understandings of social actors
themselves. In other words, the use of the adjective 'family' is not something
inherent in any particular structure but is part of the very process of shaping
family living itself.

Life events and the everyday

The first category we may refer to as 'life events'. They have two characteristics.
In the first part they are part of the experience of most human beings. Even if
we take as given that all people are born and all people will die, most people
will also witness or take part in the birth of another human being, will experience
some kind of sexual relationship or partnership, will encounter sickness or
infirmity in themselves or in someone closely connected to them and will
experience bereavement or loss. Some of these experiences are part of the frailty
which Bryan Turner has recently identified with the human condition and human
rights (Turner, 1993) or the disappointment which Ian Craib (1994), writing
from a psycho-analytical perspective, also identifies as a key fact of human
existence. Thus Turner writes:

> *Human beings are frail, because their lives are finite, because they*
> *typically exist under conditions of scarcity, disease and danger, and*
> *because they are constrained by physical processes of ageing and decay.*
> (Turner, 1993: 501)

Craib writes of the inevitability and importance of disappointment in human
life; the fact of death and the limitation of the life span constitutes a central
feature of this argument (Craib, 1994).
    The second characteristic of these events is that they are frequently
experienced as something special. This may seem to contradict the first point
but the contradiction is only superficial. In part we are looking at a difference
of levels, between the general world of statistical probabilities and the individual
level of experience. Childbirth is part of the experience of most women, but
that familiarity is not a reason for playing down the importance of that
experience to the women themselves and to others closely connected to them.
The precise character of the significance of childbirth may, of course, vary
between social settings. In a modern society, for example, the special character
of giving birth may be linked to ideas of the special character of the individual
being produced. We all die, but (with some exceptions) few societies or
individuals are indifferent to this universal fact.

It is important to avoid essentialism here. It is true that many of these events seem to be linked to what are conventionally called the facts of life and constitute the raw material of demographic analysis. However, in modern society there are many other such events which are less obviously connected. The experiences of divorce and co-habitation now enter demographic statistics and increasingly become 'talk-about-ables'. Further, and more importantly, it is not the events themselves which are significant, but the way in which they are shaped and given meaning in everyday life through talk, ritual and cultural representations. In their different ways and through a diversity of social processes these events come to be seen as 'what life is all about'. The fact that many of these life events and experiences have strongly gendered connotations is itself a matter of some significance.

The way in which dramatic or extra-ordinary events may become part of everyday life may be explored further. Births and deaths may take on a non-everyday character under particular circumstances. In the case of death one only has to think of massive natural catastrophes, train and plane crashes or September 11th 2001 in Manhattan. Most societies make some kind of distinction between 'good' or 'normal' deaths and their opposite. Distinctions between 'normal' and 'abnormal' births are more difficult to draw (and are often shaped by normative expectations) but it is likely that such distinctions are made. This underlines the point that there is no necessary or straightforward passage from the biological 'facts of life' to constructions of everyday experience, as well as making the point that such events may come outside the ambit of everyday life. It may, in fact, be suggested that it is at these points that life events become connected, however indirectly, to 'History' as understood by Braudel in the quotation that heads this chapter. Nevertheless, the fact that such events so frequently and routinely form part of everyday conversations warrants consideration in relation to 'everyday life'.

It is also clear that these life events have strong linkages with family practices. Some of them – birth, marriage, death, divorce – refer to the processes through which families and households are seen to be formed and re-formed. Others – sickness and ageing, for example – are frequently occasions for the mobilisation of informal care within family based networks. Some of them are the occasion for family based rituals and it is on these occasions when family boundaries are defined or redefined.

Again, it is important not to overstress the idea of family here. For one thing it is not simply the family on its own but the interplay between family, religious and moral practices and values together, increasingly, with state interventions, that are important. Further, these events are rarely simply just about family life, and do not necessarily concern simply all those who may be connected by family ties. Nevertheless it can be argued that, despite some increasing complexities, family relationships not only provide the context and occasion for these events but are also constructed and reconstructed through them.

Life's regularities

Many family practices have the quality of being 'ordinary' or 'routine'. Family life is frequently organised around regular and repeated routines (Felski, 2000) to do with getting up and going to bed, meal-times, shopping trips and so on. This routine character, together with the fact that so many of these tasks seem to be imposed by others or from outside often leads to the fear that they might seem 'boring' to others even if they do not necessarily appear that way to the participants themselves. Family researchers are sometimes asked by the people they interview: 'surely you don't want to hear about this?'

Family, after all, is related linguistically to the 'familiar'. Family practices are organised around the regular deployment of bodies, time and space and material culture. These constitute the routines of family living, the repeated patterns associated with waking up, going to school or work, meals, returning home and going to bed interwoven with the performance of tasks associated with the daily maintenance of the household (see Chapter 4). Regular events such as weekends, holidays and birthdays also underline a particular model of time where the clock and the calendar merge with domestic routines. If life events belong to that class of events which are worth talking about, life's regularities rarely come into this category. However, they are frequently connected within the framework of family practices; the life event of childbirth, for example, may result in the routines of childcare.

There is perhaps an affinity here with that genre of paintings known as 'still life'. Art historians have noted how this genre has been accorded relatively little attention from critics partly, perhaps, because of its subject matter and partly because of its association with women artists. Nearly a century and a half ago, George Eliot presented what is, by now, a familiar contrast between this sense of the everyday and the heroic:

> *It is for this rare, precious quality of truthfulness that I delight in many Dutch paintings, which lofty-minded people despise. I find a source of delicious sympathy in these faithful pictures of a monotonous homely existence, which has been the fate of so many more among my fellow-mortals than a life of pomp or of absolute indigence, of tragic suffering or of world-stirring actions.*
> (Eliot, 1985[1859]: 179)

Norman Bryson argues that still life exists at the interface between three cultural zones of which the first is the one that concerns us here:

> *... the life of the table, of the household interior, of the basic creaturely acts of eating and drinking, of the artifacts which surround the subject in her or his domestic space, of the everyday world of routine and repetition, at a level of existence where events are not at all large-scale, momentous events of History, but the small-scale, trivial, forgettable acts of bodily survival and self-maintenance.*
> (Bryson, 1990: 14)

Writing of the painter Chardin, Bryson argues:

> *But in these narratives which tell only of brief journeys across a corner of everyday life, nothing significant happens: there is no transfiguration or epiphany, no sudden disclosure of transcendence. The eye moved lightly and without avidity: it is at home.*
> (ibid: 93)

'At home' here is surely a significant metaphor, pointing to something at rest and in familiar circumstances. Elsewhere we may think of the Swedish painter Carl Larsen whose detailed paintings, often reminiscent of the illustrations in children's books, lovingly depict the details of domestic interiors and safe worlds of childhood.

Of course, such routines are not confined to family life. Education and employment frequently provide the opportunities for the construction of a sense of regularity and repeatedness and everyday routines may well be part of the experiences of individuals or couples who define their relationships as being at some distance from 'conventional families'. However, it is interesting to note that many of these other daily routines exist at the borders of family and employment or family and education. These would include getting to work on time and returning from work or taking the children to school or to extra-curricular activities. In Marxist or functionalist terms we may see these routines as helping to maintain or reproduce wider regularities in work or education.

Even without a specifically Marxist framework we may see this sense of the everyday as being closely linked to the material conditions of life. We are dealing, therefore, with the regularities brought about by the business of earning a living, feeding, clothing and sheltering and the continuation of human life. In some cases these material conditions will be direct and unrelenting. In other cases, the ones with which we are more likely to be familiar, these conditions are less direct and more mediated. To say that they are everyday, 'not worth talking about', is not to deny their deeper significance.

We are, as has been suggested, likely to overlook such regularities. However, as Berger and Kellner (1964) argued in relation to marriage, such regularities help to build up a sense of ontological security. We may leave the house at the same time each day even if the trains are not always there for us. Janet Askham (1984), also writing about marriage, has written about the importance of both identity and stability while indicating the possibility of a degree of tension between these two life goals. Garfinkel's students demonstrated the importance and character of such routines through the artful breaching of everyday rules and expectations (1967). Adolescents who may literally treat their home as a hotel may encounter some very puzzled responses. The disturbing character of being burgled may in part be due to the fear of the crossing of the boundary between the public and the private, and having parts of one's everyday existence open to the gaze of unwelcome strangers (Chapman, 1999). Finally, it may be noted that people who experience major disruptions in their domestic life (the sudden onset of a seriously disabling illness, for example) may be even more concerned to establish a sense of normality through everyday routines (e.g. Voysey, 1975).

What these last examples also demonstrate is the fragility of this particular understanding of everyday life. While, on a day-to-day basis everyday life seems unquestionably real, so real in fact that it is not worth talking about, it may be easily breached, disrupted or challenged. Anne Tyler shows how easily this can happen in a characteristically insightful passage:

> Rebecca always put the shells back in the carton when she was working.
> In fact, she'd assumed that everyone did. This was what happened when

> *people came to stay: they forced you to view your life from outside, to*
> *realize that there was, come to think of it, something faintly mocking*
> *about a carton full of empty shells.*
> (Tyler, 2001: 94)

Anne Tyler's Rebecca is currently unmarried but can hardly be said to be living alone. She is at the centre of an increasingly complex extended family for whom she is always organising parties and get-togethers. Here she is about to prepare breakfast at the early stage of one of these gatherings. Her reflections on her habits and routines emerge when she sees herself under gaze of her kin.

Normative life

The normalities and regularities already outlined may sometimes merge with a third more normative understanding of everyday life. This is where these life events and routine practices together provide the basis for defining normality. The regularities not only come to define what human life as a whole is about or individuals' shifting identities as members of families and households, but also a collective sense of 'people like us'.

This construction of the normative is achieved in a variety of ways. We are familiar with the various ways in which the home becomes a model or symbol for the nation and distinctions between 'them' and 'us' move back and forth across these two socially constructed entities. The meeting of the domestic and the local or national merges with the meeting of the male and the female. Cultural and social theorists have become interested in the way in which Freud wrote about 'the uncanny', using the term '*unheimlich*' which literally means unhomely. While there are complexities in this analysis which we cannot go into at this point (in some ways the '*unheimlich*' may be located within the home; Chapman and Hockey, 1999) the familiarities of routine domestic life, life as we know it, may become the basis for distinctions between 'them' and 'us'. The concern with 'pretended family relationhips' in the 'Clause 28' controversy in Britain (Weeks, 1991) seems to reflect a concern with relationships which are constructed as striking at the heart of proper family life however many attempts might be made at 'normalisation'. Switching the frame of reference can, of course, provide a critique of the taken-for-granted sexual normalities (Dunne, 1999; Weeks *et al.*, 2001).

There are many ways in which the links between home and nation are achieved with the consequent marking off of the normal from the strange. The already cited paintings of Carl Larsen may provide a benevolent example. These paintings of domestic life become identified with a particular area of Sweden, Darlena, and with Swedishness itself. In a different Scandinavian context, Gullestad writes:

> *The Scandinavian concept of everyday life thus has an implicit*
> *institutional anchoring. The institutional anchoring in the home has its*
> *roots in a more general focus on the home in Scandinavian ... cultures.*
> (Gullestad, 1992: 48)

This is but one example of the equation of home and home-land. Food and feeding practices are also important here. National identities are often popularly defined by food and eating habits and food itself has a particular strong linking with ideas of home. Memories of food often constitute a key part of memories of home and these too merge with a sense of regional or national identity.

Another way in which everyday life is given a normative edge is through what is left out in representations of home or the private sphere. Thus Hockey (1999) reminds us about what is left out in most representations of home: old age, death and dying. Feminists have stressed the ways in which ideological constructions of home edit out themes of domestic violence or the loneliness and isolation experienced by some housewives. Normal everyday life is constructed in favourable terms. As well as the darker aspects of family living mentioned above, there are also discrepant household practices associated with gay and lesbian households, single mothers, and sometimes the households of migrant or alien groups.

It is, however, possible to overstate these representations of the more normative constructions of everyday life. Models of family life or the everyday practices of people like us may include notions of hospitality. This may be literal, a recognition of the needs of strangers or a set of understandings that, as in the French language, see the terms for host and guest as interchangeable. Or the hospitality may be more metaphorical including an openness to food and artefacts from different cultures. These more positive aspects of everyday domestic life should not be ignored. Similarly we might speculate that some of the fluidity which many people have identified with modern family living may contribute to a blurring of boundaries and a consequent weakening of the identification of home and nation. Nevertheless, it remains plausible to argue that understandings of everyday life continue to include this more normative element.

Everyday family life

I have suggested three overlapping meanings of 'everyday life', referring to life events, life's regularities and the normative. Clearly, these different meanings overlap with each other although they do not necessarily constitute a unified whole. Thus life events, especially the more unanticipated events associated with serious illness or disability or premature death, may upset the everyday regularities, although in the long run there will often be attempts to regularise these untoward events within a domestic context. Similarly, as I have suggested, normative constructions of everyday life do not necessarily have room for some of the darker aspects of individual or family life. However, it is likely that these different meanings do, on a day to day basis, constitute some kind of unity.

I have also suggested that these three, overlapping, meanings of everyday life do have strong links with ideas of the home (see Felski, 2000: 22–6), the family and family practices. In addition to the points made already we may stress that all three understandings of everyday life require significant others to define them and to provide them with meaning. These significant others need not necessarily be family members or people linked to us through birth or marriage but they frequently are. Thus, while birth, death and sickness happen to everyone, whether they are in family based households or not, they require their significance and meaning to be underlined and confirmed through interaction with others. It is the social and collective meanings that are given to birth, sickness or death that are important and these meanings continue to be frequently elaborated within family settings. In some cases, indeed, these life events bring about an alteration in the family identities of others, creating grandparents, uncles or aunts for example. Similarly, regular routines require significant others – indeed they are frequently conducted in response to these others – for them to merge into the on-going process of the construction of social worlds. Without these others, such routines might, under extreme circumstances, be viewed as signs of obsessiveness or individual pathology. Finally, the more normative definitions of everyday family life require and receive their affirmation in family contexts, although they may be underlined in political speeches or public rituals.

These constructions of everyday life have particular relationships with time. In some cases they reaffirm a sense of repeated or cyclical time whether we are talking about the major events of birth, death and marriage or whether we are talking about the daily or weekly routines of family living. These understandings of time may, it can be argued, merge with another sense of time as stretching back far into the past and far into the future, as something relatively unchanging. This is not only what 'we' have 'always' done but this is what others like us have done down the centuries. One only has to think of the inventions of tradition associated with Christmas celebrations to realise how illusory this sense of time is; nevertheless the sense of the naturalness of everyday family living often seems to entail this long view of time. Even the social dramas associated with unexpected death or major sickness may be linked, through cultural representations, to this long sense of time.

Similarly, these understandings have to do with place and with a sense of place. This place is usually described as 'the home', a site of complex and interlocking meanings (Chapman and Hockey, 1999). However, these understandings of everyday life are never wholly identified with one place, especially if we identify the home with a particular dwelling or piece of land. It might be advisable, indeed, to replace the potentially fixed idea of 'the home' for a more fluid sense of 'the domestic'. The sense of the domestic and the everyday may well include the street or the square and a particular home may merge with a particular locality. Or we may be dealing with a set of linked spaces, the homes of several people within a family network, the movement between separate dwellings following divorce or separation or the summer homes characteristic of many Nordic families. In the case of more 'nomadic' individuals in the modern world, the sense of place may be locked into familiar objects and familiar ways of being in the world.

Other sites

I have already indicated that the family is not the only site for the construction of everyday life and it may be helpful to consider some other sites where this work takes place. In a sense the question is a little unreal. Human life is frequently experienced as continuous and seamless and the sense of living in the everyday world is built up through numerous interactions and encounters. At this more phenomenological level it would appear that family living has no particularly privileged position. However, as has already been suggested, people do have a sense that certain life experiences or activities are more important than others and my attempt to distinguish between different meanings of 'the everyday' was an attempt to move to some clearer assessment of the place of the family in these processes.

One candidate for an alternative site for the construction of everyday life is the world of work. Clearly this can still be very important as the characterisation of work as a 'central life interest' or the recognition of the way in which people may become absorbed in or wrapped up in their work demonstrates. Work has its own familiar objects and repeated routines as well as often being a site where the familiar themes of sexuality, birth, marriage, sickness and death are explored through informal conversations.

Yet in many cases the role of work here may be somewhat paradoxical. If we take work to mean, as the conventional understanding would seem to stress, paid employment and if we assume that the idea of alienation still has some meaning, then work need not necessarily provide that sense of 'what life is all about'. In terms of the now classic sociological formulation, such work may be instrumental, a means to an end. Further, in more recent decades, the alienating tendencies associated with work may be augmented by changes in the workplace itself such as trends towards flexibility and casualisation as well as the growing emphasis upon consumption and consumerism.

We could extend this discussion to considerations of community and religion both of which have, at least in the past, been significant in the construction of the everyday in the senses discussed here. But there are good reasons to suppose that their significance has diminished in modern societies despite some important exceptions mostly associated with ethnic communities. However, it is important to give some emphasis to looser networks of friends or 'personal communities'. Pahl sees these as a possible source of a 'social glue', becoming more important as family ties become weaker along with more traditional understandings of community (Pahl, 2000). Such networks may be important in the processes of building up a sense of the 'everyday' in terms of all the meanings outlined here. Further, it may be that the relative looseness and openness of these personal communities might lead to changes in conventional understandings of everyday life.

Such other sites have to be remembered if only to underline the argument that family life does not have a monopoly in the construction of any of these senses of the everyday. Nevertheless it may also be argued that family is a thread that runs through and links work, community, religion and social networks. Family practices may still have an important role in building up and sustaining these multiple senses of everyday life, even where (as is highly likely) these practices overlap with other spheres of life. Indeed, my understanding of 'family practices' is one which is able to refer to practices that do not necessarily take place in the home or the household (Morgan, 1996). Talking about your children's problems at school with people at work is a family practice. Despite everything, family living still has an important place in the construction of everyday realities partly because it provides links across genders and, most importantly, across different age groups and generations. Further, in a socially mobile society, family living might also provide points of shared experience across class or educational divisions.

Questions of gender

Issues of gender have been mentioned in passing in the preceding discussion but it is now time to bring them more to the centre. In the case of the key life events, the following points may be listed:

1   The tendency for women to live longer than men.

2   The tendency for women to be more readily identified, ideologically and in terms of everyday life experiences, with caring.

3   The tendency within modern society for the parenting role to be more clearly identified with mothers, with the consequently more ambiguous understanding of what might be expected from fathers (Hobson, 2002).

What this means is that while many of the key life events are formally independent of gender, in practice the meaning of these events may vary between men and women. The consequences of this are numerous and wide-ranging. Thus the tendency to see women as being more emotional than men may reflect all the tendencies identified above and the more general identification of women with the management of some of the everyday life events. This is true both inside and outside family relationships.

In terms of the second set of meanings, dealing with life's regularities we may also note the tendency for women to be more readily identified with these practices. This identification has been noted in numerous studies from different countries although there is also clear evidence of a shift towards a more equal involvement on the part of men. There is debate, however, about the pace of these shifts and whether they represent a serious assumption of responsibilities on the part of men in households or an intensification of their 'helping', with the main responsibilities still resting with women. Again, the consequences for these familiar findings and observations may be far reaching. The relatively low status accorded to housework (and, indeed to the sociology of the family or still-life painting) may derive from this identification of women with the seemingly trivial and routine aspects of everyday life. There may be consequences for different understandings of time between men and women and for different constructions of domestic space (Davies, 1990).

The gendering of the more normative aspects of everyday life is somewhat more complex. Conventionally the sense of 'we' that these understandings imply also suggests, at the very least, a blurring of gender divisions. In some cases, as in the construction of the heterosexual norm, such a blurring, implying the unities of opposite sex couples, is almost inevitable or essential. It may also be the case that relatively clear gender divisions, underlined in the beliefs and practices of both men and women, may also constitute a major strand of the normative reality that is constructed. Here, of course, family and domestic relationships continue to play an important part where divisions of labour are not simply seen as questions of practicality but as being in some deep way related to the identities of men and women. Thus constructions of 'normal' people may stress both gender differences and heterosexuality and continue to be strongly linked to family practices.

Looking beyond the normative construction of heterosexual and gendered subjectivities within domestic relations to other normative understandings reflecting ethnic, local or national identities, the picture becomes a little more complicated. We may note, for example, the feminisation of ideas of the nation, so that there is a conflation of nation, family and gender in times of war and the male soldier is called upon to defend all three. However, the alternative representation of the fatherland points to a masculinisation of national culture although with similar consequences for gender divisions within the country. Yet again, both men and women may be called upon to play their part in national defence or national construction/reconstruction but, as the discussions of British women in two world wars clearly demonstrate (Braybon and Summerfield, 1987), in different ways and ones that sometimes call into question but do not systematically upset gendered divisions.

What is clear is that constructions of everyday life, in any sense of the word, clearly continue to involve gender divisions. This is perhaps not surprising in that gender divisions continue to be seen as a major, perhaps the major, social division and the one most resistant to forces of change. Indeed it may be that the identifications and links between family, gender and everyday life contribute to the normalisation or naturalisation of gender differences and inequality and therefore their perpetuation.

Conclusion: changing families and changing realities

I have argued that family practices play an important part in the construction of different, though overlapping, meanings of everyday life. Indeed family and everyday life might almost seem to be two sides of a coin. However, it might be suggested that what is presented here is too static. It ignores the fact that family relationships have undergone important changes, changes which might well have consequences for everyday life.

The kinds of changes I have in mind have frequently been listed and have often, taken together as a kind of package, been seen as indicators of a decline or at the very least a de-institutionalisation of family life. These changes include rising rates of divorce, increasing proportions of lone-parent households, increasing rates of co-habitation, rising numbers of single-person households and so on. To simplify a great deal (but to avoid some of the more value laden discussions associated with the words 'decline' or 'crisis') we may highlight two general features which might be important for our discussion:

1   A growing complexity in family based ties and networks. This is largely the consequence of rates of divorce and separation together with a rise in the proportion of 're-constituted' households and step-parenting. Kari Moxnes' term 'bi-nuclear' family points to some of these complexities (Moxnes, 1989). The particular complexities that arise include negotiating

the rights and responsibilities in relation to children on the part of divorced couples; exploring the differences between biological and social parenthood; and exploring the consequences for the wider kin network including former in-laws and grandparents.

2   A growing sense of ambiguity about what constitutes family life. In some cases, lesbian and gay households or cohabiting parents, for example, the definition of 'real' family life has been the subject of political or moral debate. But this is not simply a debate between different moral entrepreneurs. It is also experienced by the participants themselves when deciding whether a co-habitation is like marriage or something quite distinct or whether certain kin still count as family members following divorce or separation.

These complexities have been explored in a variety of ways in the literature including Giddens' discussion of 'pure relationships' (Giddens, 1992) and Beck and Beck-Gernsheim's (1995) discussion of individualisation. To put the matter simply, if there is a greater stress on the individual construction of one's own biography, does this necessarily weaken the association between family practices and everyday life creation discussed above? Further, the range of significant others involved in the re-affirmation of an understanding of everyday life might be more various and not confined to those who might conventionally be understood as members of one's family. These others may include lovers, friends or colleagues at work.

Turning to our three headings, we may suggest that the relationships between family practices and everyday life may have become more fuzzy or complex but still raise relevant considerations. To take 'everyday life events' first. It is not simply a question of the more or less obvious point that such events still continue to be important and matters of concern. While there have been and will continue to be considerable changes in the processes associated with birth and reproduction, life expectancy (especially in the more affluent sections of modern societies) and the control and management of sickness and disability, there seems to be little evidence of a significant departure from family relationships in providing a major part of the context for these life events and of a framework for giving them meaning. The evidence suggests that family (and gendered) relationships continue to be important in the mobilisation of much informal support and care and that friends and neighbours continue to have a different, although sometimes equal, importance as compared with family and kin. The kinds of changes that have been described above produce increasing complexities which should not be underestimated but do not sever the links between family practices and everyday life events.

In the case of 'life's regularities' again the picture would seem to be one of increasing complexity rather than a severing of the linkage. People faced with relatively novel domestic circumstances may develop all kinds of strategies to introduce some element of order and predictability into their daily lives. The title of Burgoyne and Clark's study of step-parenting, '*Making a Go Of It*' (1984), would seem to sum up this sense of managing and ordering increasing complexities of daily living. The kinds of juggling of everyday life commitments and responsibilities may have added layers of complexity following divorce or the establishment of a re-constituted household but will not be unfamiliar, especially to the women who continue to assume a large part of these responsibilities. The importance of 'coping' and being seen to be coping cannot be underestimated. What perhaps may be different is a sense of working with one's own resources and according to one's own script rather than according to something that was more taken for granted, handed down or externally imposed by custom or tradition.

The more normative aspect of the construction of everyday life is more difficult to assess in the light of these family changes. One version might suggest the development of more narrowly-based loyalties in the face of, or as a substitute for these changing or weakened family ties. Gangs or groups of male peers may, it is argued, see these peer group ties as a form of substitute family. Forms of xenophobia and racism may find their roots in the weakening or more ambiguous family structures. But it might be possible to argue the opposite case which would see increasing internationalism and openness to new or novel experiences as reflecting a loosening of ties of family and community. Yet again, in the past, strongly nationalistic movements have been identified with a strong pro-family ideology and an absence of practices which depart from the domestic norm. All one can say here is that there are important issues and connections to be explored further.

It needs to be stressed, at this point, that all these remarks are highly speculative. While it is possible to point to evidence in support of some of the arguments (discussion about domestic routines in the face of family change, for example) it must be remembered that many of these issues await greater conceptual clarification and more detailed research. I hope, however, that I have underlined their importance. Despite the far-reaching changes that have taken place and taking into account all the problems of definition it is likely that family practices will continue to play an important part in constructing and reproducing notions of the everyday world.

References

Askham, J. (1984) *Identity and Stability in Marriage*. Cambridge: Cambridge University Press

Beck, U. and Beck-Gernsheim, E. (1995) *The Normal Chaos of Love*. Cambridge: Polity Press

Berger, P.L. and Kellner, H. (1964) 'Marriage and the construction of reality', *Diogenes*, Vol. 46, pp.1–23

Brannen, J., Hantrais, L., O'Brien, M. and Wilson, G. (eds) (1989) *Cross-National Studies of Household Resources After Divorce*. Aston Modern Languages Club, Aston University

Braudel, F. (1981) *The Structures of Everyday Life*. London: Collins

Braybon, G. and Summerfield, P. (1987) *Out of The Cage: Women's Experiences in Two World Wars*. London: Pandora

Bryson, N. (1990) *Looking at the Overlooked: Four Essays on Still Life Painting.* London: Reaktion Books

Burgoyne, J. and Clark, D. (1984) *Making A Go Of It (A Study of Stepparents in Sheffield).* London: Routledge & Kegan Paul

Castells, M. (1998) *End of Millennium* (Vol III of 'The Information Age'). Oxford: Blackwell

Chapman, T. (1999) 'Spoiled home identities: the experience of burglary' in T. Chapman and J. Hockey (eds) *Ideal Homes? Social Change and Domestic Life.* London: Routledge, pp. 133–46

Chapman, T. and Hockey, J. (eds) (1999) *Ideal Homes? Social Change and Domestic Life.* London: Routledge

Craib, I. (1994) *The Importance of Disappointment.* London: Routledge

Davies, K. (1990) *Women, Time and The Weaving of The Strands of Everyday Life.* Aldershot: Avebury

Dunne, G.A. (1999) '"A passion for sameness"?: sexuality and gender accountability' in E.B. Silva and C. Smart (eds) *The New Family?* London: Sage, pp. 66–82

Eliot, G. (1985)[1859] *Adam Bede.* Harmondsworth: Penguin

Felski, R. (2000) 'The invention of everyday life', *New Formations*, Vol. 39, pp. 15–31

Garfinkel, H. (1987) *Studies in Ethnomethodology.* Cambridge: Polity Press

Giddens, A. (1992) *The Transformation of Intimacy: Sexuality, Love and Eroticism in Modern Societies.* Cambridge: Polity Press

Gullestad, M. (1992) *The Art of Social Relations: Essays on Culture, Social Action and Everyday Life in Modern Norway.* Oslo: Scandinavian University Press

Hobson, B. (ed.) (2002) *Making Men Into Fathers: Men, Masculinities and The Social Politics of Fatherhood.* Cambridge: Cambridge University Press

Hockey, J. (1999) 'The ideal of home: domesticating the institutional space of old age and death', in T. Chapman and J. Hockey (eds), *Ideal Homes? Social Change and Domestic Life.* London: Routledge, pp. 108–17

Morgan, D.H.J. (1996) *Family Connections.* Cambridge: Polity Press

Morgan, D.H.J. (1999) 'Risk and family practices: accounting for change and fluidity in Family Life', in E.B. Silva and C. Smart (eds), *The New Family?* London: Sage, pp. 13–30

Moxnes, K. (1989) 'Women after divorce: the Vienna centre project', in J. Brannen *et al.* (eds), *Cross-National Studies of Household Resources After Divorce.* Aston Modern Languages Club, Aston University, pp. 39–46

Pahl, R. (2000) *On Friendship*. Cambridge: Polity Press

Schutz, A. (1945) 'The homecomer', *American Journal of Sociology*, Vol. L, No. 4, pp. 363–76

Turner, B.S. (1993) 'Outline of a theory of human rights', *Sociology*, Vol. 27, No. 3, pp. 489–512

Tyler, A. (2001) *Back When We Were Grown-Up*. London: Quality Paperbacks Direct

Voysey, M. (1975) *A Constant Burden*. London: Routledge and Kegan Paul

Weeks, J. (1991) 'Pretended family relationships', in D. Clark (ed.) *Marriage, Domestic Life and Social Change: Writings for Jacqueline Burgoyne (1944-88)*. London: Routledge, pp. 214–34

Weeks, J., Heaphy, B. and Donovan, C. (2001) *Same Sex Intimacies: Families of Choice and Other Life Experiences*. London: Routledge

Chapter 4

Materials and morals: families and technologies in everyday life

Elizabeth B. Silva

Introduction

Writing at the beginning of the twentieth century, George Simmel (1911/12 and 1918) argued that human values do not exist other than through their objectified cultural forms. Thus, culture is the embodiment of (our)selves in various concretely represented forms. In contrast, fetishising things merely as forms, drains objects of meaning, and generates an apparently unproblematic materiality. Building on Simmel, how can we discern the processes of self-construction that are embedded in the objects of everyday living? What particular cultural practices are revealed in the study of human practices in relation to objects? Whose selves (in relation to gender, race, class, age and so on) are embodied in particular objectified forms?

We are constantly confronted by everyday discrepancies between what people claim matters to them and what they give their attention to. The research I draw on for my reflections in this chapter is an investigation of these everyday 'incongruences', as expressions of desires, negotiations, constraints and possibilities. Daniel Miller (1998) has noted that ambivalences, discrepancies and tensions are always present in examinations of material culture. Understanding and empathising with what people do with objects is a means of disclosing a world of practice as culture, he says. But feelings towards the use of objects do not simply depend on relations between user and thing. Both are inserted in a complex world of embedded meanings. While drawing on these reflections by Simmel and Miller, I confine the world of my reflections in this chapter to home living in contemporary Britain, by looking at family relationships of intimacy and a key set of technologies in the home. I discuss routines, activities and technologies in everyday home life, and the diverse moral orientations of contemporary family lifestyles. I draw on an in-depth study of 23 British families with school-aged children. Broad themes arising from the research include the following: (1) The research highlights the wide variety of patterns, strategies and experiments that people make in their everyday family arrangements, including people and things. (2) The care of children appears to be the key determinant of the temporal structuring of home life in homes with children. (3) While I find that conservative patterns of gender boundaries in home life are resilient, I also find strong evidence of fluid and diverse arrangements, which appear indicative of wider social and cultural trends. In this chapter I have two linked concerns. The first is with the expression of values in material life. The second is with the ways in which currently changing moralities impinge upon both the relationships between individuals living interdependently, and on the individual consumption of objects in the home. I draw on Adam Phillips' (1998: 3) understanding of morality as '... the way we set limits to wanting; the way we redescribe desiring so that it seems to work for us'. This view of morality allows for the inclusion of the other, or the perception of the other, and the perception of the 'actions' of objects, and of objects' particular morality (Silva, 2000).

In recent sociological literature, a starting point for considering the interaction of moralities and the consumption of technologies in the contemporary developed world can be found in the work of Zygmunt Bauman and Anthony Giddens. Bauman (1995) has argued that the need to become more moral increases in post-traditional societies because set rules have diminished. Thus, ordinary people are obliged to reflect upon their own actions in a world that demands that they be authors of their own biographies. The idea of self-reflexivity as a source of information for one's own actions, and the claim that behaviour is increasingly 'contingent', are both also developed by Giddens (1991). He makes a direct reference to the roles of new technologies in culture in late modernity, and sees in the construction of personal routines a way of individuals finding 'security' in an ever-changing technological and social world. However, in Giddens' (1992) ideal model of the 'contingent' relationship, conceived around financially independent childless individuals, routines appear as social events continuously open to change. My research, however, suggests that 'routines of care' are much less contingent, particularly when they involve dependents and interdependences. Taking up Bauman's general claim about the need for authorship, it is important to note that the liberty and power of individuals to choose their own paths is not the same for all, nor is the responsibility for choices made by all alike. Nevertheless, my research confirms that general cultural rules of behaviour are increasingly minimal and that people choose their own routines to fit diverse life circumstances. In this context, I find great resonance in Phillips' (1998) assertion that moral theories are stories about what is possible and acceptable for people to do. Perhaps in different events, perhaps in different periods in our lives, we experience and express different moralities. Morality is subject to innovation: you can improvise your morality within the culture's morality repertoire. Understanding that morality is about making connections to culture, I want to consider how contemporary home life arrangements express this social grasp of morality as concrete everyday matters.

The chapter falls into three main parts. Firstly, I introduce the 'ethnography of home life project', on which the discussion of this chapter is based. Secondly, I describe the routines, moralities and technologies in the home by looking at how they are incorporated into everyday life. I consider specifically the role of television because of particular research issues in this area I want to address. Thirdly, I examine a particular story of uses of the video and computer use in the home, to convey the diverse moral orientations that impregnate a plurality of contemporary family lifestyles. I focus on gender as a key category of differentiation, although I am aware that other differences are also relevant. In the conclusion I return to the issue of the interaction between technologies and family life and the contingent character of contemporary morality and raise some issues for research.

The ethnography of home life project

My project on the Ethnography of Home Life was initiated under the ESRC Research Programme 'Virtual Society?'.[1] A key concern was to investigate the relationship between people and technology in everyday life in the home. The definition of technology included artefacts and activities, involving artefacts, of all kinds relevant to everyday living. Activities included cooking, cleaning, childcare, leisure, work and education. The artefacts concerned were cookers, microwave ovens, fridges, dishwashers, washing machines, television, video, fax, computer, internet, mobile phone and any other that appeared important in specific contexts or relevant activity. Fieldwork in 23 households, all with school-aged children, was located in London (7), East Anglia (2), Lancashire (3), South Yorkshire (3) and North Yorkshire (8).

The sampling strategy aimed to cover a wide range of issues. Diversity in family life was taken into account through the inclusion of lone-parents, varied ethnic backgrounds and lesbian households. A variety of income levels was covered. Four families had annual incomes below £20,000 (two were very poor: lone parents on income support, or on student grant) and four above £40,000 (one was over £80,000). I was concerned to develop a sample to reflect the current diversity of family life in Britain. But, while my study reflects such diversity much more than some other studies of families in the UK, the majority of households in my sample (over two-thirds) still fits in with more conventional family models. Fifteen families were heterosexual, 'intact' and married, and two were reconstituted families of heterosexuals (previously divorced and with children from both previous and current marriages). Three were lone-parent families, and three were lesbian households (two of the lesbian households could be said to be 'reconstituted' families, where children did not have social parentage from birth with the partner of the biological parent). Eighteen families were 'white' (four of these were Jewish), and all were British nationals (one was Canadian/British and another was Jamaican/British). Two families were African-Caribbean, one was Asian, and two were mixed race white/African-Caribbean.

This was an in-depth qualitative study involving participant observation and detailed semi-structured interviews. In the 23 families 93 people were interviewed. The group of 42 adults included 24 women and 18 men. The 51 children included 23 girls and 28 boys. I conducted most of the interviews myself.[2] Extensive notes were made based on participant observations and relationships with interviewees. The semi-structured tape-recorded interviews covered three basic aspects: the household and the personal history, the technologies, and everyday activities. I also made use of the vignette technique, presenting participants with situations involving particular domestic problems and inviting them to consider what should be done. This technique is particularly suitable to the investigation of moral dilemmas. I detail it further in the third section of this paper.

To account for the structuring of people's everyday activities I generally asked them to tell me how a very common, average, weekday would go by from the time they woke up until they went to bed. Because some people's daily lives had different set patterns for different days of the week, we would normally talk about these differences. The use of technologies in everyday life was a central concern. The technologies spontaneously referred to by both women and men when talking about everyday affairs were mobile phone, email, telephone, internet, computer, fax machine, television, microwave oven and lawnmower. Women had a wider repertoire including also fridge-freezer, washing machine, iron, cooker, video (for entertaining children or working out), dishwasher, vacuum cleaner, tumble dryer and sewing machine. Of course, not everyone owned these technologies, nor did everyone refer to all of them. Numerous technologies that were relevant in the women's narratives of routines did not appear in men's narratives. Technologies of work predominated in men's discourses, whereas women mentioned more often *both* technologies of work (and education) and of housework. Housework technologies were talked about by all, however (generally at my prompting), in the context of talking about cooking, cleaning, laundry, childcare and leisure.

Routines, moralities and technologies in the home

The academic debate about technologies for housework has been kept largely separate from that on information technologies in the home (some exceptions are Livingstone, 1992, and Hirsch, 1992). However, the debates have much in common. They share a concern with the role of technologies in the organisation of social life. They also have commonly interpreted technology as externally structuring life in the household (Cockburn and Furst Dilić, 1994 edited collection is an exception). Feminist studies of technology have been particularly concerned with the relational aspects of gender, but for other studies of home technologies gender is less central. My study explores in-depth both technologies for housework and information technologies and looks at how they link with broader dimensions of home life.

The families in my study exhibited plurality and difference of lifestyles. Regarding domestic activities and uses of technologies the pattern of time spent in the home was particularly significant. Of the 23 families in my study there were six women and five men who were at home all day long. All of these men, but one (who was a civil servant but at the time was on disability benefit and doing a university degree), worked from home. In contrast, only one woman did work from home, although two others had some minor earning activities as well. These people who worked from home had very similar daily patterns and their routines were more fragmented than either the males who worked out of the home, or the women who were full-time home based. Looking at each of these individuals and their household patterns, I had very little sense of a traditional normative gendered pattern setting everyday routines overall. This is not to say that gender was unimportant. On the contrary, it is significant that only five men appeared to break out of the traditional mode of male routine in the home, while only five women remained in the traditional mode of female routine. More importantly, 19 women (out of a total of 24) did not operate within traditional female routine patterns of full-time housewifery, while 13 men (out of a total of 18) did still model their everyday life according to the male 'provider' model of family. Of these 13 men, five had no involvement with the care of children or housework in a normal weekday, and four had some involvement in the evenings only.

The patterns were split along lines of involvement with homely activities, mainly centred around the care of children. Normally only one adult was involved. Where the man cared for children he also did housework (but rarely the laundry), but no woman was present. Whenever a woman was present it was she who did the care of children, although a man might have helped, particularly in the evening routines (with homework, tea, play and bedtime rituals). Individuals and households showed fragmented and diverse patterns of everyday routines. Technologies did not appear to primarily structure or set any 'normal' pattern of domestic time. The key setter of routine for the women and men in my study was school hours. The second key structuring ingredient of daily life was paid-work.

These crucial setters of families' routines (school hours and paid-work) and the relative irrelevance of technologies for the time structures of domestic activities that was revealed, call into question previous claims that particular technologies have a central role in defining and sustaining contemporary routines of the everyday. Studies of media technologies, notably radio and television, have affirmed that a close dependency exists between domestic life and the time structures of broadcasting. I have therefore chosen to address the role of television in this section of the chapter, and I will refer to several previous studies that have pointed to the centrality of television in the construction of everyday routines in households, notably studies by Roger Silverstone *et al.* (1992) and David Gauntlett and Annette Hill (1999). With no disregard for the relevance of the media, and in particular, of the television for everyday life, I wish to qualify these arguments about its centrality in relation to the contemporary domestic living practices of families with children in contemporary Britain.

In *Consuming Technologies*, Roger Silverstone and Eric Hirsch (1992) assembled a rich collection of studies of media and information technologies in the domestic space. A quote in their introduction to the book, from Raymond Williams (1990: 191), says that 'A main characteristic of our society is a willed coexistence of very new technology and very old social forms'. The question for them was how to explain the paradox of the stability and 'continuity' of family relationships in face of the 'radical changes' in the consumption culture of information and communication technologies.

Williams' view was based on his work on television in the mid-1970s. But was family life stable then, or in the second half of the 1980s, as in Silverstone's own study, if it ever was? The stability of home life structured around the temporal frameworks of television broadcasting has become a common reference point in media studies of domestic space. For instance, to confirm that radio and television are part of our domestic culture, Tony Bennett (2002) reaffirms Silverstone's argument (1994: 24) that television provides '... in its programming and its schedules models and structures of domestic life'. Certainly some people's everyday lives are bound by broadcasting schedules, but this was not a dominant pattern for the families with dependent children in my study. By contrast, Silverstone (1993) saw information and communication technologies as a strong apparatus of domestic time-structuring that had a significant role in the 'forms and management of domestic life'. My research design had some similarities with his. His ethnographic study of 20 families, each consisting of two parents and school-age children, was done in the late 1980s. In another more recent study of time use and attitudes to new media, the structuring power of television is again also emphasised:

> *Certainly breakfast time is important in terms of the family coming together and then dispersing at different times to work or school, but it is the weekday early evening schedule, when the family regularly settles down to watch the news and Neighbours, before or with their evening meal, that proves to be the most reliable marker point in their discussion of daily routine.*
> (Gauntlett and Hill, 1999: 49)

What images of the family emerge from these pictures of home routines? Is there a sense of nostalgia in these accounts (perhaps a nostalgic dream of a normalised happy nuclear family life), and with them a sense of a missing appropriate replacement? How far do these accounts accurately represent contemporary British home life?

The findings of Silverstone, and Gauntlett and Hill differ significantly from my own. Though some families in my study tuned in to breakfast TV, after school children's television, and evening programmes, the media was by no means a central apparatus in the structuring of domestic time. Breakfast was not particularly important. The morning routines were quite separate for partners living together, with each one going about their own affairs. Only in four households did partners mention getting up at the same time; five women went to work earlier than their children's breakfast time; seven men left home without having any involvement with their children or even seeing them. Families did not regularly settle down together to watch evening television. The evening saw the appearance of the television in the narratives, mostly after the children went to bed. Watching daytime television figured very little in the routine accounts of either women or men. Two exceptions were Nancy, who turned the telly on first thing in the morning when coming into the kitchen and left it on until she went to bed, and Phil, who worked from home and timed his lunch break by the BBC *One O'Clock News*. Certainly the markers of daily routine in my study were mostly not media related. The fact that radio or television programmes provide some punctuation marking the day for some people (see also Hobson (1982), who remarked on the connection between housewives' domestic activities and the schedule of broadcast programmes, although the lives of most women changed considerably since the time of her research in the 1970s) does not mean that the media structures the time routines of everyday life.

All the homes had video-cassette recorders (VCR) (one had four sets, three had three sets each) but in two of them it had been broken for some time. All children watched video-tapes regularly, or occasionally. Adults had much less regular patterns. In 13 households some video-tape recording was done, mostly of children's programmes, but also for programmes that showed late at night, when there were clashes, or commonly when people were unable to watch a favourite soap or football match. Recordings were done selectively. Only Nancy said she recorded a lot (she was taping *Dallas* from a cable channel while we talked about media watching in her kitchen). The operation and use of the VCR seemed to be fairly split for women and men. The operation of video recorders has become easier in the past 15 years or so and the use of recorded material more widespread, but also gender relations in the home have become less stereotypically gendered. In the early 1980s, when Ann Gray (1987) did her study of video recorders, she found that they were largely the possession of fathers and sons. She then argued that uses of technology were not simply a matter of technical complexity, and suspected that women might have developed a calculated ignorance of operating the video, so that another domestic task would not be expected of them. Changes in lifestyle of women and men have made more evident the fact that video technology makes it possible to de-link broadcasting time and personal time, increasing the flexibility of individuals in relation to the temporal structures of the media. The ability of technologies like the video, answerphones and microwave ovens to 'store' and 'shift' time was noted by Silverstone (1993: 305–6). Yet, writing in the early 1990s, he saw these new technologies as having a possible effect on family life 'in the future' ('a *challenge* [either] to increase the *strains* … or to *master* them' – my emphases). This future may have been very near, as my data from the turn of the century show. I will explore further the gendered uses of video recording in the home in the next section of this chapter. For now, though, let us return to the pattern of television use found in my study.

Children in ten households watched TV before going to school. The television served adults as a kind of 'electronic nanny'. However, the television was on for most of the day in nine homes. Having the television on did not mean that people were watching any programmes in particular. For Katie the TV was on as 'background', for Nancy it was 'company', Lynn left it on so as 'not to feel alone', or, as in Richard's account: '… a lot of the time I'm not really watching TV, it's just things drifting over in my mind.'

Evening television watching fitted this mode for most people. TV was placed within a personal time of relaxation or of relating with one's partner. This was the everyday pattern for 28 (out of 42) of the men and women. Occasional evening viewing was mentioned by three other adults. It was often a 'time of one's own'. However, six women and four men did not report television watching as part of their everyday lives. This does not mean they did not ever watch television. Four of the households were generally TV-free, although only in one of them had people made a conscious decision not to have a television in the home.

There were particular characteristics about these four virtually TV-free households. They were among those with relatively unconventional lifestyles. In one household Tracy, an architect, was the only woman in this study who worked from home. She looked after two sons out of school hours. Her husband, Gabriel was also an architect. They both caught up with work in the evenings. In another household Phil, an actor and writer, worked mostly from home and was in charge of the daytime care of his four children. Chris's various jobs ('lollypop lady', school playground supervisor, hairdresser) meant that she came in and out of the house at various times of the day and evening. In the evening they both shared the care of the children and had some time together. In a third household a conscious decision of not having a television set had been taken. Marc worked from home and looked after the two younger children out of their school hours. Diane worked long hours and did not get directly involved in the home's daily affairs. In the fourth household Rebecca sometimes worked from home and Eleanor out of the home. Evening routines changed depending on whether Rebecca's daughter was there (usually half of the week), but for both women time was mostly spent to replenish the self or the relationship.

How could the divergent pictures of my study and those referred to above be understood? I have argued elsewhere (Silva, 1999), along with other feminists, that social research has often not accounted effectively for changes in family life and forms of intimacy because of the limited research questions being asked. In the studies of information technology in the home I have referred to, it is assumed that 'the family' occupies a relatively isolated sphere and operates as a system with consensual internal dynamics. In this context technologies appear to be imposed externally into people's daily home lives. In my study the ways people live home life show that technologies and relationships are imbricated into each other. Machines and objects are inserted within ways of living, in personal wants and interdependencies. It is significant that Silverstone (1993) identifies the family/household with a private sphere, which is weak because it is where only 'tactics' can operate, as opposed to the powerful public sphere, which is capable of a 'strategy'. Following Michel de Certeau (1988), the distinction between tactics and strategy implies that the realm where 'the family' operates allows only for the manipulation of events (tactics) in a wider context where the rules are pre-defined and imposed by external power (that of strategy). Interestingly, in de Certeau's book (1988: xix) the first example used to explain tactics is that of a housewife in a supermarket, 'confront[ing] heterogeneous and mobile data – what she has in the refrigerator, the tastes, appetites, and moods of her guests, the best buys and their possible combinations with what she already has on hand at home ...'. The housewife appears in a web, pulled into different directions by varied data and information demanding her to provide satisfaction for them all. The power of the consumer, of the cook, of the feeder, her ability to transform data into a dish and satisfying or not (this may be her choice!) the appetites of various mouths belongs, in de Certeau's model, to the world of the weak. The association of an assumed powerlessness with women and with 'the family' invites one to question de Certeau's assumptions. Would a male 'head of a household' be seen as a subject of will and power calculating and/or manipulating relationships (as in the definition of strategy – cf. p. 36), rather than as an actor confined to a repertoire of 'tactics'? The analysis is silent about power relations within families and regarding gender.

Against these assumptions, feminist theory has emphasised the interdependence and circularity of public and private spheres. A basic argument against the separation of public and private is that this distinction implies a hierarchy since the different spheres were designed to map on to differences of power between men and women. As David Morgan (1996) remarks, it is perhaps more useful to see the spheres of men and of women as each having their public and private faces. Particularly in home life, the distinction between what is public and private is ambiguous, and the boundaries between them are fluid and changeable. It is important not to lock the family in and away from wider social changes, or to see such changes simply as impacting upon family life. It is common to contain care, gender and particular moral issues within the walls of the home. However, the household is not an isolated structure nor are the moral issues raised in the home circumscribed to private life. Nor are these moral issues (despite their traditional depiction) beyond – or beneath – political concerns (cf. Tronto, 1993: 96). Shifting boundaries of contemporary family life imply the inclusion of different issues at different times and circumstances. The delineation of a private and public sphere is part of this and it requires that the position of 'the family' be reconsidered. Certainly, there is some stability in family life, which exhibits both continuities and diversity. This is why the picture that family life has been eroded by fast changes in wider society is as false, and as dangerous, as the one that the family remains the same in a context of rapid social and technological changes.

Moral orientations

One of the themes of my wider study is that household roles and divisions of labour do not simply reflect economic rationales but are based on negotiations involving moral issues of what was 'proper' for partners and children to do. Patterns of earning and caring were established in relation both to concrete situations in the labour market and in interaction between partners. They might have been more or less conventional in terms of gender relations, but they also involved reflexive choices regarding how to deal with issues relating to the individuals' particular life stage circumstances. They represented moral choices.

The morality I refer to here, while engaging with Bauman's (1995) argument that we are all becoming more moral, is based on moral sentiments (Phillips, 1998; Tronto, 1993), not on reason. This means, following Carol Gilligan (1982), that morality is not formal and abstract, but that it is tied to concrete and material circumstances. This echoes Bauman's concerns, although it points more firmly towards practices and concrete actions. Morality is not based on a set of principles, but is an activity: it is the acting out in culture of our wants. For Gilligan, morality is grounded in the daily experiences and moral problems of real people in their everyday lives. She disputed the dominant western ethical code of objectivity and rationality associated with the masculine experience and argued that to reflect a more feminine experience a more adequate morality needed to include an ethics of care based on connectedness and a desire not to harm. Gilligan's stress on gender as a key category of difference in moral thinking was criticised for offering an essentialist view of women's morality, and from 1986 on she emphasised different gender perspectives in moral reasoning as framing problems differently. While concerned with gender differences in expressions of morality, I believe it may be more relevant to consider 'social' morality (Finch, 1989) as a wider frame of reference for the ways in which people live their lives under different social circumstances. Like gender, class has also been an invisible but crucial distinction in universalistic moral reasoning. When arguing that 'racialising culture is ordinary', Gail Lewis (Chapter 7 in this book) also makes a claim that another key category of moral thinking is race.

The part of my research specifically concerned with issues of morality included the use of a set of vignettes (four for the adults and two for the children). In practical terms this involved reading the stories of the vignettes to women, men and children and asking their opinion. I started with my own set stories, but this resulted in further related stories being told by participants about themselves, their friends and families.

In this section I will consider the issue of the moral orientations of my adult participants in relation to gender and technology in the home by using one particular vignette. This is a long vignette about two hypothetical characters in a particular circumstance. The interviewee (women and men were interviewed separately) was invited to respond to these characters' dilemmas. As a method, the use of vignettes recognises that meanings are social, while allowing an interviewee to define the meaning of the situation for her or himself. Also, it assumes that morality may be specific to particular situations (Finch, 1987).

The vignette technique brings out both the personal and the public morality of relationships, allowing for my concern with the exploration of individual wants within the perception of the other (persons and objects) and in culture. I used a method of building in a temporal dimension and altering the circumstances of the hypothetical characters at a later stage. Respondents were invited to make a choice about what 'ought to' happen in the first and second stages. What happened in the second stage was independent of a respondent's view of the first stage. This increased the complexity of my stories. I read out my vignettes at the end of a long conversation (sometimes over the course of more than one day) about the home, activities, technologies and personal life.

The first part of the vignette ran as follows:

Jane and Andrew had been married for 15 years and had two children. Jane wanted to buy a VCR. Andrew didn't. Eventually they acquired one. At first Andrew ignored it. But Jane learned how to operate it and used it very often. One day Andrew wanted to watch a football match but was unable to do it at the time it was shown. He asked Jane to record it for him. Jane did it. Then, it happened a second time and Jane thought Andrew should learn how to record programmes and taught him how to do it. But instead of doing it himself, Andrew kept asking Jane to record things for him. One day she refused and Andrew claimed that, since she wanted the VCR, she ought to record programmes for him. Do you think that:

(a) Jane should maintain her refusal.

(b) Andrew was right and Jane should record the programmes.

(c) Jane should carry on doing it until Andrew learns to operate the VCR.

I often probed responses by asking 'why?' following each choice made. The issues addressed in the vignettes were often also addressed elsewhere. Before talking about the vignettes I had invariably talked with respondents about the technologies in the home, and the use of video recorder, computer and internet had been particularly addressed. Comparing the statements of the partners, there were collusions, 'false' accounts and contradictory statements. Of course, the vignettes only disclosed beliefs, but they triggered accounts of actual happenings, or complemented accounts given previously.

I constructed this particular vignette in a way that would trigger responses taking account of gender, use of resources and claims on partner's expertise, time and interest. The elements of my vignette so far were: (1) A heterosexual couple with children in a long-term relationship. (2) Conflict over purchase, followed by agreement and acquisition. (3) Female technical expertise combined with male non-expertise and male demands of female technical services. (4) Female refusal resulting in conflict. The story ended ambiguously. What views emerged?

Most men thought Jane should have carried on recording programmes for Andrew until he had learned, but most women thought that Jane should have refused to carry on doing it. While only four men thought Jane should have refused to tape record programmes for Andrew, nine women thought Jane should have refused to do it. No one thought Andrew was right in thinking that Jane should have carried on tape recording for him indefinitely. All thought he should have learned to do it himself.

The opinions were not gendered in any traditional way:

> It's like he's saying to her: 'it's yours'. Like: 'You've had the kids, you should do all the chores for the children ye know, I'm just sort of in the background and I don't want to learn to change nappies ...'. You have to share the jobs. In a situation with me I'd say to Phil ... 'I feel you should do it'.
> (Chris Webster)

> It's incredibly annoying: this was the situation I was in with Karen: she decided she couldn't do it, so I had to do it ... she couldn't be bothered to learn ... it makes you nervous because you think if it doesn't work, I'm going to be in trouble. It's not just men who do this!
> (Rebecca Turner)

> ... having a situation similar to this in our house where Robert doesn't know how to programme the recorder and I'm the one who does it, I don't mind doing it ... but if ever he complained to me ... I should say: 'Well, that's it, you learn to do it yourself!'.
> (Frances Gibson)

Of course, issues of masculinity emerged: some remarked that there was role reversal in the story, others identified with Andrew remarking on a possible technophobia, in some cases undisclosed. Robert Gibson, for instance, did not tell me that he did not know how to record video-tapes. I talked to him about this after talking to Frances and asked him why he did not tape things. 'Cos I'm not normally here for what's recording', he said. I said: 'But you could pre-programme the video'. He replied: 'Oh, Frances does it.' Yet, he thought Andrew should have learned.

> ... like most men ..., I mean, you ask my husband to video something – zilch, he doesn't really know how to work it ... I suppose I'm more logical, I can see what's got to be done ... say, like – the dishwasher that's new ... I can see how it's got to be done ...
> (Rena Rock)

> ... when it comes down to technical equipment like working a VCR to record something don't ask me! Rena very much says – 'Oh well, if you wanna watch a programme you'd better do it yourself!' ... There have been occasions when I've come home, and what I've found is that one of the boys has done it ... But we're having the same arguments with the PC... I just don't know how they can do it so quick and actually know where they're going, click, click, click ...
> (John Rock)

> ... I ended up doing stupid things, like Andrew, because I wanted to cover the fact that I didn't know to use it ...
> (Richard Bartholomew)

> Not everyone is technically minded.
> (Ray Wells)

> I'm a bit easy going ... I tend to leave it all to Ray. I'm an Andrew! Ha ha ha.
> (Lindsay Wells)

However, not everyone is at ease with not knowing about technologies. Disclosing technical incompetence was not just a problem for men like Robert Gibson. At the Mitchells', Nancy did not tell me that her husband bought a new VCR with 'video plus' ('so easy, you just tap in the number of the programme from *TV Times* and it's done for you'). According to Alfred: 'She wouldn't learn how to do it in the old one'. But Nancy's comment on the vignette was, in the light of her husband's comment, one of faked technological ability:

> Well, it wouldn't happen in our household, whatever we buy we've all got to know how it works really ye know, especially – but they're so easy to use and – we've had videos for years so – I couldn't comment on that because it wouldn't arise ...
> (Nancy Mitchell)

The women and men, and women and women, living in the same home had generally different views about what should be done. Only three couples expressed the same views. The Goodmans were the most traditional, but the men in both the Wells and Webster homes worked from home and were the principal carers of their children on a daily basis. While I cannot explain the accident of agreement between men and women in these three households, it is important to remark that morality in households is commonly diverse, with individuals taking different views about what to give, what to take and what to ask for in particular circumstances. I will come back to this point.

The second part of the vignette presented a resolution of the previous dilemma and brought in a time dimension and a newer dilemma.

Eventually Andrew learned to operate the VCR.

One year later Andrew decided to buy a computer with internet connection. Jane was not too keen on the idea but accepted it. After the computer was first installed Andrew used it all the time. But then Jane learned how to use it and discovered many things that interested her in the net. In the evenings she would spend time navigating instead of watching TV with Andrew or keeping him company while he was having his dinner. Andrew resented this. Do you think that:

(a) Jane should not do the net and keep Andrew company.

(b) Andrew and Jane should come to an agreement about when they each should use the computer.

(c) Andrew should veto Jane's use of the net.

In this part the elements of the story were: (1) A new potential conflict over purchase, followed by agreement and acquisition. (2) Male technical expertise and female expertise. (3) Female concentrated focus of interest away from husband. (4) Husband's resentment. What views emerged?

Respondents were overwhelmingly in favour of Jane and Andrew reaching an agreement. Only Brenda Addison (a quasi-full-time housewife) found that Jane should not do the net to keep Andrew company. Two men thought Andrew should veto Jane's use of the net. Interestingly they were both self-defined 'technophiles'. One, Scott Bird, was married to a quasi-full-time housewife, who was supportive of his homely needs. The other, Ronald Chambers, who had a relationship committed to gender equality, identified with Jane in gender role reversal:

> ... I identify. Sometimes I will be so tired she would watch TV, I leave her and do surf the net – it takes me away ... It's a very real problem. But, what do I think about this?... the simple thing to do is to negotiate time ...

Rose Chambers also identified with the situation:

> We had the same problem. We talked, now I say when Ronald spends too long with the computer.

Gabriel White also identified. His wife worked full-time from home as an architect and they both used the computer and the internet for work, and sometimes recreation.

> *I go intensely in the net when I do something related to a job. You have to go browsing. Andrew should give her time to become experienced. If he's concerned they need to discuss.*

Fear of addiction was also a reason why use should be curbed even if in a negotiated and not imposed manner.

> *... [the internet] it's so addictive ... you hear about internet widows and widowers and you can see why that happens so ... go on it for a certain length of time and then make yourself come off it 'cos I think it is an addiction in many ways, just like television can be.*
> (Irene Hays-Field)

Mike Goodman, living in a relationship of traditional gender divisions said he 'wouldn't restrict, apart from the cost'.

Another outcome, a negative one, might be divorce:

> *Ian Hays-Field took a long pause, grumbling, smiling and then he said: 'I think Jane should use it less.'*

> *Elizabeth:*   *'Should Andrew ask her to do that?'*

> *Ian:*   *'No, Andrew should realise ... he would go out to the pub, leave her to it.'*

> *Elizabeth:*   *'He should go out to the pub and leave her doing the net?'*

> *Ian:*   *'Well, yeah, the problem seems to be that he wants her company and she's not letting him have it, but his company is available to her if she wants it so ... remove that availability.'*

> *Elizabeth:*   *'And you think that ...'*

> *Ian:*   *'This marriage is going to end in tragedy!'*

A similar view was presented by Daniel Seaman:

> *They don't seem to have that much in common, do they? I think there's a divorce in there!*

The context of the story of my vignette was interpreted and judged by respondents. The needs of the people in the story and my narrative were not taken as absolute. 'The proper thing to do' emerged from respondents' own construction of the situation outlined. There was clearly more than one 'true' way of reading these accounts. Respondents filled in the gaps about their knowledge of the conditions of the characters by making their own (mostly undisclosed) personal assumptions. Respondents' moral reasoning seemed to fit in very closely with Janet Finch's (1989) argument that moralities are not fixed but that they change with changes in the life course and with different situations. It also clearly confirms Phillips' (1998) assertion that morality is subject to innovation: you can improvise your morality within the culture's morality repertoire, since morality is about making connections to culture.

One inherits morality, one also is taught morality, and moreover, one chooses morality through an inventive process, commonly in relationship with others. Relationships with objects and the moralities we input into our uses of objects are also part of our cultural morals.

As stressed by Selma Sevenhuijsen (1998), in practically all contexts of behaviour we are confronted with questions of judgement and responsibility. In reflecting on 'how to act' our agency has all to do with interpretation. Clearly, the work with morally thinking and acting persons requires a conceptual framework of moral subjectivity. Studying families, Janet Finch (1989) and with Jennifer Mason (1993) have stressed that moral values are not political or cultural conflicts, but that ideas about moral obligations derive from the wider culture and from very personal circumstances. Janet Finch (1989) refers to these notions as normative guidelines and negotiated commitments. She argues that people mobilise obligations through the responses of other people. An individual's understanding of the social order helps to reproduce it accordingly because, in acting, she (or he) makes specific claims about which rights and obligations are going to be recognised in a particular situation. This is broadly how individuals interpret normative guidelines. These normative guidelines about how one should act have a role in the process of negotiations, which is not necessarily free of coercion, persuasion and manipulation. Often negotiations between men and women imply different power based on different gender positions and pre-suppositions in society and culture. In the moral orientations of the participants in my study there was an understanding that in family relationships people are dependent, needy, have complementary abilities and are interdependent (Griffiths, 1995). This is why the conditions in which people make decisions entail certain difficulties. In the opinions of participants in my study there was rarely a hint of a correct moral position. Mostly, there was no fundamental or judgemental position. This was also the way they organised their daily routines.

My findings resonate with evidence in recent feminist literature about family life in Britain in late modernity. Finch and Mason (1993), for instance, remarked that senses of responsibility develop over time, through interactions, where people balance the giving and receiving. Even in marriage, or parental relationships, responsibilities do not flow automatically from a formal tie. However, the fluidity and contingency of family living that appear in my research firmly point in a direction different from the one in the study by Silverstone (1993, and with colleagues, 1992) referred to above, and suggest a different way of looking at the interaction of the material and the moral.

Silverstone *et al* (1992: 15) develop the concept of 'the moral economy of the household' as a means of 'understanding the nature of the relationship between private households and public worlds and the role of communication and information technologies in that relationship.' While this work importantly recognises the role of moral reasoning in consumption decisions and the distinctive culture of home life, an idea of a 'generic family' is typically taken for granted. Families are regarded as having 'necessarily conservative cultures', which are disrupted by the consumption of new technologies.

There are conflicts over use and location; ownership and control; rights to access ...

There are anxieties to be dealt with: anxieties about the disruption a new technology might create for the security of familiar routines and rituals, the challenges it might present to an individual's competence or skill; or the threat it might pose to the moral values of the family. (Silverstone, 1996: 224; my emphases)

Of course, emotions accompany changes in life. They may be triggered by technologies or by any other non-human or human factor. Also emotions towards novelties can be of joy, expectation or pleasure, contrary to the battle camp idea of the family struggling against impositions of the external world, which emerges from Silverstone's vision. Certainly households domesticate technologies, but not just because these are perceived as threats, disruptions or causes of anxieties. Moreover, as my research insists, 'the family' does not have a single morality and different technologies are related to users in varied manners. A consequence of conceiving the family as a weak private sphere, separate from the powerful public one, is to place technologies as *external* to everyday life. Information and communication technologies appear to impact upon but not to be a part of everyday life. Yet, interactions with technologies are pervasive in ways people relate to each other. New technologies generate new ways of relating in a continuous transformation of everyday life.

Conclusions

My discussion of domestic routines and technologies in everyday life and the diverse moral orientations connected to contemporary family lifestyles shifts the debate on material and moral dimensions of home life away from an interaction between 'external' technologies and a 'unitary' family life. I have done this by following two complementary routes to emphasise the diversity of patterns of living and the moral orientations that are linked to these patterns.

Firstly, I demonstrated empirically the *diversity* of internal patterns of family life and temporal routines. I also stressed the scope that families and individuals have for negotiation and allocation of two essential family activities of caring and earning. I argued here, as I have done elsewhere (Silva and Smart, 1999), about the need to accept diverse forms of intimacy and caring as legitimate forms of family life in order to account for the process of cultural change so evident in contemporary everyday experiments in family practices. Traditionally established family 'rules' based on a Beveridge-style model of a male breadwinner with dependent children and wife have been strongly challenged by an evident diversification of family practices.

Secondly, I have employed a literature on *moralities* to open up ways to explore choices in how technology and gender relations are shaped within families. Clearly the new models of living are not generated in a vacuum, nor are the new technologies. They are both part of the same social process of transformation of contemporary social life. While choice is not unconstrained, the scope to choose has increased in a social context that demands continuous reflexive choices about how to live. As researchers and policy makers we need to take seriously people's stories about how they get by and about what they need to live well. These stories, together with their incongruences, ambivalences and discrepancies, do not just reveal culture but also produce culture.

Movements between external and internal worlds of individuals, small groups or societies at large are difficult for the researcher to apprehend. External pressures and constraints exist, and certainly individual agents cannot act as if 'anything goes', even in our contemporary culture, where personal choice and personal responsibility have increased as certainties about prescribed modes of living are eroded. This study stressed two major constraints on how everyday life is organised and negotiated: school hours and paid work. Individuals' scope for facing up to these constraints is minimal within a particular life course phase. Yet, there are significant emerging practices that reveal more varied ways of combining resources and choices. In this combination materiality and morality can be seen, and understood, as both resource and choice.

Notes

1   ESRC award no. L132251048. Sixteen families are part of a study carried out with colleagues from the Institute of Communication Studies at the University of Leeds. I also benefited from funding from Sociology at the University of Leeds, where I worked at the start of this project, and from the National Everyday Cultures Programme in Sociology at the Open University.

2   Emma Heron helped me with the study of four households, and Pippa Stevens with another three households. Pauline Windsor transcribed the audio-taped interviews. Their assistance was invaluable. I am grateful for all participants in this study. They are here identified by pseudonyms.

References

Bauman, Z. (1995) *Life in Fragments*. Oxford: Blackwell

Bennett, T. (2002) 'Home and everyday life', in T. Bennett and D. Watson (eds) *Understanding Everyday Life*. Oxford: Blackwell

Cockburn, C. and F,rst Dilic, R. (eds) (1994) *Bringing Technology Back Home*. Buckingham: Open University Press

de Certeau, M. (1988) *The Practice of Everyday Life*. Berkeley, CA: University of California Press (original English translation: 1984)

Finch, J. (1987) 'Research note: the vignette technique in survey research', *Sociology*, Vol. 21, No. 1, pp. 105–14

Finch, J. (1989) *Family Obligations and Social Change*. Cambridge: Polity Press

Finch, J. and Mason, J. (1993) *Negotiating Family Responsibilities*. London: Routledge

Gauntlett, D. and Hill, A. (1999) *TV Living. Television, Culture and Everyday Life*. London: BFI and Routledge

Giddens, A. (1991) *Modernity and Self-Identity. Self and Society in the Late Modern Age*. Cambridge: Polity Press

Giddens, A. (1992) *The Transformation of Intimacy*. Cambridge: Polity Press

Gilligan, C. (1982) *In a Different Voice*. Cambridge, MA: Harvard University Press

Gilligan, C. (1986) 'Reply', *Signs*, Vol. 11, No. 2, pp. 324–33

Gray, A. (1987) 'Behind closed doors: women and video', in H. Baehr and G. Dyer (eds) *Boxed In: Women on and in Television*. London: Tavistock Books, pp. 38–54

Griffiths, M. (1995) *Feminisms and the Self*. London: Routledge

Hirsch, E. (1992) 'The long term and the short term of domestic consumption: an ethnographic case study', in R. Silverstone and E. Hirsch (eds) *Consuming Technologies. Media and Information in Domestic Spaces*. London: Routledge

Hobson, D. (1982) *'Crossroads': The Drama of a Soap Opera*. London: Methuen

Livingstone, S. (1992) 'The meaning of domestic technologies: a personal construct analysis of familial gender relations', in R. Silverstone and E. Hirsch (eds) *Consuming Technologies. Media and Information in Domestic Spaces*. London: Routledge

Miller, D. (1998) 'Why some things matter', in D. Miller (ed.) *Material Cultures*. London: University College London Press, pp. 3–21

Morgan, D. (1996) *Family Connections. An Introduction to Family Studies*. Cambridge: Polity Press

Phillips, A. (1998) *The Beast in the Nursery*. London: Faber and Faber

Sevenhuijsen, S. (1998) *Citizenship and the Ethics of Care: Feminist Considerations of Justice, Morality and Politics*. London: Routledge

Silva, E.B. (1999) 'Transforming housewifery: dispositions, practices and technologies', in E.B. Silva and C. Smart (eds) *The 'New' Family?* London: Sage, pp. 46–65

Silva, E.B. (2000) 'The cook, the cooker and the gendering of the kitchen', *The Sociological Review*, Vol. 48, No. 4, pp. 612–28

Silva, E.B. and Smart, C. (1999) 'The "new" practices and politics of family life', in E.B. Silva and C. Smart (eds) *The 'New' Family?* London: Sage

Silverstone, R. (1993) 'Time, information and communication technologies and the household', *Time and Society*, Vol. 2, pp. 283–311

Silverstone, R. (1994) *Television and Everyday Life*. London: Routledge

Silverstone, R. (1996) 'Future imperfect: innovation and communication technologies in everyday life', in W.H. Dutton (ed.) *Information and Communication Technologies. Visions and Realities.* Oxford: Oxford University Press, pp. 217–31

Silverstone, R. Hirsch, E. and Morley, D. (1992) 'Information and communication technologies and the moral economy of the household', in R. Silverstone and E. Hirsch (eds) *Consuming Technologies. Media and Information in Domestic Spaces.* London: Routledge

Simmel, G. (1911/12) and (1918) 'The concept and tragedy of culture' and 'The conflict of modern culture', in D. Frisby and M. Featherstone (eds) (1997) *Simmel on Culture.* London: Sage

Tronto, J.C. (1993) *Moral Boundaries. A Political Argument for an Ethics of Care.* New York: Routledge

Williams, R. (1990) *Problems in Materialism and Culture.* London: Verso

Chapter 5

Sexual technologies/domestic technologies: pornography as an everyday matter

Jane Juffer

Pornography hardly conjures up images of the everyday. Its articulation to seedy arcades and unsavoury internet prowlers is due in part to policy debates that oppose pornography to the everyday in order to legitimate its regulation. Furthermore, participants in the porn debates often extract it from the mundane conditions in which it is produced, circulated, and consumed in order to represent political positions that have very little to do with the everyday uses to which pornography is usually put.

Historically, these positions have been framed in terms of repression and liberation. In their uneasy alliance, moral conservatives and anti-porn feminists have argued that porn turns all men into oppressors/potential rapists and all women into victims of either physical violence or objectification. Answering these charges, the pornography industry asserts that actors 'choose' to perform, invoking a voluntarism that ignores social conditions and that presumably frees consumers to enjoy a wide variety of texts because they need not worry about the conditions in which porn is produced. Another version of autonomy appears in civil libertarian arguments that champion the rights of individuals and admonish opponents of porn to simply 'not buy it if you don't like it'. More complex arguments have been articulated by 'pro-sexuality feminists'; however, these critics often take refuge in a politics of transgression that relies on interpretation to make claims about the unpredictability of the sexual psyche. In some of these arguments, pornography is worthy of academic study precisely because of its ability to evade materiality, and in this evasion to better comment on norms regarding gender and sexuality.[1]

In the nearly three decades of debates around porn since second-wave feminism raised it as a primary concern, we remain largely mired in a fruitless back and forth about the status of women in relation to the genre: hapless victims or transgressive agents? The question is no longer a useful one, if indeed it ever was. The effects of pornography have been given the power to shape the lives of women, children, and men. This inflational rhetoric has kept us from considering a much more important, albeit less dramatic, set of questions: what are the material and discursive conditions in which *different kinds* of porn are produced, distributed, obtained, and consumed? What is the relationship between these different sites, and how do these relationships shape women's access to porn? Rather than a politics of identity based on a removal from or transcendence of the everyday, I propose a politics of mobility and access – a spatial understanding of porn within the routines of everyday life. In the Foucauldian spirit, then, the question becomes not one of liberation/repression but rather of practices: 'Isn't the problem rather that of defining the practices of freedom by which one could define what is sexual pleasure and erotic, amorous and passionate relationships with others. The ethical problem of the definition of practices of freedom, it seems to me, is much more important than the rather repetitive affirmation that sexuality or desire must be liberated' (Foucault, 1984: 283). Accordingly, I am interested not in what women *experience* when they consume porn but rather in the routes/paths they have to travel in order to find the time and space for consumption at home.

Tracing these paths in pursuit of a politics of access requires us to consider the home as a primary site of determination. Porn and the home have been antithetical in regulatory discourses, and in part because of this articulation, much feminist work on porn has not considered the home or sexually explicit texts that jive with domestic routines – such as sex education videos, popular literary erotica, and soft-core cable for couples. Much feminist and queer work on sexuality has favoured transgressive sexual acts and public performances, such as Annie Sprinkle's 'public cervix announcements', works that defy attempts to contain sex to private sites. Without dismissing the importance of work on sex and the public sphere, I argue that we must not cede the territory of the home to conservatives nor dismiss texts that try to fit within conceptions of domesticity just because they do not correspond to academic assumptions about what constitutes a transgressive/public act. The home, in all its manifestations, is, after all, where most women consume sexually explicit texts; my emphasis on the everyday is meant to capture the materiality of the home while retaining its constant connection to other sites.

Sites of porn's circulation have multiplied via new media technologies in a manner that blurs the public/private distinction even as it preserves the specific materiality of the home as a site of consumption targeted in the global porn economy. AT&T, Time Warner, and many other 'reputable' companies are now bigger players in the porn industry than *Hustler* and *Playboy*. In sometimes ironic fashion, then, the globalisation of porn increases its contact with the everyday. For example, the British-based company Gold Group International owns Ann Summers, the chain of middle-class women's sex shops, as well as Birmingham City Football Club. Blockbuster, the bastion of family values, is now stocking erotic series by Playboy, Ambrosia Productions, Zalman King's *Red Shoe Diaries*, and others in the 'couples' porn' genre. In this relative normalisation, the consumption of porn has become more of a consumer choice for various demographic groups and less a marker of morality.

What we might identify, then, as a shifting moral economy around the consumption of porn must also be situated within a shifting moral economy around the shape of the household. In both the USA and Britain, there are indications of a greater acceptance of alternative family structures, such as lone mothers, gay and lesbian parents – although that 'acceptance' also prompts calls for the renewal of the traditional family.[2] I cannot do justice here to the complex developments in contemporary family life; however, my argument is premised on a notion developed in nuanced fashion by Elizabeth Silva in Chapter 4 in this book, that '"the family" does not have a single morality and different technologies are related to users in varied manners'. I would argue that when household economies shift to accommodate gender roles and sexual practices not predicated on sex as procreative or even partnered and on the mother as exclusive caretaker, the chances increase that domesticity will not be posited as antithetical to sexual pleasure. This means that domestic technologies for women no longer include just the washing machine, microwave, and dishwasher but also the vibrator, the porn video, the on-line sex catalogue, and a volume of literary erotica.

In this chapter, I focus on mothers and access to erotica/porn, constructing what Foucault calls 'an archaeology of sexual fantasies'. He says, 'I try to make an archaeology of discourse about sexuality, which is really a relationship between what we do, what we are obliged to do, what we are forbidden to do in the field of sexuality, and what we are allowed, forbidden, or obliged to say about our sexual behaviour. That's the point. It's not a problem of fantasy; it's a problem of verbalization' (Foucault, 1982a: 125–6). What can be said about mothers and sex? Obviously, there is some connection between 'what can be said' and 'what can be fantasised', but the point is not to draw some falsely linear connection. The point, rather, is to expand what can be said such that the *possibilities* for the expression of fantasies and sexual practices also proliferate. We must analyse, thus, the rules that forbid certain behaviour; one way to do that is to analyse policies that govern mothers and sexuality. I will trace a history of porn regulation in the USA that until very recently has positioned women as either vulnerable creatures in need of protection or moral guardians of the domestic sphere. Then, I will consider how other policy spheres regulate women's sexuality – namely welfare reform and immigration policy. Moral and economic issues weigh especially heavily on women targeted by various state policies; the sexuality of women receiving welfare and immigrant women, for example, continues to be policed by the state. These policy realms in turn help shape industry decisions about whom to target as erotica and porn consumers. Here, I consider three sites – Blockbuster, Borders, and Barnes and Noble bookstores, and sex toys sold through women-friendly catalogues and internet sites. All represent, in different ways, the mainstreaming of porn for women – the transformation of the domestic sphere into one of sexual pleasure. However, access is still uneven, predicated on an economic self-sufficiency that translates into 'good morals'; if these conditions exist, the consumption of erotica/porn is more likely to become a 'choice' women make in the interest of healthier, fuller personhood.

Finally, it must be acknowledged that what mothers are 'obliged to say about sexual behaviour' is a matter exceeding sex. In other words, there is often simply no time to say anything about sex, because there is too much work: childcare, housework, jobs, cars, gardens, pets, shopping, etc. How is mothers' sexual mobility determined by practices not related to sexuality? How are paths to sexual practices determined by labour, especially childcare, which leaves little time and space for care of the erotic self, for practices of freedom?

Little girls and mothers

Great Britain established the legal precedent for the protection of women in the private sphere with the passage of its first anti-obscenity legislation in 1857, the *Obscenity Publications Act*; it sought to protect young middle-class women whose pornography consisted of the romantic novel. In 1868, the *Regina v. Hicklin* case, which was to become the basis of much early US obscenity law, arose from similar concerns. In it, Lord Chief Justice Cockburn remarked, 'This work, I am told, is sold at the corners of the streets, and in all directions, and, of course, it falls into the hands of the persons of all classes, young and old, and the minds of the hitherto pure are exposed to the danger of contamination and pollution from the impurity it contains' (quoted in Kendrick, 1987: 122). The texts in question thus represented a class and gender violation of the accepted circulation of pornography, which, as historian Walter Kendrick notes, was mainly among upper-class men who owned private collections.

In the USA, in the late nineteenth and early twentieth centuries, the infamous Comstock Law was used to police circulation through the mail of anything deemed obscene – which included 'any article or thing designed or intended for the prevention of conception or procuring an abortion' (quoted in Kendrick, 1987: 134). In this manner, the law's zealous enforcer, Post Office special agent Anthony Comstock, linked sex outside procreative purposes to obscenity. Women were prohibited access to any sex-related materials while men were allowed access to porn in private, for example via stag film viewings in male-only clubs. Even court cases that are hailed for their recognition that certain literary works should be freed from regulation implicitly excluded women from consumption.[3]

The 1950s marked the gradual recognition of the need to address women's particular pleasures. The Kinsey report of 1953 noted the importance of the clitoral orgasm, which suggested that women were not fulfilled through traditional intercourse. In the 1960s, legal decisions that freed more explicit materials for circulation, the women's and gay rights' movements, the birth control pill, and the growth of the porn industry all contributed to an environment in which women were acknowledged as sexual beings and, by the early 1970s, as consumers of porn. Porn's increasing public presences and legitimation had the potential to redefine domestic relations; as Linda Williams notes, there was a moment in the 1970s when 'pornography became a household word' (Williams, 1989: 99), and a governmental commission (the Lockhart report, 1973) actually endorsed the consumption of porn as a 'healthy' practice.

It was a relatively brief moment, however, and in some areas of the country, the proliferation of porn only increased attempts to restrict its dissemination. Many cities deployed zoning regulations that limited porn to certain areas that were far removed from 'family' zones that had homes, churches, and schools. And during the 1980s, a new presidential-appointed investigation into porn, popularly known as the Meese Commission, returned to the standard of woman-as-little girl in need of protection from porn's pervasiveness. In the attempt to squash porn's public presences, the conservative commission found a group of strange bedfellows in anti-porn feminists Andrea Dworkin and Catharine MacKinnon. Yet the rhetoric of the porn-in-public threat was belied by the commission's continual infantilising of women, which revealed that the commission was equally if not more concerned with using porn as a way to restore patriarchal relations in *both* public and private. For example, the commission argued that the porn industry exploited young women: 'perhaps the single most common feature of models is their relative, and in the vast majority of cases, absolute youth' (US Commission, 1970: 229). The commission then used this concern to homogenise all women as victims. After hearing anecdotal evidence from selected porn performers, the commission conflated their lives with the lives of all women: 'the evidence before us suggests that a substantial minority of women will at some time in their lives be asked to pose for or perform in sexually explicit materials ... if our society's appetite for sexually explicit materials continues to grow, or even if it remains at current levels, the decision whether to have sex in front of a camera will confront thousands of Americans' (ibid: 839–40). Women – all of whom are either porn performers or potential performers – thus need the protection of the state, justifying regulation that is purportedly about cleaning up the public sphere but actually works to legitimate traditional gendered relations premised on women's sexual purity.

With the explosion of the video market in the 1980s and the subsequent growth of new technologies in the home, regulation has had to shift correspondingly. Conservatives have found themselves in an awkward position: how to regulate the home, the site of so-called privacy – when pornography enters via cable wires, satellite dishes, and the internet, who should be held responsible? This has led to an intensification of rhetoric focusing on pornography's threat to children on the internet, which also reinforces the role of mothers as guardians of the domestic sphere. Consider, for example, the historical shift between the 1986 Meese Commission's focus on women as victims and the 1995 debates on the *Communications Decency Act* (CDA) of the *Telecommunications Act*. In debates leading to passage of the CDA,[4] the regulatory rhetoric was no longer women as porn victims but rather mothers as moral guardians of a home under siege by internet porn. This fear was fuelled by an infamous Carnegie Mellon study – later largely discredited – released in spring 1995 that purported to document the widespread use of internet porn; the cover of *Newsweek* featured a terrified child, with the headline 'Cyberporn: A New Study Shows how Pervasive and Wild it Really is. Can we protect our kids – and free speech?' Senator James Exon, the primary sponsor of the CDA, was one of several who recounted during congressional debate anecdotes about mothers horrified by the discovery of how their children could find internet porn, and reasserting their desire to police computer technology for the benefit of the entire household.

Welfare and immigration policy

At roughly the same time that Congress was debating porn on the internet, it was pushing through the so-called 1996 *Personal Responsibility Act* (PRA), which abolished the nation's 60-year commitment to helping poor families via the *Aid to Families with Dependent Children* programme and substituted block grants to the states to distribute as they choose – with five-year limitations on aid. The PRA gained support in part because of the representation of welfare mothers – their sexuality not contained by the nuclear family – as dangerous to the nation. Conservative guru William Bennett proclaimed that 'illegitimacy is America's most serious social problem' (Bennett, 1994: A14). Charles Murray wrote in *Commentary* that the answer to babies born 'out of wedlock' is not sex education and counselling but rather threats such as 'my father would kill me' (Murray, 1994: 31). Murray repeatedly blamed women for not controlling their sexuality and excused fathers who shirked responsibility, even though, ultimately, for him, fathers are the alternative to a welfare state. Women should do whatever it takes, Murray argued, to convince their children's fathers to marry them.

This conservative logic undergirds the PRA, which, even as it gradually eliminates aid, continues to blame the sexuality of applicants. For one thing, the PRA denies aid to children unless paternity is established. Congress also created what it called the 'illegitimacy bonus' – $20–25 billion a year for three years to be shared by the five states that lower their non-marital birthrates the most without increasing their statewide abortion rates above 1995 levels (Abramovitz, 2000: xv). Welfare reform also earmarked $250 million in matching funds for states that run abstinence-only programmes in public schools and prohibit sex education (ibid: xv). Furthermore, welfare reform is linked to immigration policy in an insidious manner, leaving the most vulnerable of women – single immigrant mothers, many of whom are undocumented, without recourse to public assistance for their children; almost half of the projected $54 billion savings in welfare cuts was achieved by restrictions on immigrants.

So-called reforms in immigration policy are often fuelled by a rhetoric similar to welfare propaganda: undocumented women, especially from Latin America, are said to come to the USA in hordes to have their babies born as citizens and then take advantage of social services. In California prior to the passage of the anti-immigrant *Proposition 187* in 1994, for example, much blame was cast on unwed mothers having large families and soaking up governmental resources; Governor Wilson's office claimed that Latina immigrants have a welfare dependency rate 23 per cent higher than the rate for all other women – a statistic clearly disproved by numerous studies showing that immigrant women, both documented and undocumented, use social service programmes at very low rates.

As with welfare reform, immigration 'reform' unfairly penalises immigrant women based on the myth that they can't control their sexuality and hence won't be able to become 'self sufficient'. For example, the 1986 *Immigration Reform and Control Act* offered amnesty to undocumented people who had been in the country since 1982. However, it included a provision that denied amnesty to anyone 'likely to become a public charge' and included a five-year ban on welfare and food stamps for anyone who did qualify for amnesty. Hence, if women had ever received welfare, they would not qualify for amnesty; and if one wanted to apply for amnesty, she was then disqualified from applying for welfare for the next five years. Under this policy, women remain in exploitative conditions because they are undocumented, retaining a low-wage employment force for factories, domestic, agricultural, and sex work. The assumption is that immigrant and poor women have fewer rights as mothers to care for their children because they carry more 'value' in terms of their labour capacity.

The combined effect of immigration and welfare policy is to sanction as good mothers middle and upper-class women who are either part of a nuclear family or who prove their worth through economic self-sufficiency and moral respectability; indeed, in this discourse, it is impossible to be morally respectable without being economically self-sufficient. Working-class and immigrant mothers find it much more difficult to join this class. They are assumed to be unworthy because of the inability to control their sexuality and their subsequent dependency on the state. Access to and consumption of sexually explicit materials within the routines of everyday life seems remote for women in these economic conditions; the stigma associated with sexuality that is not a choice also reinforces the binary through which other women frame their consumption of erotica/porn as another aspect of self-sufficiency, a route to 'healthier' personhood.

Porn as big business

The above policy analysis reveals some of the conditions that limit women's sexual mobility – conditions that are masked in the myth of global capitalism's erasure of borders. The myth of unlimited access extends to pornography, which has become a profitable venture for many multinational corporations; it is a $10 billion industry in the USA alone.[5] Increasingly, corporations legitimate porn through the neo-liberal articulation of the self-regulated individual defined by consumer choice. As any commodity, porn is a choice, which, if made responsibly, need not indicate moral depravity. Companies make it clear that part of this choice is keeping it away from children. A spokesperson for AT&T Broadband defends the company's involvement in porn: "'We call it choice and control", says spokesperson Tracy Hollingsworth. "Basically, you use your remote to block out any programming you don't want. But if you want it, we offer a wide range of programming that is available in the market we're in"' (quoted in Egan, 2000). The corporate belief that enough consumers want the porn option has led to the gradual normalisation of at least certain kinds of porn for certain consumers.

The question remains, however: to what degree has the expansion of porn included women consumers? Despite the growth in kinds of porn, much of the internet, video, and pay-per-view porn still targets men as the primary consumers. This is not to say that women can't also enjoy this porn but rather that in its marketing, framing, and textual practices, this porn continues a long history of addressing men's pleasures within their leisure routines. Furthermore, most households are still defined by an uneven division of labour, with women doing most of the household chores and childcare; single mothers of course do all the work and generally have more limited mobility than women with partners. Without suggesting that 'pornography' can only appeal to male consumers, then, I argue that it is important to analyse the growth of porn for women – which often goes under other, more women-friendly labels, such as erotica and sexual self-help. Although some feminists have critiqued the erotica/porn distinction as one based on essentialist assumptions about female and male desire, I am more interested in how the distinctions shape the distribution and circulation of sexually explicit materials, making some texts more accessible than others for women, many of whom are justifiably reluctant to enter a porn video arcade or rent a porn video from the local store.

Women's ability to domesticate porn, so to speak, depends not only on what is available but also on a wide range of other conditions: Where must you go? Is there any stigma attached to its place of purchase? How much it is? What happens if someone sees you buying porn, or if one of your kids finds it at home? Is there time to read/watch it, and then to masturbate? Do you have access to the necessary technologies, such as the VCR or the computer? In answering some of these questions, domesticated porn will necessarily be shaped by the very regulatory conditions described above that, in some respects, have worked against women's sexual expression; for example, the very need to market an explicit text as 'erotica' rather than 'porn' draws on the same essentialist assumptions that guide governmental decisions to protect women from hard-core porn. However, while these marketing strategies may in fact make texts more accessible because they are perceived to be more legitimate, to note how women's erotica participates in these essentialist assumptions is not really to draw any conclusions about how women consume the products, for erotic texts are open to a wide variety of uses and fantasies that may have nothing to do with marketing. There is, in other words, as Silva argues in Chapter 4, a complex and ongoing interaction between technologies from the 'public sphere' and everyday life in the home that contradicts the idea that technologies act *on* a static home life.

It is useful as well to deploy Foucault's notion of 'technologies of the self', which he defines as those technologies 'which permit individuals to effect by their own means, or with the help of others, a certain number of operations on their own bodies and souls, thoughts, conduct, and way of being, so as to transform themselves in order to attain a certain state of happiness, purity, wisdom, perfection, or immortality' (Foucault, 1982b: 225). To be able to perform these operations is one aspect of the care of the self, which Foucault finds in Greek philosophy, and which he contrasts to the Christian philosophy of 'know thyself'. While the latter is based on self-renunciation as a means of salvation (the true self that can be liberated), care of the self requires one to emphasise how the subject is constituted through the practices of everyday life. Also, to care for one self is the first step towards the care of others. Although Foucault takes no account of gender in his analysis, this description is especially important when thinking of mothers' care of the self and sexuality. Because mothers constantly care for others, often feeling pressure to neglect their own needs and pleasures – a kind of self-renunciation – there is little time for care of the self; in fact, such care may seem selfish and inefficient. The valorisation of household technologies that function as both domestic and sexual thus holds promise for an economy that allows more time and space for mothers to care for their sexual selves – to constitute the sexual self through everyday practices – without feeling guilty or harassed; and ultimately, then, to be better able to care for others. These technologies – such as the vibrator, the erotic book, and the erotic video – interrupt an asexual, self-sacrificing moral economy.

Vibrators as domestic appliance

Since their first use in the USA in the late 1800s, vibrators have been applauded for their efficiency within household economies. Doctors considered massage a valid treatment for hysteria[6] and found that vibrators made house calls more expedient. By the early 1900s, vibrators were advertised quite widely as home appliances that could improve health, induce relaxation, and polish the furniture! One 1906 invention 'could be used on the face, head, and body' and, 'in its larger or heavier forms for rubbing down and polishing all kinds of woodwork, furniture, etc., that are given a rubbed or polished finish' (Swartz, 1980: 58). Sears, Roebuck's *Electrical Goods* catalogue for 1918 advertised, under the headline 'Aids that Every Woman Appreciates', a 'vibrator attachment for a home motor that also drove attachments for churning, mixing, beating, grinding, buffing, and operating a fan' (Maines, 1999: 19–20). This shift from the medicalisation of the vibrator to its status as household appliance corresponds with the historical shift from women as sickly creatures (who could not use their vibrators on their own) to managers of efficient households (who could use vibrators under the auspices of housework).

Vibrators did not begin to acquire relative mainstream legitimacy as sexual technologies until the 1960s, with the proliferation of information about women's bodies and pleasures (especially clitoral orgasm), ranging across sexology, sex therapy, and various strands of feminism. Much anxiety accompanied the 'new' technology, often because the vibrator promised women sexual self-sufficiency – perhaps the vibrator would be so efficient, women would reject their husbands! Sex therapists struggled to acknowledge female pleasure yet to still defend the household economy that relied on heterosexual partner sex. Noted sex therapist Helen Kaplan said in a 1976 article, 'In therapy we suggest the vibrator as a last resort, and if your partner objects, you should not use it' (quoted in Safran, 1976: 86–7). In lesbian communities, debates about vibrators and especially dildos centred on whether enjoying penetration indicated a level of false consciousness about heterosexual desire. As writer Dorothy Allison notes, 'In 1979, the idea of using dildos was still anathema to most feminist lesbians. *Male-identified* was a bigger insult than ever' (Allison, 1994: 132).[7]

Mainstream women's magazines worried about the vibrator as a potentially addictive machine, raising the spectre of dirty homes and neglected children; writer Claire Safran warns in *Redbook*, 'Reports are that over the course of an hour or so a woman can have as many as 50 consecutive orgasms using the machine' (Safran, 1976: 86). Vibrators threatened the essentialist conception of women wanting romance and emotional engagement; Virginia Johnson (the sexologist of Masters and Johnson fame) warned, also in *Redbook*, that 'women who use vibrators over a long period of time ... feel that a great deal of richness has disappeared from the ideas, thoughts and emotional meanings for them.' They are left, says Johnson, with a 'great yearning', asking themselves, 'like the old Peggy Lee song, "Is that all there is?"' (Johnson, 1976: 136). Even by 1980, in an *Esquire* article documenting the decade-long growth in vibrator sales, writer Mimi Swartz inquires, 'Has the vibrator become a sort of microwave oven of the bedroom, a fast, efficient means of getting sexual pleasure? Is the most efficient orgasm the best orgasm? Is the bedroom really the place for a time-saving device?' (Swartz, 1980: 63).

Fear of technology has dissipated over the course of the 1980s and 1990s – perhaps because, as it turns out, few women have chosen vibrators over partners. Furthermore, gendered disparities in the use of household leisure technologies have decreased; as men and women share access to technologies such as the VCR and computer (in some households, at least), the threat of woman as cyborg declines. However, a significant percentage of women in several sexological studies in the 1990s still report guilt about masturbation,[8] suggesting that buying a vibrator in a sex store may not be the easiest thing to do. Furthermore, many women simply don't have access to the women-friendly sex stores that have sprung up in various locations: Good Vibrations in San Francisco and Berkeley, Eve's Garden in New York, the Ann Summers chain in Britain, to name a few.

Many of these stores, however, have on-line sites and mail-order catalogues, and thus introduce an important link between the technology of the vibrator and the technology of the computer. Shopping for vibrators and other sex toys as well as getting information on the internet represents a virtual link between private and public spheres; it is a kind of sexual mobility that recognises mothers' limited physical mobility outside the home (you especially cannot go to a porn video arcade with children) and links women to a virtual community of women interested in supporting each other. Women are still positioned as the primary household consumers – continuing in the long history of radio and television assumptions about women at home – but this time, the shopping is for their own masturbatory pleasures: for the production of orgasms. Furthermore, women-friendly sites usually do not play on women's insecurities about beauty and body type, and they don't suggest that vibrator usage should ultimately lead to a better sex life with your partner. Some advertising acknowledges the interplay of everyday routines with sexual pleasure. One *Good Vibrations* catalogue, for example, is organised around the theme 'A Day of Erotic Pleasure': 'Instead of hitting the snooze button on your alarm clock, why not reach for a vibrator instead? Meet your lunch date for an afternoon quickie or attend your next staff meeting wearing one of our quietly vibrating toys', says the opening page. The rest of the catalogue features toys for different times of the day: a butt plug for the long commute, a set of three Black Lace novels to read on the subway, the Auto Arouser vibrator which plugs into the cigarette lighter of a car. And the Orbit is a remote-controlled vibrating egg that 'allows you to tickle your lover's fancy from across a crowded room'.

Shopping for sex toys on-line could very well lead to further exploration of sexual spaces on the internet (or vice-versa). Although the extent to which women are finding friendly on-line sites is beyond the scope of this article, it is important to note the vast potential of the computer as a sexual/domestic technology. It can work as a technology of the self that claims the material site of the body as one of pleasure, within the privacy of the home, yet allows one to escape the (working) body and the home momentarily. Both situated and liberating, placed and (momentarily) placeless, it expands women's paths outside the home even when they are tied to that material site.

The book as erotic technology

The commodification of sex toys, in part via the internet, has helped transform the domestic sphere. However, it is critical as well to analyse more public spaces, to ask whether 'society' is willing to accept the public display of erotic works aimed at women to the degree that the public display of magazines such as *Hustler* and *Playboy* has been accepted or at least tolerated for years. Access is not just a matter of material availability but also of the unashamed representation of the sexual self, which in turns facilitates sexual mobility across sites. If porn is readily accessible in some ways, it is prohibited in others, as in the ongoing belief that mothers should not be openly sexual, especially around their children. To return to Foucault, it is not about the fantasy but about the verbalisation: what is it possible to say in public about mothers and sex?

For the past 30 years, authors of women's literary erotica have been able to say quite a lot about women and sex, taking advantage of the relative privilege accorded the 'literary' and of the feminist valorisation of a 'woman's desire' linked to writing that distinguishes erotica from porn. Erotic foremothers such as Anais Nin and Pauline Reage paved the way for other women to begin writing erotica. The 1977 publication of Nin's *Delta of Venus* is often cited in subsequent women's erotica anthologies as a moment that legitimated women's erotic production as truly literary, in turn sanctioning women's consumption and helping produce a genre of women's erotica that has become increasingly popular even as it retains its links to literary distinction. The past 20 years have seen a veritable explosion in identity erotica defined by gender, sexuality, race, ethnicity, even religion. Despite the reliance on the identity category 'woman', however, literary erotica as such often defies stereotypes about women's desires as more nurturing, egalitarian, etc. The double protection granted by the 'literary' and identity politics, both distancing erotica from porn, has made the technology of the book one of the more explicit that is nevertheless readily available for women.

The space of the US superstores Borders, and Barnes and Noble, like the erotica itself, is built around a simultaneous appeal to the artistic and the popular. The stores attach middle-brow cultural capital to the practice of reading – great literature, that is. In the Barnes and Noble café where 'Starbucks coffee is proudly sold', one sips lattes surrounded by drawings of T.S. Eliot, Virginia Woolf, James Joyce, and other canonical cronies – figures that also decorate the plastic bags of purchases. Discriminating taste in coffee complements literary taste. Large comfortable couches and chairs are scattered throughout the store; unlike the more low-brow B. Dalton stores in shopping malls, the superstores are for people of leisure and hence intellect.

Furthermore, the superstores bring this cultural capital into line with community values, counteracting the image of the large chain with local involvement. Both stores regularly sponsor appearances by local authors and artists, reading groups, children's story hours, and other events with community tie-ins. They are simultaneously cosmopolitan and local, literary and popular, leisurely and expedient. In terms, then, of women's access to erotica, the superstores represent a very safe space: large stores, easily accessible, with events for children, and aesthetic legitimation for any purchase. It is perhaps one of the few places where a mother can purchase a volume of explicit fantasies for as little at $6 and the latest book in the Magic Tree House series without feeling like a 'bad mom'.

The categorisation of erotica differs between the stores. Barnes and Noble stocks erotica in three sections: literary anthologies, sexuality, and gay and lesbian literature; Borders adds to those possibilities a fourth section of directly marked 'Erotica', usually next to the literature section. A wide variety of texts is available at both stores, although Borders clearly has the more explicit commitment to stocking erotica and making it easily accessible (however, for some women, going to the 'Erotica' section may be more embarrassing than simply perusing the 'Literary Anthology' section). Anthologies by major publishing houses as well as books by independent houses are available, representing different kinds of fantasies and levels of explicitness. Because of the legal history that has more often granted legitimacy to print than film, these mainstream bookstores fear no legal consequences for selling even the raunchiest fantasies that in other contexts have been labelled pornographic. The appeal to erotica as a literary category works to normalise its production and circulation – to make it accessible within the terms and spaces of women's everyday lives.

Although content is very diverse, we can discern the attempt by book editors, publishers, and writers to integrate elements of the everyday into the erotic; this tactic distinguishes erotica from the more placeless and timeless world of pornography. Women's erotica picks up on the bodily discourses that legitimated the use of the vibrator with a specific attention to women's orgasms; the clitoris is perhaps the most frequently featured body part – but the body takes form within everyday routines. The challenge, thus, is to eroticise and 'everyday' the body without collapsing the two, making sex too mundane, a negotiation evident in the British erotic series for women, Black Lace, published by Virgin Publishing and marketed as 'erotic fiction by women for women'. Surveys at the end of many Black Lace novels inquire into the kinds of female and male protagonists readers find appealing ('do you like a female protagonist who is dominant, submissive, naive, kinky', etc?). Female protagonists combine sex with careers; a recurrent theme is the successful career woman who searches for a space to express her masochistic desires. The mundane is intertwined with the erotic; in some novels, the intersection becomes quite bold precisely because women's roles as mothers, for example, are not supposed to be erotic. In *Like Mother, Like Daughter* (Brown, 1999), 50-year-old Liz seduces her daughter's boyfriend and other twenty-something men, discovering that middle age can bring new forms of sexual pleasure. Her daughter, Rachel, is initially chagrinned: 'Mothers and sex don't mix, do they?' she asks her boyfriend upon suspecting he finds her mother attractive (Brown, 2000: 150). Eventually, however, Rachel comes around to seeing things her mother's way, and the family (including the husband/ father) is happily united around their various sexual practices, rearticulating 'family values'.

These erotic books travel easily, much easier than adult videos – especially in a bag adorned with the face of Virginia Woolf (used at Barnes and Noble). Many volumes have 'tasteful' covers, suggesting they can be read in subways, left out on coffee tables; indeed, one of the questions on the Black Lace reader survey asks, 'Would you read a Black Lace book in a public place – on a train, for instance?' Literary value facilitates women's mobility between different sites – the bookstore and the home, for example. Returning home with a volume of erotica indicates a certain degree of sexual agency, one defined by everyday routines and yet possibly exceeding them as well.

The family video store

If Barnes and Noble, and Borders are family friendly sites that nevertheless lend themselves to erotic accessibility for women, to what degree can we say the same about Blockbuster, the world's largest video retailer and the most insistent on its family values? Since its inception, Blockbuster has refused to carry X- or NC-17 rated videos; recently, however, in the face of technologies such as DVD and satellite threatening the video market, Blockbuster has had to consider new strategies, including the incorporation of more sexually explicit fare. That is why Blockbuster becomes an important site to consider: a place that has from its inception defined leisure activity for mothers as one of clearly delineated family values has expanded that definition to include the possibility of sexual pleasure and children's activities coinciding at one site. Convenience is an important ingredient in the care of the erotic self for mothers.

Blockbuster's policy of not renting X-rated videos actually began before the well-known entrepreneur Wayne Huizenga bought into the company and started eating up independent stores throughout the country. Blockbuster started as a small Dallas chain in 1985, a time when video stores were booming as the VCR became a household appliance (video retail stores grew from 7,000 outlets in 1983 to 19,000 by 1986 (De George, 1996: 95)). Many video stores garnered a significant portion of income from porn rentals; Blockbuster decided to distinguish itself through a family values theme. Blockbuster continued the theme in 1987 when Huizenga bought into it and then quickly became its chairman; at the 1988 Video Software Dealers Association convention in Las Vegas, Blockbuster showed video clips of its bright, well-lit interior, contrasting it to outlets represented as dark and dingy, suggesting porn outlets (De George, 1996: 110). Blockbuster also emphasised its 'kids first' theme and named itself 'America's Family Video Store'. These were the Reagan–Bush years, and the Meese Commission had just prompted a crack-down on porn. In 1988, Blockbuster implemented a 'youth restricted viewing programme' which went one step beyond the no-X policy, 'reviewing and restricting the rental of videos deemed inappropriate to children under age 17' (De George, 1996: 127). Then, in 1991, Blockbuster announced it would not carry NC-17-rated videos; the new rating was intended to allow more flexibility for 'artistic films' that were explicit but distinct from 'X-rated'.

The consolidation of family values policies happened during incredible growth years for the company. When Huizenga bought into Blockbuster, it was a $7 million chain of 19 stores; by 1994, when Huizenga sold it to Viacom, it was a $4 billion enterprise with more than 3,700 stores in 11 countries and 50 million card-carrying customers (De George, 1996: ix). But in 1994, Huizenga thought he saw the writing on the wall – that Blockbuster would not be able to keep up with new technologies – and he turned out to be right. Video rentals have levelled off in the face of cable, satellite television, and the internet. In fact, Blockbuster struggled so much in the mid-1990s that its new parent company, Viacom, was reportedly close to spinning it off. Since 1998, however, Blockbuster has recovered through a number of strategies that have re-consolidated its hold on the market; for example, the company has itself expanded into new technologies, now offering DVDs and DirecTV satellite systems.[9]

Blockbuster has also begun stocking more sexually explicit videos (Lewis, 2000: 292), although it still will not carry NC-17 and X-rated films, a policy that has helped stymie production of NC-17 films, given the fact that success at Blockbuster is one of the primary determinants of studio production profits.[10] Ironically, then, Blockbuster has managed to eviscerate the NC-17 rating system while simultaneously maintaining the moral high ground even as it profits off the more palatable genres of erotic thrillers, cable erotic series turned into videos, and now, through its collaboration with DirecTV, more explicit porn offered on pay-per-view.

My point is not to revert to evaluation and dismiss the erotic videos Blockbuster carries as simply co-opted because they are less daring/explicit. Rather, the point, again, is to expand possibilities for care of the erotic self through an expansion of what can be said about mothers and sex, which includes both easy access to porn and the wider social acceptance of the fact that mothers can be sexual without posing any threats. Given this objective, it must be acknowledged that Blockbuster holds considerable potential to multiple practices of sexual freedom. Blockbuster's continued self-representation as family friendly makes it an innocuous and easy site for mothers with little time away from children. Furthermore, there is no stigma attached to going into a 'porn section' because there is none: the sex videos are scattered through new releases and drama – which also makes them somewhat more difficult but not too hard to find.

The question, though, is how the video box covers and video content represent women and sex, and here we can say that Blockbuster's propensity to carry videos made for the heterosexual couples' market returns to a more traditional conception of how sex fits in the household economy, in contrast to the kinds of pleasures encouraged, for example, in catalogues for sex toys and literary erotica. The greater historical burden on visual representation to be less explicit in order to avoid regulation (such as NC-17 ratings) works well, whether intentionally or not, to reinforce the myth that women's pleasures are fulfilled through heterosexual intercourse. Attention to the clitoris that dominates women's literary erotica and sex toy catalogues is replaced by breast shots and simulated sex in the missionary position, the obligatory moaning and facial expressions indicating the woman's pleasure. The problem is not heterosexual sex in itself but rather that its representation in these videos elides women's pleasures.

Furthermore, many of the erotic videos for rent have first appeared on premium cable channels; Cinemax and Showtime in particular have found a profitable niche market in late-night couples' programming that is explicit but not hard-core, distinguishing these programmes from offerings on more hard-core channels such as Playboy and Spice. For example, the made-for-cable Showtime series *Red Shoe Diaries* frames women's desires in terms of a male narrator's attempts to understand women. Blockbuster carries many copies of the cable series, usually three episodes per tape. Former *X-Files* star David Duchovny is the series' narrator; he is desperately seeking answers to his own lost love by running an advertisement in the newspaper that solicits erotic diary entries: 'Women. Do you keep a diary? Have you been betrayed? Have you betrayed another? Man, 35, wounded and alone, recovering from the loss of a once-in-a-lifetime love. Looking for reasons why. Willing to pay top dollar for your experiences. Please send diary to Red Shoes.' In a nostalgic rejection of such modern-day technologies as the internet, Duchovny receives the hand-written entries at various post office boxes, accompanied by his loyal dog Stella. He reads a few lines of the letter; the scene then shifts to the enactment of the sexual predicament, told in the woman's voice, as she struggles with how to negotiate love and sex within some kind of everyday context, not unlike the Black Lace series. The episodes always contain a steamy sex scene, although rarely is it very explicit. At the end of each episode, Duchovny returns us to the position of voyeur/moral exemplar, commenting cryptically on the dilemma, offering a version of 'what does woman want?' Hence, although the series stresses women's sexual agency in that she is always the protagonist, it does so within the framework of male narration and desire. Although this positioning does not determine consumption, it represents in a public site a fairly traditional articulation of sex and romance.

Conclusion

It is difficult to generalise the 'everyday life' of any mother; yet we can say without too much hesitation that it is characterised by numerous tasks that involve the mastery of various domestic technologies: making microwave macaroni and cheese, vacuuming, listening to the weather report on the radio, getting a glimpse of headline news on the television, helping your child do research on the internet, answering email in the 30-minute time slot allotted by a children's television show. In this context, it seems that sexual technologies should take on a different valence – as a kind of liberation from the mundane technologies that overwhelm the possibilities of pleasure. Yet liberation from household chores via domestic technologies will never happen, simply because household work is never done, and children always require care. Moreover, positing sexual pleasure as a matter apart from the routine only reinforces the dichotomy that positions household chores as worthy tasks and sexual pleasure as a secondary matter, to be turned to only when everything else is finished. To care for oneself as a mother is to see that domestic technologies must also include sexual technologies, and that the mastery of the vibrator within household routines is just as important as a clean house or a well-behaved child. To say this is not to make the fantasy or sexual practice itself mundane, but rather to make room for its practice within the routines of everyday life.

Notes

1   Laura Kipnis argues in *Bound and Gagged* that 'pornography provides a realm of transgression that is, in effect, a counteraesthetics to dominant norms for bodies, sexualities, and desire itself' (1996: 166).

2   In the USA, for example, the year 2000 census statistics showed that while the number of married-couple families with children grew by less than 6 per cent in the 1990s, households with children headed by single mothers, increased by 25 per cent, and now account for nearly 7 per cent of all households.

3   For example, Judge John M. Woolsey's 1933 decision to free *Ulysses* for distribution in the USA instituted a new legal standard – not the danger to 'little girl' but the capacity to arouse lust in the 'average person' (de Grazia, 1992: xxi). The 'average person', it turns out, was based on Woolsey and two male friends.

4   The Supreme Court later ruled that the CDA was so broad as to be unconstitutional; it ruled that speech on the internet should be accorded the same First Amendment rights as books and newspapers.

5   General Motors, the world's largest company, now makes more money on graphic sex films through its DirecTV subsidiary every year than does Larry Flynt, owner of the Hustler empire (Egan, 2000: 2). AT&T Corp., the nation's biggest communications company, offers a hard-core sex channel called the Hot Network through its broadband cable service and owns a company that sells sex videos to nearly a million hotel rooms. Time Warner, EchoStar Communications, Liberty Media, Marriott International, Hilton, OnCommand, Rupert Murdoch's News Corp., all have big stakes in the porn industry.

6   In her history of vibrators, Rachel Maines notes that 'massage to orgasm of female patients was a staple of medical practice among some ... Western physicians from the time of Hippocrates until the 1920s' (1993: 3).

7   It is important to note, as Allison's quote suggests, that vibrators, unlike dildos, are not necessarily penetrative but rather can be used for different kinds of stimulation; some vibrators come with attachments intended for clitoral stimulation.

8   For example, a 1993 study by the University of Chicago, released in a document called *Sex in America*, found that 47 per cent of women who said they masturbated between one and five times a year reported feeling guilty about it. In her 1994 report, Shere Hite said that 61 per cent of young women she interviewed had positive feelings about masturbation – which of course suggests that 39 per cent still felt guilty.

9   Most significantly, it has signed a series of revenue-sharing deals with the major Hollywood studios. Basically, Blockbuster gives studios a share of its rental revenue in exchange for low prices on movie titles, enabling the company to buy more copies of hit videos upon their release. Independent retailers filed a class action anti-trust suit against Blockbuster, claiming that revenue-sharing drove them out of business. However, a federal judged denied their request for class-action status. According to the National Association of Video Distributors, 4,500 small retailers have closed since 1998.

10 In fact, studios have been forced to make R-rated versions of NC-17 films such as *Showgirls* and *Bad Lieutenant* in order to sell them to Blockbuster.

References

Abramovitz, M. (2000) 'Foreword', in Grace Chang (author) *Disposable Domestics: Immigrant Women Workers in the Global Economy*. Cambridge, MA: South End Press, pp. ix–xvii

Allison, D. (1994) *Skin: Talking About Sex, Class, and Literature*, Ithaca, NY: Firebrand

Bennett, W. (1994) 'America at risk: can we survive without moral values?' *USA Today*, 11 November, pp. A14–16

Brown, G. (1999) *Like Mother, Like Daughter*. London: Black Lace

De George, G. (1996) *The Making of a Blockbuster: How Wayne Huizgena Built a Sports and Entertaiment Empire from Trash, Grit, and Videotape*. New York: John Wiley & Sons

De Grazia, E. (1992) *Girls Lean Back Everywhere: The Law of Obscenity and the Assault on Genius*.New York: Random House

Egan, T. (2000) 'Wall Street meets pornography', *The New York Times* online, http:/www.nytimes.com/2000/technology/23PORN.html, October 20

Foucault, M. (1982a) 'Michel Foucault: an interview with Stephen Riggins', in P. Rabinow (ed.) (1997)

Michel Foucault: Ethics, Subjectivity, and Truth, New York: The New Press, pp. 121–33

Foucault, M. (1982b) 'Technologies of the self', in P. Rabinow (ed.) *Michel Foucault: Ethics, Subjectivity, and Truth*. New York: The New Press, pp. 223–51

Foucault, M. (1984) 'The ethics of the concern of the self as a practice of freedom', in P. Rabinow (ed.) *Michel Foucault: Ethics, Subjectivity, and Truth*. New York: The New Press, pp. 281–302

Johnson, V. (1976) 'What's good – and bad – about the vibrator', *Redbook*, March, pp. 85, 136

Kaplan, H. (1974) *The New Sex Therapy: Active Treatment of Sexual Dysfunctions*. New York: Brunner/Mazel

Kendrick, W. (1987) *The Secret Museum: Pornography in Modern Culture*. New York: Viking.

Kipnis, L. (1996) *Bound and Gagged: Pornography and the Politics of Fantasy in America*. New York: Grove Press

Lewis, J. (2000) *Hollywood v. Hard Core: How the Struggle Over Censorship Saved the Modern Film Industry*. New York: New York University Press

Maines, R. (1999) *The Technology of Orgasm: 'Hysteria,' the Vibrator, and Women's Sexual Satisfaction*, Baltimore: Johns Hopkins University Press

Michael, R., Gagnon, J.H., Laumann, E. and Kolata, G. (1994) *Sex in America: A Definitive Survey*. Boston: Little, Brown

Murray, C. (1994) 'What to do about welfare', *Commentary*, December, pp. 26–34

Safran, C. (1976) 'Plain talk about the new approach to sexual pleasure', *Redbook*, March, pp. 85–7, 136

Silva, E.B. (2004) 'Materials and morals: families and technologies in everyday life', in E.B. Silva and T. Bennett (eds) *Contemporary Cultures and Everyday Life*. Durham: Sociology Press

Swartz, M. (1980) 'For the woman who has almost everything', *Esquire*, July, 56–63

US Commission on Obscenity and Pornography (1970) *Report of the Commission on Obscenity and Pornography*. Washington, DC: Government Printing Office

Williams, L. (1989) *Hard-Core: Power, Pleasure, and the 'Frenzy of the Visible'*. Berkeley, CA: University of California Press

Chapter 6

Living 'difference' in the everyday: non-heterosexual people and the interrelationship between intimacy and material constraint

Gillian A. Dunne

Introduction

An increasingly dominant feature of late-modern society is the experience of uncertainty in people's everyday lives (Beck, 1992). Traditional pathways, often gendered, that guided people through major life-course transitions, are now less apparent and easy to follow. Unbridled global capitalism, de-industrialisation and new technologies are rapidly transforming the meaning and experience of work. Ideologies of tradition, and collective responsibility – which suffered a major blow from Thatcherism and even under New Labour – are being gradually replaced by those of individualism (Beck and Beck-Gernsheim, 1995). The power of heterosexual romance, and even parenthood, as the stuff that binds women and men together 'for ever' appears to be less assured as more people, particularly women, find themselves able and/or willing to create lives outside marriage. Although women's identities have expanded, and a general aura of gender equity has begun to inform the popular imagination, the advantages of challenging the tyranny and limitations of 'hegemonic gender identities ' (Connell, 1987) seem less clearly apparent to men. While some have willingly embraced the chance to interrogate and transform the limitations of traditional masculinity, others remain insecure, bemused, and angry.[1] Sociologists are increasingly focusing on intimacy in search of wider understanding of the meaning and consequence of contemporary change (Smart and Neale, 1999). Social theorists such as Giddens (1991, 1992) see a softening of the glue that binds traditional webs of gender, work and intimacy, offering actors new opportunities to be more reflexive about their actions and to experience greater agency in the construction of individual biographies. On the other hand, there is much wringing of hands as our political leaders struggle to retain the status quo. As such, popular, political and media interest has increasingly shifted to a preoccupation with 'the family', intimate relationships and morality in an attempt to regain a semblance of order (France, 1996).

It is puzzling then, that just as the family has become 'interesting again' (Smart and Neale, 1999) and some of the world's leading social theorists, Giddens (1992) and Beck and Beck-Gernsheim (1995) have placed gender and intimacy at the centre of their analysis of the social world, the dominant focus of mainstream feminist theory has become the disembodied text (Jackson, 1998; Maynard, 1995; Ramazanoglu, 1995; Smart and Neale, 1999). This is particularly ironic given the major and contrasting predictions that these social theorists offer. On the one hand, Beck and Beck-Gernsheim (1995) argue that we are on the brink of 'a long and bitter battle' between the sexes, as women become more aware of the contradictions between their egalitarian ideals and the everyday realities of the labour market and the home.[2] On the other hand, Giddens (1992) speaks of harmony and reconciliation. He suggests that couples are already beginning to experience greater democratisation in their intimate relationships and that, gradually, the outmoded foundations of gender divisions will dissolve. Once achieved, he predicts that the economy could change beyond recognition (1992).[3] Of course neither Giddens (1992) nor Beck and Beck-Gersheim (1995) have escaped criticism. Giddens (1992) in particular, has been criticised by feminists for assuming that contemporary egalitarian discourses actually reflect everyday practice (Jamieson, 1999; Smart and Neale, 1999).

At a time when mainstream cultural certainties have become more visibly eroded, it is worth remembering that certain groups in society have always experienced their everyday lives in this context, namely non-heterosexual people. This paper explores some of the creative solutions that are emerging within lesbian and gay communities. It draws on four detailed research projects on lesbian, gay and bisexual (LesBiGay) experience to sketch out some alternative models for work, intimacy and family life. Employing a materialist-feminist analysis, it argues that much of this creativity arises in their different location in an everyday social context which is partially founded on the logic of outmoded gender differentiated identities and practices.

Sexuality, difference and everyday life: a materialist analysis

My research extends mainstream feminist debates on the impact of gender on people's experience of work and intimacy, by focusing on non-heterosexual experience. Like Weeks et al. (2001) I am critical of the extent to which the mainstream has assumed a heterosexual subject. This has intellectual as well as a political cost, insofar as the illuminative potential of the practices of this population of differently positioned women and men is lost. To be fair, the heterosexual colonisation of the routines and practices of 'ordinary' everyday life is partly the result of the contemporary preoccupations of some of those working in the sexualities field. With notable acceptations (for example, Plummer, 1995; Weeks et al., 2001), recent sexualities literature tends to capture 'difference' in non-heterosexual lifestyles in two contrasting ways – either emphasising the exotic dimensions of non-heterosexual lifestyles (Butler, 1990) or (of obvious importance) the difficulties and disadvantages associated with constructing sexual identities against the norm (Epstein, 1994). Thus portrayed, the experiences of LesBiGay people can remain safely 'other', often remote from mainstream concerns. Thus I suggest there exists an under-explored joint middle ground, a middle ground that is as profoundly intellectually challenging as either perspectives of exoticism or victim-hood. I argue that much *illuminative* value comes through relating the 'difference' of non-heterosexual people to this middle ground: rather than in the *bedroom* – it is in the *kitchen, the nursery and the workplace* and in the routines and practices of everyday life that their radicalism lies. It is here where we are all, heterosexual and non-heterosexual alike, getting on with our lives, that the implications of 'difference' become most visible. I contend that significant insights come when we confront 'other' as familiar, and it is in this confrontation that we learn as much or more about the workings of the mainstream as we do about the experience of people 'living difference'.

The observation that there may be something radically distinctive yet socially illuminating about non-heterosexual experience has not entirely escaped the notice of mainstream social theorists. Giddens (1992) comments on the head start that lesbian and gay people have in the construction of democratic intimacy. However, the full implications of this insight have yet to be developed, and may even have been impeded by recent intellectual and political transformations in sexualities scholarship. Earlier insights from sociology, history and materialist feminism appear to have been lost (Jackson, 1998, 1999), superseded by post-modern notions of (unlimited and context-less) performance, and fluidity and fragmentation of the subject, which dominate cultural studies and queer theory. Given that my approach to the study of sexuality is informed by the former traditions, I want to take a moment to summarise some of the problems that have been identified in the latter[4] before moving on to illustrate some of the value in a more inclusive position towards the study of gender and sexuality.

Importantly, there are theoretical inadequacies in post-modernist concepts of the social, and serious limitations in approaches that conceptualise identity only in relation to fragmentation and fluidity, focus on discourse as the sole source of meaning and regulation, and look to deconstruction as the primary route to emancipation. These ultimately lead to voluntaristic understandings of people's gender identities and sexual preferences (for example, Butler, 1990). The study of sexuality has been crucially advanced through social constructionist insights (see for example, Parker and Aggleton, 1999) – shifting the origins of sexual identity (heterosexual and non-heterosexual alike) from the *natural* to the *social*. However, in taking these insights forward it is important to remember that the social is an immensely powerful force. Sociology has always warned against naive assumptions about choice: if difference is socially constructed, that does not mean that we all necessarily have equal access to it. Social location – with respect to gender, class, ethnicity, and indeed geography – has an enormous influence on the construction of opportunities and people's capacity to imagine alternative ways of living. This is as relevant in the study of sexuality as it is in the study of any other social phenomena. When pushed on this point, post-modernists such as Butler (1993: 10) retreat by falling back upon the significance of 'regulatory norms'. However, because of the post-modern denial of social structures she and they face a problem in explaining the origins of these norms (Jackson, 1995; Ramazanoglu, 1995). This emphasis on difference at the expense of commonalities obscures and denies patterns of social organisation and disadvantage which, while not having their origins in discourse, also demand explanation (Walby, 1992). Thus, while it is crucial to recognise diversity and the value of deconstruction, for feminists it is also important to understand how and why, for example, structured inequality persists.[5] As Ramazanoglu (1995: 31–2) notes, male power remains '(with considerable variations) more or less effectively entrenched at all levels from private sexual relations to the political system, state and economy.' For material feminism the discursive is but one medium for the operation of power; the inclusion of the material[6] is crucial in the formulation of adequate accounts of the structural basis of oppression and the limitations and possibilities in relation to identity formation.

For me, coming from a materialist-feminist position, post-modern approaches to sexuality bypass or leapfrog over two of the most interesting and significant questions that can be asked about difference. First, given the dominance of heterosexuality as a socially constructed outcome, how is it that some people come to interpret their sexuality differently? Second, given that heterosexuality is central to the reproduction of gender inequalities (Jackson, 1995; Rich, 1984) as post-modern feminists can accept (Butler, 1990) but cannot explain, what are the social consequences when women and men construct their identities and lives beyond heterosexuality? These questions extend the analysis of the everyday lives of lesbian, gay and bisexual people into the particularly interesting terrain of social reproduction. In asking these questions I hope to provide an alternative lens through which some of the more oppressive and intransigent aspects of mainstream practice can be interrogated.

I now want to turn to my research on LesBiGay experience to illustrate the importance of relating identity formation and everyday social practice to the material world. I shall be referring to four studies to explore some of the social consequences of 'living difference'. In this I do not assume that difference automatically equates to disadvantage, for that would be to imbue the mainstream with a perfection that is clearly unwarranted, at least from a feminist perspective. Instead, I suggest that difference in relation to sexuality serves to reposition actors in the social world, and in doing so encourages (or almost demands) the construction of alternative practices and approaches to problem solving. In the first section I shall consider the interrelationship between identity formation and the material world by focusing on intimacy and patterns of employment for lesbian women. In the second section I shall focus on the experience of women parenting with women to explore their solutions to the contradiction between time to care for children and time to earn a living. The third section focuses on fatherhood to ask whether gay men may be at the forefront of finding new ways to father. Finally, I explore the experience of differently empowered young LesBiGay people to interrogate the notion of freedom in relation to the construction of alternative sexual biographies.

Women, work and the politics of sexuality

Women's opportunities remain heavily constrained by the gender dynamics of both the labour market and structures of intimacy. The domestic division of labour seems highly resistant to change as women continue to retain the bulk of domestic and caring responsibilities when they are in relationships with men (Abbott, 2000). Drawing on Janet Siltanen's work (1994, 2002) my research on the everyday lives of lesbian women starts with the observation that it is unusual for women to earn a living wage, and as such the great majority of women are, to some extent, financially dependent on their families, partners and/or the state.[7] Any discussion either of the dominance of heterosexuality as a sexual outcome for women (see also Jackson, 1995) or post-modernist conceptions of 'performing' sexuality must take such material facts into account.

This life-history study (Dunne, 1997) set out to illuminate the ongoing significance of gender in shaping adult capacities to be economically independent. Firmly grounded in a materialist feminist perspective, it extends debates on gender and work by showing how women's difference in relation to sexual identity can lead to novel outcomes with respect to employment. It illustrates the need to appreciate the inter-relationship between gender and sexuality if we are to fully understand women's disadvantage in the labour market, and the reasons why the performance of femininity seems to require the performance of so much housework (Dunne 1999; Jackson, 1995). As Jackson (1995) points out, the transition into heterosexuality is not just a matter of *sex* – it involves absorption into a logic upon which many gendered practices and ideas are based: a deeper logic guiding everyday interactions. Drawing on a social interactionist approach to gender, (Connell, 1987; Fenstermaker *et al.*, 1991; West and Zimmerman, 2002) I view gender as an ongoing active social accomplishment, something that we *both do and have done to us* – in our social interactions, through the manipulation of objects and in the performance of tasks.

As the reproduction of heterosexuality is linked with the accentuation (Butler, 1990) and hierarchisation (Jackson, 1995) of difference along lines of gender – *something that is an active ongoing accomplishment* – I argue that the exploration of the everyday lives of people who have made a different transition may be particularly revealing. I contend that there is a need to extend notions of gendered personhood by recognising that gendered experience is filtered through the lens of sexuality (Dunne 1997, 1999).

The study explored continuity and change for 60 non-heterosexual women (aged 17–60) and encouraged respondents to speak of their journey through and beyond heterosexuality. Despite the complexity of respondents' life-narratives, commonalities could be identified – one of the most striking being the relationship between lesbianism and empowerment.[8]

By focusing on their ordinary everyday experience of earning a living, of the routines of domestic life and intimacy, it became clear that 'coming out' presented respondents with a major problem (one that is rarely discussed in the literature): going beyond heterosexuality swept away implicit, yet taken-for-granted, expectations of an economic alliance with a man. At the same time, neither could they imagine being financially dependent on another woman. Therefore 'coming out' reinforced for many or introduced for some a more explicit awareness of the necessity for lifelong financial self-reliance and often had serious implications for their paid working lives. This repositioning in the social world, which involved the necessity for financial self-sufficiency, was reflected in respondents' occupations and earnings. In contrast to the female workforce more generally, they were employed full-time, and only a small proportion of the sample was located in traditionally female-dominated occupations/levels in an occupational hierarchy. The Armed Forces and male-dominated craft occupations appealed particularly to working-class lesbians, offering career opportunities and relatively good pay (Dunne, 2002). Gaining self-sufficiency was a struggle for many, particularly those who were not educationally advantaged. Thus their life histories showed that sustaining their capacity to live difference was often associated with retraining, the return to education and/or occupational change. Income levels were also illuminating, for while not particularly high as compared to their male counterparts, it was striking that most (86 per cent) earned 'full-wages', and the wages of the rest usually came fairly close. This is a very important finding in light of the disadvantaged circumstances of women more generally. While I do not say that there are no poor lesbians (Hyman, 2001), this finding demonstrates how material circumstances have an important bearing on the extent to which women can imagine and construct sexual identities against the norm and suggests that those living their lives as lesbians may represent the tip of the iceberg.

Women in the study also spoke of what might be called the 'emotional economy' of the advantages of navigating the gender dynamics of the labour market in partnership with a woman. These advantages were seen and articulated particularly clearly by those in the sample who had previously been married. Speaking of their liberation from gendered straightjackets about 'who did what' in the home (see also Heaphy *et al.*, 2002) they described their achievement of more egalitarian and less-time consuming domestic arrangements with pleasure. Moreover, partners took for granted the right of the other to have paid employment, and consequently there tended to be mutual support and encouragement as each negotiated employment opportunities (Dunne, 1997).

Thus, I make a theoretical and empirical case for lesbians representing a different kind of worker for sociological analysis. I argue that because their engagement with the *gender dynamics of employment opportunities* is less distorted by the *gender dynamics of their intimate relationships* a middle ground, or more authentic relationship to paid work, is achieved (Dunne, 2000a). This comes about because lesbians' relationship to the labour market is less constrained by discourses and practices which construct women as secondary workers, and because it is less likely to be *inflated* by those that support the notion that men are main providers. That by transcending heterosexuality, women tend to navigate the home–work interface on more favourable terms than women more generally, and on less favourable terms than men, has important implications for theories of gender and work by bringing the significance of the institution of heterosexuality into sharp relief. I now want to illustrate this further by drawing on two additional pieces of research, starting with the experience of lesbian mothers, and then gay fathers.

Balancing acts: women parenting with women

My research on parenting further tested issues of empowerment in lesbian women's everyday experience of employment and domestic life by exploring whether such factors hold for lesbian couples[9] with dependent children?[10] For the purposes of wider comparison, I was particularly fortunate in my sample. The majority of the 37 co-habiting couples interviewed chose to have children within their lesbian relationships and most had children of pre-school age – a time when gender divisions are often at their most polarised in heterosexual partnerships. Most respondents became parents via donor insemination, usually in collaboration with a gay male friend (Dunne, 2000b). As the women intended to bring up the children together, biological fathers usually, but not always, had little involvement in the care of their children.[11] There were, however, some interesting examples of biological fathers sharing the childcare with the mothers.[12]

Again the central focus of this study was the everyday ordinary routines of social life and how these had evolved and changed over time. I was as interested in those mundane and often time consuming areas of domestic life – who put laundry away, who did the grocery shopping, who cooked evening meals, who remembered birthdays and dental appointments, and who put children's toys away – as much as I was in the evolution of the women's careers. My concern was with how women bringing up children together would resolve the seemingly intractable problem experienced by heterosexual couples: the contradiction between time to earn a living and time to manage a home and care for children. Mainstream debates on this topic have reached something of an impasse because heterosexual couples with young dependent children continue to 'solve' this contradiction through some degree of specialisation. It remains mothers, rarely fathers, who balance these competing demands, which they do by temporarily withdrawing or reducing their labour market participation. In this way women's often already marginal position in the labour market is reinforced. It seemed theoretically plausible that because of their similarities, in terms of gender – structural and experiential – together with their positioning outside conventionality, lesbian couples were in a position to bring fresh thinking to bear on this old conundrum.

This prediction proved correct, although not in all the ways I had anticipated.[13] A major finding was that lesbian mothers in the study with pre-school aged children did not reject ideologies of being a 'good' mother, and they did what other mothers of young children do – they balanced their time between income generation and childcare. However beyond this they radically diverged from everyday practice in that *both partners* usually aimed for and often achieved this outcome (Dunne, 1998). They did this by adopting a strategy of avoiding specialisation, with both partners sharing care and reducing hours of paid employment, or by taking it in turns to have time-out for mothering. They did not see their approach to co-parenting as unusual – in the absence of gender-differentiated ideologies to inform, and legitimate specialisation, traditional arrangements simply did not make sense or seem fair. Respondents further reversed conventional wisdom by rejecting the idea that the lower earner should 'obviously' take the dominant share of childcare. With a completely novel but disarmingly obvious logic they suggested that it was actually the partner with *a higher paid, more established job* who had greater power over the conditions of their employment and who could therefore take time out with fewer penalties.

Unlike many heterosexual fathers (see Dermott, 2001), all respondents – biological mother or not – spoke of the importance they attached to participating in the everyday routines of domestic life and childcare as well as the strategies they developed to facilitate this. However, this was set against a concern not to restrict their identities to the kitchen and the nursery, and most were keen to retain a measure of financial self-reliance. While it could be argued that these practices are a luxury that most cannot afford, it is worth pointing out that the economic penalties for couples who combined practical mothering with paid employment were no greater than one would expect to find in many heterosexual households which rely on one income (usually the income generated by the male partner alone). This more integrated approach brings other more obvious longer-term benefits, including women's greater scope in operationalising egalitarian ideals and the limiting of employment marginalisation. Importantly, their choices in balancing work and care had been greatly extended because they had not foreclosed options by basing earlier employment decisions on gendered ideas about future practice and who constituted the main earner.

   The study demonstrates how in negotiating the contemporary time/space constraints of caring for children and earning a living from a position of relative gender symmetry in the home, women together can construct different and viable solutions from the norm. By prioritising their egalitarian ideals in the performance of the familiar routines of nurturing, housework and breadwinning, respondents' practices challenge the logic of the gender division of labour. I suggest that their 'solutions' have wider transformational implications. In their engagement in the pleasures, concerns and constraints of motherhood they bridge the gap between the known and the unknown. Motherhood represents a common currency and by relating their difference to these familiar activities and routines we gain an alternative reference point to reflect back on mainstream practice (Dunne, 2000b). Thus, ironically, their sexuality which places them in contradiction to dominant gender arrangements, can be sidelined. This is why I contend that significant insights come when we confront 'other' as familiar, and it is in this confrontation that we learn as much or more about the workings of the mainstream as we do about the experience of people 'living difference'. Specifically, the solutions negotiated by women together highlight three critical constraints on more widespread change.

   First is the ongoing relevance of cultural gender norms that differentiate parenting expectations and practices in such a way as to enable fathers to view themselves, and be viewed, as equally engaged and caring parents despite limited practical everyday involvement. Research shows the extent to which heterosexual couples describe their parenting as equally shared despite empirical evidence to the contrary (Dermott, 2001; Jamieson, 1999). This holds even when, as is true in many cases, fathers are absent from the home for 50 or 60 hours a week when their children are young (Ferri and Smith, 1996). Within the logic of heterosexual gender norms it appears that even in such fundamentally impossible circumstances, so long as fathers are supportive and make family-life central *outside* of paid working hours, their arrangements can appear egalitarian.[14] Without this logic to shape evaluations, two sharing mothers simply hold much higher standards of what constitutes a fair distribution of responsibilities, tasks and activities. As such they are both active participants in monitoring who does what, ensuring deeper notions of equity and reciprocity within the relationship.[15]

Second is the extent to which the 'masculine model of employment' (Bradley, 1989) lies in contradiction to egalitarianism in the home. This model is dependent on the notion that a committed worker is free from the time constraints of managing a household and caring for children. If women simply, and uncritically, join men in the existing system rather than urge men to challenge it, we run the risk of extending inequalities between households on the basis of social class, as less privileged women take on the role of main carer to the children of the more affluent.

The study also vividly highlighted a third constraint – the extent to which the logic of consumption shapes desires and limits the creativity of more affluent people. Within limits the lesbian mothers in my sample were prepared to experience a reduction in their standard of living to enable more equitable sharing, noting that (in addition to its obvious benefits) sharing also reduced the need to buy care, labour-saving goods and services, and expensive toys to make up for their absence. The prioritisation of career and consumption over care and nurturing is beginning to be challenged by some highly-paid professional couples. Recent American research identifies the emergence of a 'neo-traditional' division of labour, whereby (you have guessed!) *mothers* have chosen to prioritise time over income, taking a break from their careers to care for their children and manage the household (Norton, 2000).

An awareness of these contradictions, arising as they do through the interaction between patriarchy and capitalism, reminds us of why the erosion of gender hierarchies has been so piecemeal. Their continued existence must be accounted for in feminist debates about whether equality is best achieved by asserting women's similarities with men, or by asserting their differences.[16] Evidence from this study suggests that rather than (1) *aiming* to achieve what privileged men have, or (2) *asserting* the distinctive qualities of the sexes, we need to transcend this binary thinking and remove the contradiction itself. Rather than women becoming more like men, I suggest the need for men to become more like women. Thus, undermining the significance of 'difference' and in so doing re-conceptualising what we mean by 'equality'. This requires sustained interrogation of masculinity, the 'masculine model of employment', and the choices and constraints facing men. Up against a labour market where the logic of reward has been constructed to reflect *male* experience of the division of labour, we need to challenge the way we think about work. Faced with the dominance of the market in creating our value system, we need *also* to *vigorously assert* the value of caring, and in doing so, facilitate men's engagement in nurturing their children so that they too might develop 'maternal' thinking (Ruddick, 1990). Based on this research, I tend to agree with Giddens (1992) when he says that true equality between the sexes would transform the economy (see Note 3).

Gay men and the 'remaking' of fatherhood?

No account of change can ignore constraints upon men and the significance of gender in their everyday lives. Of course, contemporary value systems make it less easy for men to see the advantages of challenging the embedded gender identities and practices that are perceived as having empowered them. Connell (1987) has opened up notions of diversity amongst men by stressing the existence of masculini*ties*. Importantly, he shows how in a patriarchal society the construction and maintenance of the 'properly' masculine individual rests on the creation and devaluation of *otherness*, most particularly women and to some extent gay men (Connell, 1987). The 'othering' of gay men, together with the gender dynamics of their intimate relationships with men (which, for example, are less easily based on the appropriation of the unpaid labour of a partner) can serve to reposition them in relation to both the privileges and constraints of hegemonic masculinity. It would seem theoretically reasonable to suggest that gay men's possibly more favourable position in relation to 'remaking masculinity' may also place some in the vanguard of those who are 'remaking fatherhood'. Here too, we might find alternative visions of how women and men could relate as parents in such a way as to reflect greater harmony and equality between the sexes.

In this study of the different dimensions of gay fatherhood,[17] certain commonalities could be identified in the diversity of the circumstances of the 100 men who shared their stories with me. Half of the sample were either currently married (n=11) or divorced (n=39). Interestingly, divorce tended to mark a *transition* in a relationship rather than an *ending point*, and there were examples (n=8) of marriages evolving to incorporate a husband's gay identity (Dunne, 2001). Underpinning the positive relationships that married and divorced men often reported was an expressed affection, with half of these men describing their wives or ex-wives as their best friends. Their level of involvement in the lives of their children post-divorce further contrasts with trends for divorced fathers more generally (Smart and Neale, 1999). Few of the divorced gay fathers had abandoned their parenting responsibilities and contrary to expectations, few had been expelled from them either (although eight did have horrific stories to tell). Instead they tended to remain actively involved in the everyday care of their children, often co-parenting with their ex-wives (n=9) or taking on the role of main carer (n=9). Reasons given for this were simple – most described having been active and involved fathers when married. While I could not verify this in interviews with the women concerned, both of these observations have been made in one of the few studies to consider gay fatherhood (Gochros, 1989). This North American research which focused on the ex-wives of gay men noted that the women often described their marriages as unusually egalitarian, as well as how common it was to find that couples had retained strong bonds of friendship post-divorce (Gochros, 1989).

The other half of the sample had opted into fatherhood in non-heterosexual contexts, through surrogacy or adoption, as foster carers or, more usually, through donor insemination. Again these men tended to describe their experience of fatherhood as heavily slanted towards nurturing. One respondent had become a social father by joining forces with a disabled lesbian friend who had recently 'come out' and, following abandonment by the biological father, had become a lone mother. He portrays this as a 'for life' commitment and describes taking a full role in everyday care of his young daughter. Another, who had been a donor father for a lesbian friend but had limited involvement because of geographical constraints, enjoyed the experience so much that they had a second child. This time he took on the responsibilities as main carer. Novel strategies were often constructed to enable co-parenting between the father and the mother. For example, the father above resigned from his job to live full time with the mother while she was breast-feeding the infant and made arrangements to work from home, while his child was young. Other fathers set up households in the same apartment block, street or neighbourhood as the mother.

While I could not pursue this in great detail, it seemed that those in the sample who had active involvement in childcare often made changes in their level of employment participation, especially when respondents were main carers. Some balanced care with part-time employment while others withdrew from the labour market altogether. These men sometimes mentioned the difficulties they experienced as they struggled to have their parenting commitments recognised by employers and colleagues. Actively involved fathers often commented on how qualitatively different their experience of fatherhood was from other fathers, gay or straight.

I believe that a gender analysis is essential for making sense of these findings. As I suggested earlier, gay men may be engaged in remaking masculinity and this may have an impact on how they interpret and negotiate the everyday experience of fatherhood. Certainly many respondents, particularly those who had lived as heterosexual men, described 'coming out' as reinforcing/supporting a critique of traditional masculinity – encouraging the embracement of a wider range of human qualities. One divorced main carer described the thinking involved in 'coming out' as a 'PhD on life'. Another, who was in the process of divorce, spoke of his relief at no longer having to 'play at straight masculinity'. Having confronted his gayness, this powerful policing mechanism of the parameters of a 'properly' masculine identity dissolved. Over a series of interviews, he told with excitement of a consequent chain of thinking which led him to challenge his understanding of how he should express his fatherhood. While gay men may not put their alternative take on masculinity at the top of their list of the advantages associated with being gay, the mothers of their children may well do so. Certainly, it was an appreciation of these wider human qualities that encouraged the lesbian mothers in my earlier study to include gay men in their children's lives, as parents and/or role-models (Dunne, 2000b). Ironically, it may be that gay men are at the forefront of constructing new forms of masculinity that are more in step with the raised aspirations of many contemporary women. This is perhaps why there were some examples of heterosexual women combining with the men participating in this study to have and raise children.

Finally, the research illuminates an almost completely neglected consequence of hegemonic discourses that conflate heterosexuality with motherhood and fatherhood – *the privileging of romantic love, and the sexual as the foundation stone for the parenting relationship*. Given the fragility of marriage, friendship may well have a more enduring quality than romance. Importantly, it may also support the construction of more enlightened and egalitarian forms of intimacy between women and men. However, while the power of heterosexual romance to sustain relationships is being eroded, its power in constraining imagination seems intact and this may be a major stumbling block to the broadening of mainstream thinking about parenthood.

Thus far I have sketched out some of the insights that can be gained when we confront the 'other' as familiar and focus on the ordinary everyday routines and pleasures of work, care and intimacy for non-heterosexual people. In doing so, I hope to have illustrated that much of what is interesting and radical about LesBiGay experience relates to the way that their sexuality acts to reposition them in a social world that takes much of its form and logic from the operation of gender through heterosexuality (Dunne, 1997, 1999). While non-heterosexual people may choose to emulate existing practice, I argue that it is simply easier to develop more innovative strategies. Throughout this discussion I have also retained an awareness of the significance of the material world in shaping action as well as the role of action in transforming material constraints. I have illustrated that within the context of gender hierarchies, living as a lesbian can be viewed as an economic achievement for women. Gay men may experience fewer material constraints on their capacity to negotiate a sexual identity against the norm. However, when gender loses its power to differentiate identities and practices in relation to care we find that women parenting with women find new, more integrative, 'solutions' to old problems and we find some evidence of men becoming more like women as they struggle to balance care around income generation.

On 'coming out' and issues of empowerment for young LesBiGay people

The impact of material constraint on identity formation becomes more clearly apparent when we consider young people who are negotiating alternative sexual identities at a time when young people are increasingly dependent on their families for making a successful transition to the independence associated with adulthood. I want to illustrate this by drawing on our current study of young (aged 16–22) LesBiGay people.[18] Interested in the experience of transition for this population, we selected two theoretical samples of differently empowered young people – those who were homeless and those who were in higher education.[19] Comparing and contrasting the life narratives of these two samples revealed some surprising commonalities which we believe have important consequences for understanding the extent to which young people may choose alternative sexual lifestyles today. These commonalities demonstrate the pervasive influence and effects of negotiating an identity in a world hostile to difference. At their most extreme, these include being thrown out of home because of their sexuality (Dunne et al., 2002). Our analysis also reveals that no aspect of everyday life, with friends, at school and at home, can be taken for granted by these young people.

Four relevant issues emerged from this study. These concern: (1) the meaning and consequences of difference; (2) the existence, or not, of a light at the end of the tunnel; (3) the 'dark side' of family life; and (4) the potential for this group to gain alternative, and possibly empowering, perspectives.

(1) The meaning and consequences of difference

I have noted that people in the studies discussed above have tended to 'come out' well beyond adolescence. An early suspicion of difference, evident for many, was unlikely to have had the label lesbian or gay attached until further along the life-course – by the mid to late 20s or later. Their experience has to be seen in a social context whereby powerful processes of naturalisation and legitimation serve to support heterosexuality as the identity of default and render alternatives invisible or undesirable (Dunne, 1997; Epstein, 1994; Foucault, 1978; Rich, 1984). As respondents' experience and confidence developed, they came to acquire knowledge that placed them in contradiction with dominant beliefs and sexuality, and this enabled them to evaluate and move beyond heterosexuality (Dunne, 1997).

Interpretations of sexuality, however, have to be seen in their historical and cultural context (Foucault, 1978). Sociologists such as Giddens (1991) have characterised late-modernity as offering greater freedom in the construction of individual biographies. The proliferation of sexual knowledge (Giddens, 1992; Holland *et al.*, 1997; Plummer, 1995; Weeks *et al.*, 2001) in which alternative 'narratives' of gay lives are coming to be more widely available, enable greater agency to young people as they negotiate their identities. Consequently, we argue (Dunne *et al.*, 2002), it is likely that more people will come to question and move beyond heterosexuality and they may do so at a younger age than in the past.[20] This is an important observation – greater opportunities to 'come out' in the teenage years rather than further down the life course – because it raises the crucial question of what resources are available to a person of this age who seeks to negotiate an identity against the norm.

One striking commonality across our two samples is that, unlike most respondents in the studies above, the great majority identified as lesbian, gay or bisexual during their mid to late teenage years. Our young people usually did not immediately attach a name to their difference. For our young men in particular, names were usually supplied by bullies. Naming almost always arose because they did not quite fit in with prevailing gender stereotypes – the boys' dislike of football, their pleasure in the company of girls, their interest in school-work, or their avoidance of 'the lads'. Discovered in this way, the labels lesbian or gay appeared both tantalising and horrifying, supporting their initial rejection of these labels as applying to them. Immensely attentive and sensitive to the reactions of others (parents, teachers and peers) and to any representation of gay issues, most struggled with their suspicions in silent turmoil. Thus, for almost all of the young people in our study, the social frameworks of understanding available to them at a key time of sexual exploration both facilitated gay identification and at the same time signified that it could only be a source of trouble, exclusion and possible danger. Ironically, the greater visibility of alternative sexualities in popular culture which may facilitate the questioning of heterosexuality, appear also to provide powerful weapons for others to more effectively police identity. For example, homophobic bullying may actually be more widespread than it was a decade ago (Douglas *et al.*, 2000; , 1995).

(2) A light at the end of the tunnel?

A second commonality relates to the pushes and pulls shaping respondents' desire to leave their home-base, as well as their choices of where to go (Dunne *et al.*, 2002; Prendergast *et al.*, 2002b). For many these two factors overlap: in experiencing the neighbourhood/home as landscapes of fear from which they seek to flee, our young people were often drawn to areas with visible gay communities. Others found the experience of a home-life predicated on hiding their emotions, lying about relationships and policing all manifestations of a gay or lesbian identity intolerable. Thus, a common and powerful theme – their quest for an authentic sense of their own sexuality – united our two samples.

Here again, material and social circumstances shaped the solutions available to our two samples. At some crucial moment of crisis, young people with little support or reason to stay at home and with no sense of an independently viable future had cracked. With little to lose they had simply upped and left – homeless, often by their mid-teens or earlier. Importantly, they commonly spoke of this as their first experience of agency – exchanging the constraints and sometimes dangers of home-base and locality for the opportunity to find alternative communities where they could experience and live more authentic lives. This quest was often punctuated by trauma and danger as they set about exploring their new identity in a strange city. Cut loose from their home-base, with no other means of support, they had fallen through the welfare safety-net, ending up in hostels and relying upon the mercy of strangers. Although homelessness was a dire step, as one of our young women commented, 'nothing could be as bad as staying put'.

In contrast, for our higher education sample, going to university could be seen to represent a light at the end of the tunnel and was often a spur to greater school achievement. With these plans in mind, respondents spoke of having initially put their sexuality on the back burner. Thus university provided a 'marker' beyond which they would gain more freedom to 'be themselves' – they would not have to wait forever. Certainly our higher education sample interviews resonate with images of 'hanging on', being patient, biding one's time until this moment arrived. Their choice of university usually reflected their desire to explore their sexuality away from home and was often influenced by whether there was a known gay community within the university or in the locality. However, the achievement of a place at university did not guarantee the end of anxiety. Respondents were aware that the withdrawal of parental financial support was always a possibility and knew other LesBiGay students to whom this had happened.

(3) The 'dark side' of family life

A third commonality was both the fear and the reality of negative reactions to their sexuality and subsequent loss of emotional and/or financial support from family members. This can have serious consequences. Most young people experienced deep levels of anxiety about this possibility while others took extreme actions to ensure their parents (and others) did not find out. Others experienced the withdrawal of financial and practical support once their parents knew of their sexuality, and some the equally damaging withdrawal of emotional support. Yet others found their worst fears came true: they suffered physical violence and/or were completely rejected and thrown out of their home.

Most of the young people in the study had experienced anxiety about parental reactions from an early age. They may also have experienced parental or carer abuse which made them fearful of coming out to their families. Thus, for a variety of reasons, far from being able to explore early feelings of difference, almost always these had to be kept hidden. Crucially, anxieties about parental responses meant that they usually kept silent about homophobic bullying at school, both to parents and to teachers. To complain might elicit unwanted questions about their sexuality: no smoke without fire, as one interviewee said.

They reported a variety of strategies for concealing these feelings of difference and minimising their vulnerability at home and at school. Some had become 'loners', and for boys, opting out of games or spending time mostly with female friends was a common strategy. Others engineered conspicuous heterosexual relations as a cover. Few were able to be openly out about their sexuality, and if they were it was likely to be at Sixth Form College, 'when the bullies had left', and a more liberal and mature ethos prevailed.

Thus, because of their sexuality, almost all of our respondents experienced degrees of alienation and isolation in the two environments where young people are meant to feel most protected and supported: home and school. Ironically however, some of our higher education sample reported strategies which may have enhanced their school career – like becoming lunch-time library monitors, attending homework sessions or (for boys) avoiding 'lads' groups – while our homeless sample had often opted out of school completely.

Thus, high levels of anxiety dominated the everyday teenage years for both samples. Those in higher education tended to keep silent rather than lose financial support, and once exposed some of our interviewees did indeed lose support – financial, practical and emotional, forcing them to leave university. Continued support was often predicated on playing 'straight' and returning to the closet at home. Unable to talk about who they fancied or put a poster of a gay icon in their room, even the everyday act of watching television with the family could be rendered problematic: a chance image might elicit a homophobic comment or a row. For some of our homeless sample, there had not even been this choice. Seeing little to hang on for they risked the streets in pursuit of their identity. For up to one third of young homeless people, their sexuality was the major factor in their leaving home; it was usually the experience of physical violence that precipitated the crisis of an immediate and unexpected departure (Dunne *et al.*, 2002; Prendergast *et al.*, 2002a). Unable to activate or stripped of parental support because of their sexuality, many young people in both our samples felt a real sense of abandonment. At the emotional level, in the words of one higher education respondent, 'your family was *not* there for you as families should be'.

Our findings lead us to conclude that the 'freedom to construct one's own biography' (Giddens, 1991) needs to be theorised within a framework of paradox for young people today. Often, in an enthusiasm to emphasis agency, the theoretical literature on sexualities can underplay the significance of social and material constraint (e.g. Butler, 1990). While the proliferation and wider awareness of sexual possibilities is abstractly available to all young people, this has not necessarily led to a corresponding extension of a social infrastructure so as to inform, support and validate sexual diversity. As mentioned above, homophobic bullying may have increased over recent years. Further, the impact of individualism and familial ideologies (Barrett, 1988) on State funding of education and welfare, together with changes in the youth labour market have played a major role in extending the period in which young people must rely upon parental support (Christie *et al.*, 2001; Irwin, 1995; Jones, 1995; Jones and Wallace, 1992; Morrow and Richards, 1996). This situation makes young people who, for whatever reason, are in conflict with parents, increasingly vulnerable (see Dunne *et al.*, 2002; Prendergast *et al.*, 2002b).

(4) Alternative sexualities, alternative perspectives

A final important commonality was that notwithstanding, and often because of many of the difficulties respondents had experienced in their search for an authentic identity, almost all felt they had made important gains along the way (see Prendergast *et al.*, 2002a). Most cited coming out as their greatest life achievement. Our homeless sample in particular, male and female, spoke of having gained confidence in the process of coming out and of their sexual identity making them feel special. Respondents also felt that their experiences of negotiating their sexuality had forced them to grow up quickly, had made them more tolerant and open to new ideas as well as providing important insights into the discrimination faced by ethnic minority groups in Britain. Young men in both samples tended to exhibit high levels of reflexivity in relationship to masculinity, commenting upon their uneasy relationship with traditional masculinity and the ease with which they developed close relationships with young women. As we saw earlier, they had often discovered that the price of not joining in with the 'lads' or 'sporty groups', and their preference for the company of girls at school was to be bullied. However, most took for granted the advantages of constructing more rounded masculine identities and interacting with women as equals. Our young women believed that their relationships with women should be founded upon equality: financial independence was important for them and those in higher education, and many of our homeless sample were striving to achieve this.

Conclusion

I argue that it is important to recognise that in constructing their sexuality against the norm, lesbian, gay and bisexual people are experiencing life beyond one of the most fundamental, taken-for-granted and powerfully regulated and regulating building blocks of everyday life – heterosexuality (Dunne, 1997; Epstein, 1994; Lees, 1986; Rich, 1984). The institution of heterosexuality, for example provides the logic behind the construction of differential gender identities and scripts (Butler, 1990; Dunne, 1997, 1999), and the basis for many key rights of passage. Thus 'coming out' serves to reposition an actor in the social world and imagery, placing them in contradiction with many taken-for-granted everyday assumptions and practices (see Chapter 2, regarding how this is done in other contexts). Non-heterosexual people have to make different maps of the social world. Because of this, their landmarks, their assumptions about their lives and their opportunities, may be structured differently from those of the heterosexual mainstream, particularly in relation to power and the gender dynamics of their relationships and lifestyles. As such they are less able to follow the taken-for-granted pathways and gender scripts that often reproduce the status quo. Because of their circumstances, I contend that lesbian, gay and bisexual people represent reflexive actors par excellence, and this has been the case for some time. I suggest that non-heterosexual people are on the cutting edge with respect to problem solving, and during these times of rapid change, the 'solutions' they develop may have wider resonances.

Notes

1   Increasingly we face the problem of emphasised masculinity in relation to young unemployed working-class men who have found themselves excluded from the 'civilising' identities gained in the workplace, marriage and/or committed fatherhood (Abbott, 2000).

2   Beck and Beck-Gernsheim (1995) describe the contradictions faced by women as they negotiate new opportunities in the context of outmoded feudal patterns of gender organisation. They identify shifts in women's access to education from the 1970s onwards as a key engine of transformation in gender relations:

> *Education opens the trap door: it allows the woman to escape from the restrictions of her existence as a housewife; it deprives inequality of its legitimation; it sharpens her sense of self-confidence and willingness to take up the battle for prizes long denied; her own earnings strengthen her position within the marriage and free her from the need to remain married for purely economic reasons. All of this has not really removed the inequalities but it sharpens our awareness of them, and makes them seem unjust, annoying and politically motivated.*
> (Beck and Beck-Gernsheim, 1995: 8–9).

According to them recognition of disadvantage marks an important prerequisite for change and heralds the beginning of 'a long and bitter battle' between women and men (Beck and Beck-Gernsheim, 1995: 14).

3   Giddens (1992) focuses on the significance of love and intimacy in the 'reflexive narrative of self'. Contemporary women enter relationships as equals, and hold higher emotional and sexual expectations than in the past. Importantly, the myth of living 'happily ever after' has been undermined, and romantic love has been superseded by confluent love whereby couples need only stay together as long as the relationship works for them (ibid: 61). Women have power because the endurance of relationships can no longer be taken for granted, and as such they are in the position to either negotiate more democratic partnerships or leave an unsatisfactory relationship. While he acknowledges the ongoing relevance of gender divisions (ibid: 131), it is through the medium of love rather than war that he sees these being eroded. Giddens' predictions are as profound as those of Beck and Beck-Gernsheim (1995).

> *The transformation of intimacy might be a subversive influence upon modern institutes as a whole. For a social world in which emotional fulfilment replaced the maximising of economic growth would be very different from that which we know at present*
> (Giddens, 1992: 3).

4   See Jackson (1995, 1998, 2000), Ramazanoglu (1995) and Walby (1992) for critiques of post-modernism and discussion of material feminism.

5   See Walby (1992) for just such an attempt to integrate diversity into materialist explanations of systemic gender inequality.

6   By material I mean 'events, relations, social and economic formations and bodily experiences which have conditions of existence and real effects outside the sphere of the discursive' (Maynard and Purvis, 1995: 5).

7   Siltanen (1994, 2002) has devised a method for relating pay to the cost of living and makes a distinction between *full* and *component* wages. Full wages enable a person to support a household of one or more persons, while component wages do not. When overtime is taken into account, 85 per cent of male and only 53 per cent of female *full-time* workers earn a full-wage. If we include women who are in part-time employment, it is safe to say that the great majority of *employed* British women must be to some extent financially dependent – on family, a partner or on the state.

8   See Dunne (1997) for extensive elaboration.

9   My focus on couples relates to my interest in contributing to feminist debates on gender divisions of labour. Other research (for example, Lewin, 1993) suggests that lesbians bringing up children on their own experience similar difficulties to single mothers more generally.

10 I am grateful to The Economic and Social Research Council for funding this three-year project (R000 23 4649).

11 See Dunne (2000b) for discussion of the process of becoming, and the experience of being, parents and respondents' relationships with biological fathers.

12 Interestingly, in cases where a biological father (and partner if relevant) was involved, his parenting took the form of active care-giving, rather than financial support (Dunne, 2000b). In one situation a father collected his seven-year-old son from school each day, brought him home and made his tea, and the school had his rather than the mother's mobile number in case of an emergency. In another, the biological father and his partner were responsible for the care of their two very active primary school aged sons from Thursday to Sunday evening, providing the mothers with a welcome break.

13 I had initially assumed that their caring practices might veer towards a 'gender equality via the denial of difference' model of buying in childcare and aiming for uninterrupted 'careers'.

14 Recent research on the attitudes of British fathers to parental leave (Dermott, 2001) suggests that men's ideal for balancing care and paid employment includes several months leave on the birth of a child (to encourage bonding) and greater employment flexibility to enable their presence at important events in children's lives. They tended not to want further opportunities to engage in routine childcare and few saw the sense in extended leave or part-time employment.

15 Lesbians appear to be remarkably sensitive to the operation of power and (potential) sources of inequality in their relationships. I argue that this has much to do with the absence of the gender-differentiated norms that serve to justify, obscure and sustain inequalities between women and men (Dunne, 1997, 1999). While this sensitivity is essential for the construction of more equal relationships, it can encourage dissatisfaction with current arrangements. I have found this evident for couples with children, perhaps because the decision to have children and share parenting requires a greater sense of the partnership working well. Nonetheless, respondents were much more likely to underestimate the extent to which they had achieved egalitarian arrangements. This mismatch became apparent because methods used in the study were designed to illuminate respondents' household strategies to myself *and participants*.

16 See Squires (1999) for a useful overview of sameness-difference debates.

17 Because of the scarcity of research on gay fatherhood, this study was exploratory in nature. I am grateful to the ESRC for funding this one-year project (R000 22 2557).

18 I am conducting this research with Shirley Prendergast and David Telford. We are grateful to the Economic and Social Research Council for funding this two-year project (R000 23 7995).

19 Our knowledge about the experience of young LesBiGay people in our two samples was gained in a number of different ways. These included focus groups and 19 in-depth life-history interviews with young homeless LesBiGay people, as well as the analysis of the records of two organisations that specialised in supporting young LesBiGay people in a housing crisis. In-depth life-history interviews were conducted with 20 young LesBiGay students – 10 women and 10 men from a range of old and new universities. An email survey was completed by 117 LesBiGay students in universities across Britain.

20 A recent national survey (Johnson et al., 2001) of the sexual behaviour of 11,161 adults in Britain, aged 16–44, strengthens our confidence in this argument. This research found that by the age of 24, one in 19 men, and one in 20 women had experienced a gay relationship; representing a substantial increase from similar research conducted in 1990.

References

Abbott, P. (2000) 'Gender', in G. Payne (ed.) *Social Divisions*. Basingstoke: MacMillan

Barrett, M. (1988) *Women's Oppression Today: Problems in Marxist Feminist Analysis*. London: Verso

Baxter, J. and Western, M. (1998) 'Satisfaction with housework: examining the paradox', *Sociology*, Vol. 31, No. 1, pp.101–20

Beck, U. (1992) *Risk Society: Towards a New Modernity*. London: Sage

Beck, U. and Beck-Gernsheim, E. (1995) *The Normal Chaos of Love* (translated by M. Ritter and J. Wiebel). Oxford: Polity Press

Bradley, H. (1989) *Men's Work, Women's Work*. Cambridge: Polity Press

Butler, J. (1990) *Gender Trouble: Feminism and the Subversion of Identity*. New York and London: Routledge

Butler, J. (1993) *Bodies that Matter*. New York and London: Routledge

Christie, H., Munro, M. and Rettig, H. (2001) 'Making ends meet: student incomes and debt', *Studies in Higher Education*, Vol. 26, No. 3, pp. 363–83

Connell, R.W. (1987) *Gender and Power*. Cambridge: Polity Press

Dermott, E. (2001) 'Combining work and family? British fathers and parental leave', Paper presented at the European Sociological Association Conference, Helsinki, Finland, 28 August–1 September 2001

Douglas, N., Kemp S., Warwick, I. and Aggelton, P. (2000) *Sexuality Education in Four Local Secondary Schools: Learning From Local Initiative*. London: Institute of Education, University of London

Dunne, G. (1997) *Lesbian Lifestyles: Women's Work and the Politics of Sexuality*.London: Macmillan

Dunne, G. (1998) '"Pioneers behind our own front doors": New Models for the Organization of Work in Partnerships', *Work, Employment and Society*, Vol. 12, No. 2, pp. 273–95

Dunne, G. (1999) 'A Passion for "Sameness": Sexuality and Gender Accountability', in E.B. Silva and C. Smart (eds) *The 'New' Family?* London: Sage

Dunne, G. (2000a) 'Lesbians as authentic workers? Gender, sexuality and the reproduction of the status quo', *Sexualities*, Vol. 3, No. 2, pp. 133–48

Dunne, G. (2000b) 'Opting into motherhood: Lesbians blurring the boundaries and re-defining the meaning of parenting and kinship', *Gender and Society*, Vol. 14, No. 1, pp.11–35

Dunne, G.A. (2001) 'The lady vanishes? Reflections on the experiences of married and divorced gay fathers', *Sociological Research Online*, Vol. 6, No. 3 (http://www.socresonline.org.uk/6/3/dunne.html)

Dunne, G. (2002) 'Lesbians in manual jobs', in S. Jackson and S. Scott (eds) *Gender: A Sociological Reader.* London: Routledge

Dunne, G., Prendergast, S. and Telford, D. (2002) 'Young, gay, homeless and invisible: a growing population?', *Culture, Health and Sexuality*, Vol. 4, No. 1, pp. 103–15

Epstein, D. (ed.) (1994) *Challenging Lesbian and Gay Inequalities in Education.* Buckingham: Open University Press

Fenstermaker, S., West, C. and Zimmerman, D.H. (1991) 'Gender inequality: new conceptual terrain', in R.L. Blumberg (ed.) *Gender, Family and Economy, The Triple Overlap*. London: Sage

Ferri, E. and Smith, K. (1996) *Parenting in the 1990s*. London: Family Policy Studies Centre

Foucault, M. (1978) *The History of Sexuality*, Volume 1: An Introduction (trans. R Hurley). Harmondsworth: Penguin

Giddens, A. (1991) *Modernity and Self Identity: Self and Society in the Late Modern Age*. Cambridge: Polity Press

Giddens, A. (1992) *Transformation of Intimacy: Sexuality, Love and Eroticism in Modern Society*. Cambridge, Polity Press

Gochros, J.S. (1989) *When Husbands Come Out of the Closet*. Binghamton, NY: Harrington Park Press

Heaphy, B., Donovan, C. and Weeks, J. (2002) 'Sex, money and the kitchen sink', in S. Jackson and S. Scott (eds) *Gender: A Sociological Reader.* London: Routledge

Holland, J., Ramazanoglu., Sharpe, S. and Thomson, R. (1997) *Pressured Pleasure: Young Women and the Negotiation of Sexual Boundaries*, WRAP Paper 7. London: Tufnell Press

Hyman, P. (2001) 'Lesbian and economic/social change: Impacts of globalisation on our community(ies) and politics', *Lesbian Studies*, Vol. 5, No. 1/2, pp. 115–33

Irwin, S. (1995) *Rights of Passage – Social Change and Transition from Youth to Adulthood*. London: UCL Press

Jackson, S. (1995) 'Gender and heterosexuality: A materialist feminist analysis', in Maynard, M. and Purvis, J. (eds) *(Hetero)Sexual Politics*. Bristol: Taylor and Francis

Jackson, S. (1998) 'Feminist social theory', in S. Jackson and J. Jones (eds) *Contemporary Feminist Theories*. Edinburgh: Edinburgh University Press

Jackson, S. (1999) 'Feminist sociology and sociological feminism: Recovering the social in feminist thought', *Sociological Research Online*, Vol. 4 No. 3 (http://www.scresonline.org.uk/4/3/jackson.hlml)

Jamieson, L. (1999) 'Intimacy transformed? A critical look at the "pure" relationship', *Sociology*, Vol. 33, No. 3, pp. 477–94

Johnson, A.M., Mercer, C.H., Erens, B., Copas, A.J., McManus, S., Wellings, K., Fenton, K.A., Korovessis, C., Macdowall, W., Nanchahal, K., Purdon, S. and Field, H. (2001) 'Sexual behaviour in Britain: partnerships, practices, and HIV risk behaviours', *Lancet*, Vol. 358, pp. 1835–42

Jones, G. (1995) *Leaving Home*. Buckingham: Open University Press

Jones, G. and Wallace, C. (1992) *Youth, Family and Citizenship*. Buckingham: Open University Press

Lees, S. (1986) *Losing Out: Sexuality and Adolescent Girls*. London: Hutchinson Education

Lewin, E. (1993) *Lesbian Mothers*. Cornell: Cornell University Press

Maynard, M. (1995) 'Women's studies', in Maynard, M. and Purvis, J. (eds) *(Hetero)Sexual Politics*. Bristol: Taylor and Francis

Maynard, M. and Purvis, J. (1995) 'Introduction: A context for hetero(sexual) politics', in Maynard, M. and Purvis, J. (eds) *(Hetero)Sexual Politics*. Bristol: Taylor and Francis

Morrow, G. and Richards, M. (1996) *Transitions to Adulthood: A Family Matter?* York: Joseph Rowntree Foundation

Norton, C. (2000) 'Pressures of life force married women out of careers', *The Independent*, 18 October 2000, p. 10

Parker, R. and Aggleton, P. (eds) (1999) *Culture, Society and Sexuality: A Reader*. London: UCL Press

Plummer, K. (1995) *Telling Sexual Stories: Power Change and Social Worlds.* London: Routledge

Prendergast, S., Dunne, G.A. and Telford, D. (2002a) 'A story of "difference", A different story: young homeless lesbian, gay and bisexual people', in *Sociology and Social Policy*, Vol. 21/22, pp. 64–91

Prendergast, S., Dunne, G.A. and Telford, D. (2002b) 'A light at the end of the tunnel? Experiences of leaving home for two contrasting groups of young lesbian, gay and bisexual people', in *Youth and Policy: The Journal of Critical Analysis*, No. 75, pp. 42–62

Ramazanoglu, C. (1995) 'Back to basics: heterosexuality, biology and why men stay on top', in Maynard, M. and Purvis, J. (eds) *(Hetero)Sexual Politics*. Bristol: Taylor and Francis

Rich, A. (1984) 'On compulsory heterosexuality and lesbian existence', in A. Snitow, C. Stansell and S. Thompson (eds) *Desire: The Politics of Sexuality*, London: Virago

Rivers, I. (1995) 'The victimization of gay teenagers in schools', *Pastoral Care,* Issue 95, pp. 35–41

Ruddick, S. (1990) *Maternal Thinking: Towards a Politics of Peace.* London: The Women's Press

Scott, S. and Jackson, S. (2000) 'Sexuality', in G. Payne (ed.) *Social Divisions*. Basingstoke: Macmillan

Siltanen, J. (1994) *Locating Gender: Occupational Segregation, Wages and Domestic Responsibilities.* London: UCL Press

Siltanen, J. (2002) 'Full wages and component wages', in S. Jackson and S. Scott (eds) *Gender: A Sociological Reader.* London: Routledge

Smart, C. and Neale, B. (1999) *Family Fragments.* Cambridge: Polity Press

Squires, J. (1999) *Gender in Political Theory.* Cambridge: Polity Press

Walby, S. (1992) 'Post-post-modernism? Theorising social complexity', in M. Barrett and A. Phillips (eds) *Destabilizing Theory: Contemporary Feminist Debates.* Cambridge: Polity Press

Weeks, J., Heaphy, B. and Donovan, C. (2001) *Same Sex Intimacies: Families of Choice and Other Life-Experiments.* London: Routledge

West, C. and Zimmerman, D.H. (2002) 'Doing gender', in S. Jackson and S. Scott (eds) *Gender: A Sociological Reader.* London: Routledge

Chapter 7
Racialising culture is ordinary[1]

Gail Lewis

Preliminary remarks

It is November 2001 and as I sit down to work further on this chapter, Douglas Sirk's 1959 film *Imitation of Life* is being shown on afternoon television. The central characters of the film are two mothers and their (just turned adult) daughters. One mother is white – an actress – and has a white daughter. The other mother is black – runs the house they all live in – and has a daughter conceived with a white man. The white mother is called 'Miss Laura', her daughter 'Suzie'. The black mother is called 'Mama', her daughter 'Sarah Jane'. The relationship between the mothers is ambiguous, simultaneously one of beloved friends and mistress/maid. That between the daughters is one of rivalrous siblings refracted through the inequalities and psychic consequences of racially ordered femininities. Mama has played mother to them both – reliable, secure, containing, loving, present. Miss Laura's mothering has been a little less than good enough, fractured by her own conflicted desires to be both 'good mother' and successful actress. This ambivalence produces its own dynamics on the white mother/daughter relationship – including an Electra drama, resolved over the deathbed of Mama. For the black/mulatta, mother/daughter couple the murderous feelings more commonly associated with Oedipal dynamics are produced by and expressed through the prism of 'race'. For Sarah Jane 'passes' and her ambivalent love for her mother stems from her shame of her own and her mother's blackness. She denies both, over and over and over again, and after suffering a violent assault from her white boyfriend who has found out that she is 'a nigger', she runs from one down-beat dance club to another as she seeks unchallengeable and unambiguous entry into whiteness. Blackness is the colour of abjection. Blackness is the colour of her mother. Blackness is her.

Re-watching this film reminded me of the first time that I had seen it. Again as a result of afternoon television scheduling, I watched it with my own – white – mother. I wondered now how we had dealt with the scenes of denial between daughter and mother. How we had negotiated its unspoken but very present echoes of our own racial dramas. Dramas that were sometimes played out with my mother's public denials of me – on the streets, outside her place of work.

The day before re-watching Sirk's film I had been reading a twelve-page pull-out on 'Race in Britain' published by *The Observer* newspaper. Alongside some statistical mapping of the racial/ethnic landscape, what this supplement began to capture was the complexities of 'race' in the contemporary UK. It showed the porosity of cultural boundaries, the fluidity of cultural practices, the unevenness of racialised or ethnicised experiences across class, gender and regional divides. It indicated emergent hybridities of style, language, and ways of being. It showed violence alongside desire, tolerance alongside hatred, friendship alongside fear. Perhaps even hope alongside confusion and uncertainty.

In terms of the writing of this chapter I interpreted these two events (the showing of Sirk's classic and the publishing of this pull-out) as messages from the gods. The immaterial speaking through these media to the material of embodiment. Messages reminding me how difficult a task it is to capture, let alone interpret the complexities of 'race'. Messages reminding me that popular culture has the capacity to act as a vehicle for both the representation of urgent social and political issues, and the projection and displacement of collective anxieties. A capacity to point to what is at stake in processes of identification, and the opportunities these might foster or inhibit for both the individual and the wider collective. Messages reminding me just how ordinary are the complexities – and anxieties – of 'race' in the modern UK. And that this ordinariness bespeaks the degree of embeddedness in the tolerant/moderate fabric of contemporary culture rather than a circumscribed belonging only at the extreme edges of hatred and intolerance. Despite their separation by 42 years the newspaper and the film reveal just how deep a part of the everyday 'national' culture 'race' really is.

It is this 'ordinariness' that I want to consider in this chapter. I do so by using the work of Raymond Williams alongside a series of vignettes depicting racialising culture. Some will recognise that I take my title from a piece by Raymond Williams called 'Culture is Ordinary', originally published in 1958. One of Williams' key achievements was to break down the division between 'high' and 'low' culture. In destabilising this division he drew attention to the ways in which working-class people use culture as a means of mediating individual experience and class relations (Dworkin and Roman, 1993: 4). He conceptualised culture as activity – rather than simply art – and demonstrated a way of analysing class relations as involved in the process of meaning making as well as reflecting a particular mode of economic organisation. 'Culture is Ordinary', pointed to the importance of ordinary, everyday experience in the making of national culture. In this essay Williams wrote:

> Culture is ordinary: that is the first fact. Every human society has its own shape, its own purposes, its own meanings. Every human society expresses these, in institutions, and in arts and learning. The making of a society is the finding of common meanings and directions, and its growth is an active debate and amendment, under pressures of experience, contact, and discovery, writing themselves into the land. The growing society is there, yet it is also made and remade in every individual mind. The making of a mind is, first, the slow learning of shapes, purposes, and meanings, so that work, observation and communication are possible. Then, second, but equal in importance, is the testing of these in experience, the making of new observations, comparisons, and meanings ... the nature of a culture ... [is] that it is always both traditional and creative; that it is both the most ordinary common meanings and the finest individual meanings. We use the word culture in these two senses: to mean a whole way of life – the common meanings; to mean the arts and learning – the special processes of discovery and creative effort.
> (Williams, 1958: 75–6).

Like his *Culture and Society* (1961) this essay reflects Williams' concern to intervene into debates about the definition and parameters of culture, an intervention that was highly political in character. The opening of 'Culture is Ordinary' depicts a scene in a village on the Herefordshire borders between Wales and England. It begins with an account of a bus journey that stands as both description and symbol of the multifaceted, repetitive character of culture. The sites and practices of culture are the conversations on the bus, the routes the bus takes, the shapes of the hedgerows and contours of the farming valleys, the houses and pits; the dynamic of relations within them; the advertisements for television and cinema programmes. From this Williams develops what Alan O'Connor (1989) has called an 'oppositional article' that challenges ideas about the rise of mass education, espouses the capacity of the working classes for cultural critique, their involvement in democratic process and achievements in artistic creation.

More is also conveyed by this depiction of a bus journey. Its location reminds us of Williams' own 'border' status – born into and produced out of a working-class, Welsh border community. While the travel conjured up by the route the bus takes might also be seen as a metaphor for Williams' own 'travels' into England and the bastions of upper and upper-middle class culture that prevailed at Cambridge. This is not any bus journey but one that signifies the existence of insider/outsider communities that both contribute to the production of culture and might be the source of oppositional consciousness challenging hegemonic conceptions of culture.

The article reflects Williams' insistence that though excluded from the centres of power, working class people are still actively located in and productive of English culture (and English is the term he uses). In other words, asymmetrical power relations should not be taken to mean that the working classes are outside of culture. By beginning with a bus stop/journey Williams shows that it is in the symbols and interactions of ordinary life and the places where these interactions occur that culture is manifest. One reading of this approach is that Williams is presenting a view that the meanings embedded in forms of cultural activity are manifestations and sources of struggle. But a number of cultural analysts have drawn attention to the limitations of Williams' analytical frame.

There are two areas of critical engagement with Williams' work that are particularly relevant to my own concerns. One relates to the avenues of investigation that are opened up by his idea that culture is ordinary. For example, Loren Kruger (1993) notes Williams' failure to see through the political implications of his conviction that culture is more than art and should be understood as including ordinary activity. For her this limitation stems from Williams' retention of an elitist conception of art as exemplary works containing some intrinsic aesthetic value. Thus, Williams hesitates at the critical border he constructs by his insistence that culture is both 'art' and 'ordinary activity':

> *Confronted with the radical levelling implied in the phrase 'culture is ordinary', and concerned lest 'culture is ordinary' (natural, common, popular) might produce only 'ordinary (mundane, trivial, consumer) culture', Williams returns to the high ground of aesthetic **value** and the apparently inalienable concept of **art**.*
> (Kruger, 1993: 57; emphases in original)

Experience may mediate the reception of art, but both 'art' and 'experience' retain their status as objective, un-negotiated categories. Moreover, Williams' hesitation at his own critical border is reflected in his equation of cultural democratisation with increased access to the infrastructure of cultural production and the generation of a sensibility that allows appreciation of intrinsic aesthetic value.

This has two implications for my argument. First, as Kruger notes, it prevents Williams from fully recognising that cultural practices (of both the ordinary, whole way of life and the art variety) are themselves sites and expressions of struggles. Struggles over the meanings associated with particular practices and struggles over/for their legitimation. Thus whilst the depiction in 'Culture is Ordinary' of a working-class, border town community as at the heart of cultural production is a radical move, its radical potential is circumscribed by a failure to depict such a community as a potential site and source of counter-hegemonic, critical practice. This leads to the second implication in that it points to a surprising absence of agency attributed to such communities, even the form of agency required for the production of hegemonic cultural forms and practices.

This stems from Williams' reliance on an elitist conception of art alongside his idea that cultural democratisation equates to a kind of organic expansion of access to the infrastructure of cultural production. The result is a move away from an understanding that the representation of ordinary life and an appreciation of the effects of the contexts of their reception can help reveal both the contradictory experiences of subordinated groups and offer glimpses of alternative modes of being and cultural practice.

Critical engagement with Williams' work has also pointed to his inability to fully draw an analysis of imperialism into his own analytical framework and critical practice. Like Kruger, Gauri Viswanathan (1993) has argued that this limitation stems from Williams' failure to follow his own logic but this time in relation to the extension of his critique of the orthodoxies of historical materialism to colonial/imperial relations.

> *While his theory of culture has the potential to produce a reading of England's colonial adventure, his cultural analysis is seriously inhibited by the framework of economic determinism within which that reading is produced. Suspending contestation altogether, Williams's scattered comments on empire in The Long Revolution and Culture and Society suggest that Britain had achieved dominance through the power of a 'fully' formed cultural and institutional system whose values are simply transported onto the colonies. That system is subsequently identified as the 'national' culture, but it partakes little of the contingencies of the colonial situation it confronts and remains hermetically sealed from the continually changing political imperatives of Empire.*
> (Viswanathan, 1993: 223)

Unlike the working classes within the 'fully formed national', the peoples (of various classes) of the empire have no role to play in the making of metropolitan culture – conceived either as art or as a whole way of life. One effect of this was to limit Williams' ability to see and analyse the racialising effects of cultural practices, a point I will elaborate later.

Despite Williams' own failure to incorporate racialising practices into his conceptualisation and analysis of culture, we can use his idea that culture is ordinary to disrupt the prevailing notion that issues of 'race' and processes of racialisation are relevant only to the extreme edges of life in the UK. The relegation of matters 'racial' to the extreme edges can be understood as a strategy of hegemony aimed at constructing the nation – and national belonging – in a particular way. This is as a benign, post-imperial society premised on tolerance and a history of welcoming 'the stranger'. This is, of course, a deeply contested construction but even if one agrees with it issues of 'race' and ethnicity are central to the debates. Thus, to say that racialising culture is ordinary is to use Williams to point to some of the ways in which such cultural practices stand right at the heart of contemporary everyday life and mediate individual experiences and the social relations of 'race', gender, class, sexuality, and age. Moreover, as Williams was so keen to point out, hegemonic projects are never fully achieved, are always unstable, making possible forms of appropriation, destabilisation and change. Thus, whilst cultural practices of racialisation occur with networks of power and contestation, as the articles in *The Observer* pull-out so clearly show, their trajectories and outcomes are never certain, never guaranteed.

A focus on culture in this sense can bring to light some of the multifarious and complex connections between the micro-social of everyday practices and the macro-social of institutional forms, patterns and the fields of relations that inhere within and across these institutions. One major axis cutting across and articulating these dimensions of social life is the ways in which identities, solidarities and belongings are produced and experienced. This includes forms of social connection – and disconnection – imagined and experienced around sexual, gender, class, regional, age, religious and ethnic/racial identities. And, of course, intersecting articulations of connection/disconnection coalesce around individual and collective agents. Agents who are simultaneously the subject and objects of cultural practices. My deployment of the idea of agency should not be taken as referencing only a form of constructive and reflexive assertion of autonomy and power. As Paul Hoggett (2001: 43) has noted 'there is nothing *necessarily* constructive about agency and we should beware of smuggling normative assumptions into our thinking here, as if agency is good and absence of agency is bad. [For] just as we can be destructive agents so also at times we can be constructive in our dependency and powerlessness' (my emphasis). Thus Hoggett wants to distinguish between first and second-order levels of agency in which first order agency functions within the patterns of power relations, and second-order agency occurs at those moments of rupture that occur when individuals and groups challenge the patterns and relations of rule. I hope to illustrate that the impact of racialising cultures produces complex and multi-dimensional expressions of agency. These usually establish the terrain for the reproduction of racialisation, although it is occasionally destabilised by the actions of those tyrannised by such cultural practices of everyday racialising.

I am, then, concerned to think about a field of discourse and practice that, in my view, forms one of the most important contexts for a project aimed at relocating the meaning of 'Britain' in the social imaginary. This is the ubiquity, potency and *ordinariness* of racialising culture. I suggest that such culture establishes an unstable, shifting, ambiguous but nevertheless profound limit on any project aimed at the social and cultural relocation of 'Britain'. This is because it is linked to the performance of racial difference in the way in which Judith Butler (1993) has conceptualised performance as an iterative practice that instantiates normative identities and relations within the contingencies of power. The performance of racial difference is also linked to the constitution of sexual difference and practice – and their attendant anxieties – as the film *Imitation of Life* so ably demonstrates in its representation of the 1950s dominant discourse in both the USA and the UK. This discourse is that transgression of the boundaries of racial difference simultaneously destabilises the boundaries of sexual difference and leads to tragedy. In the British case at least, the racialised and gendered outcomes of such disciplinary logic are, however, obscured by another expression of power. This is the construction of the nation through a notion of tolerance and fairplay as its enduring and essential characteristics, a notion carried in the once commonly-stated phrase 'play the white man'.

Thus a project of symbolic relocation requires an investigation of the multiple sites and ways in which racialised culture is practised in the interstices of 'the quotidian' (de Certeau, *et al.*, 1984), 'the everyday' (Lefevbre, 1992) or in Schutz and Luckmann's (1974) terminology 'the everyday life-world'. They defined this as '... that province of reality which the wide-awake and normal adult (sic) simply takes for granted in the attitude of the common-sense ... [it includes] all the meaning-strata which transform natural things into cultural objects, human bodies into fellow-men (sic), and the movements of fellow-men into acts, gestures, and communications' (Schutz and Luckmann, 1974: 4–5). It must then include the ordinary practices of racialising culture.

I elaborate on these points in what follows but I want to begin by clarifying how I am using the term racialisation. Robert Miles (1989: 75–6) has suggested that 'Racialisation is a dialectical process of signification ... [and that] the concept of racialisation ... refers to the historical emergence of the idea of "race" and to its subsequent reproduction and application' (pp. 75–6). As a dialectical process it involves defining the self in the very act of defining the 'other'. Despite this emphasis on the dialectical or mutually constitutive effects of racialisation, two linked understandings about the object/subject of racialisation have become commonplace. First, in both popular and academic discourse, processes of racialisation are presented as being the preserve of what we might, in the context of an inadequate terminology, call populations of colour. Second, there is a tendency to conflate racialisation with racism itself commonly thought to be associated only with the extremes of UK society.

In contrast to the definition offered by Miles, I want to slightly modify a lead signalled by Barnor Hesse (1997: 101n), and differentiate among distinct but intersecting forms of racialisation, because I think this facilitates an analysis of the mundane quality of *processes* of racialisation and investments in its logic. Thus, we can think of racialisation as signalling three overlapping processes. First, the emergence of a discourse in which human physical and cultural variability became constructed as coterminous with, and representative of, the division of human populations into distinct races. Second, the inauguration and reproduction of 'whiteness' as the dominant 'racial' and 'cultural' category, whilst simultaneously constructing 'whiteness' in naturalised or 'non-racial' terms. In this process 'whiteness' is also constructed as being devoid of 'cultural' specificity – a move effected by its claim to the status of the universal. Third, the forms of *appropriation of and challenge* to dominant forms of racial categorisation that are themselves expressed on the terrain of racial discourse. Such practises represent the kind of first order agency defined by Hoggett (2001). Racism is an integral and mediating force running through these three processes, and signals the ways in which the structure of hegemonic systems of racial categorisation acts to define the terms of inclusion in, modes of relation among, and the horizons of the racialised social. Importantly, exploration of practices of the everyday can help unlock the ways in which the horizons of the social are structured by, and structuring of, racialised culture.

By way of a beginning

In the 1950s, when I was a child living in Kilburn in north west London, I had two ambitions. I wanted – indeed was determined – to grow up to *become* a black woman. The litmus test of my entry into adulthood would be the moment when I too could perform the acts that defined what I thought it meant to be a black woman. That is, I wanted to use my two bare hands and by their power and sound produce sheets, and towels and shirts so white and gleaming they would not only be the envy of all but a sure sign that I had entered the ranks of the women around me. The fact that the subjects of this identification were the women other than my white mother probably raises interesting points about the production of subjecthood through simultaneous processes of racial and sexual difference, and the dramas this simultaneity produced in our domestic world.

My second ambition related more directly to the immediacy of my life at that time. I wanted to be the best and most authentic 'Davy Crockett', not only in my street but in the whole of Kilburn and Harrow (the other, highly different space/place framing the geographical boundaries of my familial and intimate world). Davy Crockett was a member of the Texan army that fought for the annexation of Texas from Mexico and its incorporation into the expanding United States of America. He died in 1836 at the battle of the Alamo and, more importantly for my concerns, he became a key figure in the Anglo-American imaginary with its myths of freedom and masculine success against the ravages of both nature and the barbarians of 'uncivilised' races. In the 1950s there was a children's television programme that celebrated, albeit implicitly, his achievements as yet another victory for white, protestant supremacy. It was also a kind of Pokemon or Harry Potter of its day, sprouting a whole industry producing artefacts aimed straight at the hearts and imaginations of children. So I had my rifle – for bear hunting – and my Davy Crockett hat with its distinctive beaver tail running down my back alongside my plaits.

There are four points embedded in these two memories of childhood fantasies that are central to my concerns. First, they indicate that our imaginations, identities, and ways and visions of being in the world are structured through highly racialised and gendered discourses and positions. Second, they indicate that despite a commonsense that suggests differently, our bodies do not automatically prescribe any necessary or automatic belongings and that our conceptions of self cannot be read off from our bodies in any simple way. This is, of course, one of the key insights of queer theory and it raises many pressing questions about how we might conceptualise the link between the materiality of our bodies and our subjectivities, identities, lived experiences, and social, sexual, cultural and economic locations. For I wanted to *become* a black woman and to *become* – in what at the time was the here and now – a Davy Crockett. The racial and gender commonsense told me that the former was inevitable whilst the latter was forever unattainable. In contrast my phantasmic identifications suggested something different. The former would only emerge after I had developed particular but ordinary skills of the domestic, while the latter was, as far as I was concerned, liveable now.

This relates to a third point, in that my implicit concern with 'acts of becoming' emphasises *behaviours* – of dress, cleanliness, bodily movement – as the modes by and through which racialised gendered positions are achieved. As mentioned earlier the focus is reminiscent of Butler's notion of performance as citational or iterative practice as the constitutive ground of embodied belonging and identity. Finally, by focusing on a child's play and women's household work, these stories also show that it is in the banalities or mundane routines of everyday life that racialised gendered positions are constituted and lived. I raise these issues not just because they concern the everyday but because the ordinariness of the acts and locations carried in these memories highlights just how ordinary racialising culture is.

Like Williams' bus journeys, the scenes passed as the travel proceeds, and the conversations occur, these activities are both absolutely mundane *and* expressive and productive of British culture. They are also activities that shift across social categories and subject positions even while they attempt to effect closures around particular categories. They occurred in the late 1950s, exactly the moment depicted by Sirk's film and when Williams is writing the essay 'Culture is Ordinary' and his *Culture and Society*. Yet racialising practices such as these are outside of Williams' conceptualisation of the ordinariness of national culture. As such they are a further indication of Williams' failure to pursue to the end the logic of his own argument about culture and its analysis. Williams was particularly concerned to free Marxist-inspired analyses of culture from the constraints imposed by a rigid conceptualisation of the relation between base and superstructure. Rather than see these relations as fixed abstractions with a unidirectional flow of cause and effect, he was concerned to show how the relation was more dynamic and involved processes of mutual constitution. Yet, despite some recognition of the impact that the imperial had on the making of national culture, Viswanathan (1993: 220) has made the important observation that in Williams' analysis of the place of the colonies in nineteenth-century British popular fiction 'colonial territories remain without material presence or substance'. As actual places the impingement of the colonies 'on the lives of [those] poor characters [who appear in this fiction] in powerfully direct, immediate ways cannot be accommodated to Williams's location of conflict' (ibid: 220). Rather 'the colonies are turned into a vanishing point, the symbolic space for dissolving all problems that cannot be solved at home' (ibid: 220).

Such a vanishing point also becomes a starting point for racialising the national (or metropolitan) as white or at least as racially and/or ethnically homogeneous. And it is a move that replicates the suturing Williams effects around the class antagonisms embedded in cultural practices noted earlier. We can glean this more clearly if we turn to some of what Williams had to say in relation to imperial/metropolitan relations in his essay on Orwell's 'England, your England'. The main argument Williams makes in his piece (entitled 'England whose England') relates to what he sees as Orwell's partial and limited critique of England's class and imperial relations. For Williams this limitation derives from Orwell's own class origins *and* the fact that, as a product of the ruling classes the 'England' the latter sought was one devoid of the deformities imposed by the decadence and obsolescence of an elite and archaic class. It is this decay that Orwell writes of and wants to eliminate rather than the class itself. Thus at the end of his essay Williams writes:

> *'A foreign observer, new to England'. He [Orwell] was never, of course, that. But he came back from the periphery with a real and lasting hatred of imperialism and saw at the centre what his education and experience had prepared for him: 'a family with the wrong members in control' ... What he could tell them about, effectively, was the imperialism they ignored, the slums they neglected. But just as it is limiting to see a capitalist system without its imperialist extension, so it is limiting to see capitalism only through imperialism and through its visible ruling class. Part of the England he discovered was a real society, living under and within this order, keeping certain values going. But inseparable from this was the different England created by this order, in prejudices, compromises, adjustments, illusions. To respond to the society would be to distinguish one part from the other, to enter a necessary conflict, reaching into every area of life.*
> (Williams, 1984: 27–8)

Here we have evidence of the vision that was, in part, produced by Williams' own 'border' status as both Welsh and of working-class origin. For as he reminds us in the third paragraph of 'Culture is Ordinary' the location in which he grew up afforded him multi-directional views across diverse topographies of agricultural and industrial, rural and urban, religious and secular, class and labour.

Yet one might also turn these last comments back on Williams in relation to the 'inseparable' but 'different England' made visible through the lens of 'race', had he sought to use his cultural analysis to 'travel' there. For as both empirical evidence (then and now) and Williams' own arguments should have indicated, culture's racialising practices were as endemic to England (then and now) as the inequities tied to class (then and now). And it cannot be claimed that at the time Williams was producing 'Culture is Ordinary', *Culture and Society*, 'The Long Revolution' or *Orwell*, little was evident about the degree to which England (Britain, the UK) was a racial formation. The signs were there for anyone wanting to read them. Kelso Cochrane, a West Indian carpenter in his early 30s was murdered in Kensal Rise (near Notting Hill) in May 1959. Front windows were littered with signs reading 'No coloureds, no dogs, no

Irish'. And between 1948 and 1958 West Indian writers were publishing a veritable wave of works of fiction, some of which related to life in Britain and exposed the racial thinking at its heart. Listen to the voice of George Lamming, the writer from Barbados, writing in *The Pleasures of Exile*, first published in 1960. He is charting the connection between an institution given over to the celebration and support of art and an inner city location that had come to stand for the racial anxieties produced by the presence of colonial immigrants:

> *I think it is necessary and appropriate to establish as I best can the connection between the I.C.A. and Notting Hill. I ... feel their connection since I see them as expressions of a similar deficiency in the national life of the country ...Intellectuals take refuge in the absurd habit that it is enough for two people to share similar ideas in order to claim a certain identity of outlook ...and when the subject is race, naturally the whole matter is excluded as being no part of our agenda for serious talk. We may speak about what's to be done to stop racism in a way that plumbers may consult with each other about the defects of a pipe line; but the pipe line has nothing to do with the plumbers. [If I disagree I am charged with having a chip on my shoulder] ... It does not occur to him [my cultured interlocutor] that he is making me an offer of equality, or reminding me of his original disposition to grant me that much. He is horrified if I say that his equality ... is an abstract equality. It does not grow from a felt recognition of my capacity for experience, my particular way of seeing. Unfortunately for him, it is not possible to dismiss me by branding me ignorant of his world, for that world is also part of mine. Moreover, I am capable of situating him in it by examining the history of his relations to it.*
> (Lamming, 1984: 73–4; my emphases)

Lamming makes quite plain the quotidian, yet disavowed, character of racialising culture and how knowledge of this culture is not predicated on being educated in England but rather being formed in relation to it in the dynamic of unequal yet mutual constitution between metropole and colony. It is this relationality of racialising culture that undermines Williams' claim at the beginning of 'England whose England' that:

> *The eyes of the observer, of a man coming back to England, are eyes full of this experience of imperialism. But he is not coming to England in the same way as, say, an Indian or an African student: to a foreign country about which he has only read. He has been educated here, his family lives here. He is aware of the internal structure of English society, but from a class position which he has only theoretically rejected.*
> (Williams, 1984: 17)

It is as though the practices of imperialism were only limited to a formal political control with no extension into the fabric of everyday life and cultural practice of those subjected to its rule. It is as though it is only by being born and raised upon the land of Britain, that one can be inside the social relations and sensibilities of 'home'. Such a view is to underestimate the powerful impact imperial relations had on the formation of subjectivities. This is a point indicated by the Trinidadian C.L.R. James in his *Beyond a Boundary* when he said '... I was British, I knew best the British way of life, not merely in historical facts *but in the instinctive responses*. I had acquired them in my childhood' (James, 1963: 152; my emphasis). Indeed this claim to Britishness is further specified as being a Victorian variety and Simon Gikandi has noted that this identification by James was linked to an anti-colonial political project. By claiming the core values of Victorianism as his own, Gikandi argues (1999: 8) that James is mapping 'the process by which colonial subjects appropriated instruments of colonial rule, such as sports and literature, in order to transcend the colonisation of their consciousness'. Like Williams, James is claiming an understanding of British culture as simultaneously an insider and an inhabitant/product of the boundaries.

This juxtaposition between, on the one hand, Williams' exposition of the ordinariness of culture and the particular ways of seeing afforded by differential class location, and my own and others' memories allows us to think about the points of connection between everyday practices and different dimensions of processes of racialisation. Once we remember that racialisation is relational we can begin to see that racialising culture is a field of discourse and practice in which we are all imbricated and which is productive of diverse forms of agency. Its ordinariness includes but extends beyond racism, understood as oppressive practices of racial domination. The relationality of racialisation draws attention to the processes by which groups are constructed as racial groups around boundaries of universal/particular, majority/minority. In other words, the constitution of racial ordering, identification and belonging involves constructions of whiteness as well as blackness, Asianess, Arabness etc., even while closure around these categories is never fully fixed, is never stable.

But the idea of the ordinariness of racialising culture extends beyond the instability of racialised categories and identities. What it shows is that processes of racial ordering are structured by and structuring of, the practices of the kitchen, the washroom, the living room as much as those of the labour market. By the micro-practices of workplace relationships as much as the institutional policies of employers and trade unions; and by practices of the self and imagination as much as those of the media, the academy and the laboratory. In these ways and in these locales the parameters and 'characteristics' of nations are constructed and marked out as racial formations produced by, and productive of, everyday practices. Here we can see how we might appropriate Williams' insights and use them to extend his project of re-articulating conceptualisations of culture and its relation to issues of class and national belonging. For in his insistence that culture be seen as a whole way of life he is also making a claim to the national culture – even if this claim is somewhat ambivalent. Because for him culture is produced and expressed in lived social relationships within and across all social classes, then the diverse patterns and sensibilities associated with this whole way of life belong to both upper and working classes.

By suggesting that as a way to get to the pervasiveness and ordinariness of racialisation we look at everyday practices I am trying to push the analytic eye towards an investigation of those daily acts that are so well trodden, so repetitive that they seem almost substanceless. In drawing attention to this I do nothing new. For example, Michael Billig's *Banal Nationalism* (1995) is just such a project concerned with the way in which nations deemed devoid of nationalism are in fact saturated with nationalist practices and habits and indeed dependent on them for their reproduction as nations.

> *Daily, they are reproduced as nations and their citizens as nationals. And these nations are reproduced within a wider world of nations. For such daily reproduction to occur, one might hypothesize that a whole complex of beliefs, assumptions, habits, representations and practices must also be reproduced. Moreover, this complex must be reproduced in a banally mundane way, for the world of nations is the everyday world, the familiar terrain of contemporary times.*
> (Billing, 1995: 6)

Other writers have also pointed to the simultaneity of asymmetrical power relations and their mutual imbrication in the practices that reflect and produce these asymmetries. For example, by investigating everyday practices of the dominated, de Certeau and his colleagues (1984) have pointed to the ways in which institutions and relations of force are in fragmentary, temporary and partial ways appropriated and assimilated by those who are subjected to and by those relations of force. For them, such acts of appropriation occur in the practices of the everyday. Whilst I recognise that there are differences of approach among these writers, I want to take these insights and use them to explore the ordinary asymmetries of racialising culture as they structure everyday practice. In this spirit what follows is a series of 'scenes', or vignettes, depicting ordinary practises of racialisation and examples of 'first order agency' (Hoggett, 2001: 43).

Practices of skin – part I: becoming black

One of the effects of processes of racialisation is the production of social and cultural minorities who occupy subordinate positions in the hierarchies and strategies of power. Given this, it is necessary to look at the ways in which 'blackness' is produced by the actions of 'white' people in the ordinary, everyday dynamics of micro-social relations. This, however, is only one aspect of the investigation of racialisation. For if cultural formations are, in part, the product of those excluded from the centres of power (as Williams would put it) or shaped by those who insinuate themselves into the interstices of the force relationships that dominate at any one time (as de Certeau and colleagues would suggest), then a second and equally urgent area of analysis is required. It concerns a need to attend to everyday practices of racialisation of those constituted and subordinated as racial or ethnic minorities. For example, we need to look at the ways in which black people, or other 'racial minorities', themselves construct the limits of racial belonging and authenticity under the sign of 'blackness' and define its legitimate and legitimating practices.

To reiterate: the embeddedness in the construction of racialising culture by those groups who occupy subordinate positions in systems of racial categorisation should not be taken to mean that such systems are characterised by symmetrical relations of power. Rather, they point to some of the ways that subordination in fields of racialising discourse and racist practices are negotiated and contested. They also indicate the ubiquity of systems of racial thought and the ways in which these shape the formation of identities, processes of everyday meaning-making, and the terms of group belonging.

I want to suggest that these are practices of the skin in that they are everyday – taken-for-granted/'normal' actions that construct boundaries of belonging and give meaning to certain kinds of interaction and experience. The following are all examples of some of the dimensions of the making of 'blackness'.

Scene one: The ordinariness of being made black by the actions of white people

It is a beautifully warm and sunny evening and Ann P. and I drive back down to London after what, we both feel, has been a productive day at work. We decide to go to a café in Swiss Cottage and find one that promises good coffee and a chance for a homegirl chat. We settle in. We notice that it is the habit to leave the money for the bill on the table – having seen several groups of white people of diverse accents and nationalities do so. When we finish we decide to do the same. We notice too that as we stand to go the woman working on the tables moves carefully – and she thinks surreptitiously – across and quickly counts the money before we are out of the café. She takes up the money. On several of the other tables the money that has been left is still there. Ann and I smile knowingly at each other and I say: did you notice. Ann says, yes but let's not bother about it, otherwise we'd never get anywhere because it never stops. I say, true. And we know we have just been made into black women.

Scene two: Being 'black' – effecting racial boundaries, making masculinities

(The following two scenes are taken from interviews conducted by Tony Sewell and published in his 1997 book *Black Masculinities and Schooling*. They illustrate some of the ways in which racial discourse helps give meaning to social relationships in schools.)

A conversation with an African-Caribbean teacher:

> *TS: What do you think about the African-Caribbean boys' attitude to women?*
>
> *Mr Jones: During a Social Education class, we were talking about children's reading books and we were trying to identify stereotypes. I told them I had 10-year old twins, one boy, one girl, and my wife and I decided we would not create this gender divide in the twins.*
>
> *Then one of the [black] boys in the class said to me: 'You've only got two kids sir?'*
>
> *I said: 'Yes, that's right'. He then asked: 'What about the others back in Jamaica?'*
>
> *I said: 'I've only got two children'. He said: 'Well sir you're not really a true Yard man!'*
> (Sewell, 1997: 97)

Scene three: Policing femininity, negotiating racism

A conversation with an African-Caribbean male pupil:

> Calvin: The worst teacher in this school is Miss Kenyon. She's a bitch; she's like a man – everyone says it. She's a joker – you just laugh when she gets mad. I always tell her she's like a man.
>
> TS: What does she say?
>
> Calvin: She says, 'I don't care what you think'. I don't like her and she don't like me. She used to find me threatening. She talks to kids as if they're idiots, but she couldn't talk to me like that. She thinks she's vicious. She was also a racist; she pays nuff attention to white lads'
> (Sewell, 1997: 117)

Scene four: 'Blackness' as a practice of 'insider' control

My god-daughter goes off to sixth-form college. It is a tyranny of racialising and racist discourse and the daily negotiation of just being allowed to be sometimes takes its toll – what with the teachers' low expectations of the black students, and the students' expectations of what it is to be black. Her hair is twisted and she looks fine, like Erikah Badou and what, in the days of Black Power, we called 'natural'. The time of 'blackness' for young people now though is a very different one. Now you must have straightened hair, greased flat against the head. You must dress like you're ready for 'dancehall'. You mustn't study hard and play the viola, and like classical music alongside hip-hop and gansta rap and dancehall. You mustn't think homophobia is as bad as racism. If you do any of these things you cannot be 'black'. My god-daughter knows all this – and pays the price.

Each of these four 'scenes' depicts ordinary interactions in the context of daily life. They show something of the low level impact of stereotypes on behaviour, the relationship between racialising thought and the making of gender economies and identities, and the place of emotions such as envy in the development of racialised sensitivities. In short, they point to the pulse and patterns of racialising practice and its prevalence in the worlds of black people. Given the commonsense association of issues of 'race' with black, and other people racialised as minority, this is probably unsurprising. But what of white people? How might a notion of the ordinariness of racialising culture be applied to these groups?

Practices of skin – part II: being white

In the past decade or so writers such as Vron Ware (1992), David Roediger (1991), Ruth Frankenberg (1993) and Catherine Hall (1992, 2000) have argued that attention needs to be paid to the processes by which whiteness is constructed and deployed as a social location and identity. In their view, the analytic gaze needs to be turned towards the ways in which 'whiteness' is constructed and lived as a racial ideology, category of belonging and practice of power.

As with all racial categories 'whiteness' is simultaneously an unstable and changing fiction but it is also a position of power. It is relational – formed within the cauldron of racial thinking and at the intersections with other axes of differentiation operating in a multitude of spacialities and temporalities. 'Whiteness' is, to use Frankenberg's terminology, 'co-constructed' in relations of inequality. She writes:

> *This co-construction is, however, fundamentally asymmetrical, for the term 'whiteness' signals the production and reproduction of dominance rather than subordination, normativity rather than marginality, and privilege rather than disadvantage.*
> (Frankenberg, 1993: 237)

Thus, investigating the processes by which 'whiteness' is constructed involves analysing the context through and within which it is produced simultaneously as a non-racial, 'empty' and yet normative and dominant social location and category of belonging. Such a project involves analysis of the ways in which the racialisation of 'whiteness' is constituted by, and constitutive of, multiple spacialities and temporalities. As with the production of other racial belongings and positions this points towards an analysis of everyday culture. In part this requires that we look for the silent presences of racial 'others' – note their invocation but lack of recognition or comment upon their presence. Similarly we must look for the ways in which narratives construct different spacialities – predicated on racial discourse and perhaps racist practice – and which therefore silently act back onto the speaker to position them as 'white'. Indeed, we have already seen an example of just such racial discourse in the hands of the Welshman Williams' essay on Orwell when he suggests that only an Englishman can know England, albeit a knowledge differentiated by class. The point is that we need to actively seek out how 'whiteness' is being produced and positioned in the social relations of particular places and times. Approached in this way it is possible to identify at least three aspects involved in the analysis of the racialisation of whiteness. These are its paradoxes, its connections to the limits of national belonging, and its internal instabilities and ambiguities.

As already indicated we must first look at 'whiteness' as paradoxical; that is, as simultaneously an unmarked and unspoken position, and a universalising norm that produces an exotic other. Like all racialised positions and identities it is premised on iterative practices. However, the ordinariness of such practices disguises both its constructed and relational character and the position 'whiteness' occupies in systems of racial hierarchy.

Scene five: Whiteness: transgression and exotification

This is taken from an article by Stef Pixner, 1985:

> *At school ... I am decidedly anti-religious ... Mum has often told us about my brother's first rendering of the Lord's Prayer: 'Our father which art in Heaven, Halibut be thy name'. Her laughter says: of course! How can children understand all this hocus pocus? I'm not sure what halibut is either, if truth be told, but it's the 'trespasses' that bother me; I think they*

*must be something like 'christmasses' (a kind of Christmas tree, perhaps?)
– but why do they need to be forgiven? I stand with my eyes open in
morning assembly; why is everyone talking to someone who clearly isn't
there? In the playground one day I am taunted and called a heathen. It
hurts, but I'm proud of my difference, my unbelief.*

*I have an Indian friend at school called Himalata, whose family live in
one room in a block of houses in our street that's full of Indian families
each in one room. Her house is mysterious and smells of curry, and when
I stay the night she and her parents snore at different volumes, loud,
medium and soft, like the three bears. She teaches me how to make
necklaces from coloured birthday-candle wax that you drip into cold
water. It makes little round beads that you can thread together with a
needle. She also teaches me to move my head from side to side without
moving my neck, like Indian dancers do.*
(Pixner, 1985: 85)

Scene six: 'Whiteness' as establishing the limits of the 'British' nation and national belonging

Taken from a Metropolitan Police document:

*In Britain the word family normally refers to the immediate family group
of parents and children. By contrast, in some minority ethnic
communities, family is more likely to have a broader meaning, due to
greater involvement of other relatives in a person's affairs ...*

*In English culture, raising the voice is associated with a person becoming
angry and losing control, or with trying to impose themselves
aggressively upon a conversation or other situation ... In other cultures,
volume, pitch and manner of delivery do not necessarily convey the same
meaning.*
(Metropolitan Police, 2000: 5–6; emphasis in original)

Statements such as these have become commonplace in social policy documents
and among welfare professionals and they are important in that they are aimed
at the creation of systems of service delivery that are suitable for an ethnically
diverse population. But everything hangs on the words 'Britain' and 'English',
for not only do they conflate the two and so erase the notion of the UK as a
multi-national state that was always multi-ethnic, they also construct those
deemed to be 'minority ethnic' as outside of the nation. Since the term 'minority
ethnic' is always already 'non-white', the effect is to construct the nation of the
UK as white. This in its turn reproduces a pattern of subordinated inclusion in
the UK's social, economic, political and cultural institutions and relations.

Scene seven: 'Whiteness' as an unstable, ambiguous identity and social location, exposing its own limits and internal contradictions as the grounds for a racialised understanding of solidarity and belonging

Taken from Hickman and Walter (1997):

> *When we arrived we were staying with my husband's brother, his wife and child, and my brother's sister. When they went back to Ireland three or four months later, we found out they had been squatting, although we had been paying them rent. We were evicted.*
>
> *We were put into a B and B in Kilburn. It was terrible, four in one room. People were hitting my daughter. The Council said 'Why not go back where you came from?'. I felt it was holding us back, being Irish. We were on the list for five years. They told us to forget it. They said 'You're the wrong colour'. We need 450 points but we've only got 53. We're renting this two-bedroomed flat for £125 a week – a three-bedroom council house would be £60.*
>
> *People can't understand why they're not doing anything for us. My husband has given up. They said 'Why did you come over here in the beginning?'. My husband says 'Play on the fact that you're born here', but they say 'Where was your husband born?'. When I say 'Ireland', they say 'Well that's it then'. It isn't right. The couple round the corner, she's from Dublin, he's from Jamaica. When he went to the council it was easy. Another girl, Irish mother, black father, she's got a place by getting involved with an Englishman. You shouldn't have to ...'*
> (Hickman and Walter, 1997:168–9; interview with British-born Irish woman speaking of her return to London in 1989)

This example illustrates an attempt to summon up a discourse of whiteness and birthplace as the grounds upon which rights and belonging should be accorded. But what it also shows is that white skin is not in itself enough to ensure inclusion into a social location of 'whiteness' because it is not yoked to Englishness and to a particular gender. Like the example depicted in scene four, it shows that racialising culture constructs hierarchies of insiderness, only here within the category 'white'.

By way of a conclusion

In abstract terms I have tried to show five main points. First, that racialising culture is ordinary and saturates the everyday in multiple and complex ways. Second, that despite constructing asymmetrical power relations, in a racially ordered social formation, we are all racialised and implicated in the dynamics of racialising culture. Third, that 'whiteness' should be seen as a constructed category of belonging and social position, and that it needs to be 'outed' and dislodged as a position of dominance. Fourth, that an expanded understanding of the concept and process of racialisation is vital if we are to begin to relocate the peoples and nations of Britain in the social imaginary. And finally, that a focus on the practice of everyday cultures is a fine place to start this process.

But what of the individual that is conjured up in the ordinary practices of racialising culture? Developing an analysis of racialising culture as ordinary offers the potential to engage in the task of facing our own investments in what Michael Rustin (1991: 57) has called 'the empty category of race'. Such investments are social, political, economic, cultural and psychic and facing up to them is part of a project that has the potential to connect us – individuals and collectivities – to our pasts and each other in new ways. But it is a painful, difficult and contradictory process and we need help to do it.

And, to return to my mother's own racial dramas in the 1950s and 1960s. If we used the idea of racialising culture as ordinary we could see that her own racialising practices were no more, no less than examples of the ordinariness of white, English working-class culture. We could also see that her own ambiguous and ambivalent investments in whiteness were always open to destabilisation. Finally, we could see that when she walked with my hand held tight in hers at the time of the Notting Hill riots she was practising an act of both good enough mothering and, perhaps a second-order agency (Hoggett, 2001), or what David Roediger (1994) would call an 'abolition of whiteness'. Racialising culture is indeed ordinary, pervasive and very contradictory.

Note

1   This article is dedicated to the memory of Caroline Adams (1949–2001), a committed Open University tutor, a passionate historian, a lover of Bach and a tireless fighter against the tyranny of racial thinking and for social justice.

References

Billig, M. (1995) *Banal Nationalism*. London: Sage

Butler, J. (1993) *Bodies that Matter*. New York and London: Routledge

De Certeau, M. (1984) *The Practice of Everyday Life*. Berkeley: California

Dworkin, D. and Roman, L.G. (eds) (1993) *Views from Beyond the Border Country*. New York and London: Routledge

Frankenberg, R. (1993) *The Social Construction of Whiteness: White Women, Race Matters*. London: Routledge

Gikandi, S. (1999) 'The embarrassment of Victorianism: colonial subjects and the lure of Englishness', in J. Kucich and D. Sardoff (eds) *The Post-Victorian Frame of Mind*. Wisconsin: University of Minnesota Press

Hall, C. (1992) *White, Male and Middle Class*. Cambridge: Polity Press

Hall, C., McClelland, K. and Rendall, J. (2000) *Defining the Victorian Nation*. Cambridge: Cambridge University Press

Hesse, B. (1997) 'White governmentality: urbanism, nationalism, racism', in S. Westwood and J. Williams (eds) *Imagining Cities: Scripts, Signs, Memory*. London: Routledge

Hickman, M.J. and Walter, B. (1997) *Discrimination and the Irish Community in Britain*.London: CRE

Hoggett, P. (2001) 'Agency, rationality and social policy', *Journal of Social Policy*, Vol. 30, No. 1, pp. 37–56

James, C.L.R. (1963) 'What do men live by', in *Beyond a Boundary*. London: Stanley Paul and Co.

Kruger, L. (1993) 'Placing the occasion: Raymond Williams and performing culture', in D. Dworkin and L.C. Roman (eds) *Views from Beyond the Border Country*. New York and London: Routledge

Lamming, G. (1984) (first published 1960) *The Pleasures of Exile*. London: Alison Busby

Lefevbre, H. (1992) (first published in French 1954) *Critique of Everyday Life: Introduction*. London: Verso

Metropolitan Police (2000) *Policing Diversity*. London: Metropolitan Police

Miles, R. (1989) *Racism*, London: Routledge

O'Connor, A. (1989) *Raymond Williams: Writing, Culture, Politics*. New York: Basil Blackwell

Pixner, S. (1985), 'The oyster and the shadow', in L. Merou (ed.) *Truth, Dare or Promise: Girls Growing Up in the Fifties*. London: Virago

Roediger, D. (1991) *The Wages of Whiteness*. London: Verso

Roediger, D. (1994) *Towards the Abolition of Whiteness: Essays on Race, Politics and Working Class History*. London: Haymarket Press

Rustin, M. (1991) *The Good Society and the Inner World: Psychoanalysis, Politics and Culture*. London and New York: Routledge

Schutz, and Luckmann, T. (1974) *The Structures of the Life-World*. London: Heinemann

Sewell. T. (1997) *Black Masculinities and Schooling: How Black Boys Survive Modern Schooling*. Stoke on Trent: Trentham Books *The Observer* (2001) 'Race in Britain', special twelve page supplement, November 25

Viswanathan, G. (1993) 'Raymond Williams and British colonialism: the limits of metropolitan cultural theory', in D. Dworkin and L.C. Roman (eds) *Views from Beyond the Border Country*. New York and London: Routledge

Ware, V. (1992) *Beyond the Pale: White Women, Racism and History*. London: Verso

Williams, R. (1958) 'Culture is ordinary', in N. Mackenzie (ed.) *Conviction*. London: MacGibbon and Kee, pp. 74–92

Williams, R. (1961) (first published 1958) *Culture and Society*. London: Penguin

Williams, R.(1984) (first published 1971) 'England whose England?', in *Orwell*. London: Flamingo, pp.16–28

Chapter 8

Schooling everyday cultures: 11–14 year old boys and constructions of masculinities

Ann Phoenix

For most children and young people schools constitute the central site of everyday cultural practices. For six hours per day, five weeks per week, forty weeks per year they negotiate the expectations, rules and multiple social practices associated with the institution they attend together with other children and young people of the same ages. And they do so in contexts that afford them little privacy or breathing space to be alone. Not surprisingly, then, it is in schools that children and young people learn to negotiate the complexities of institutional cultural practices and social relationships. The potential impact of schools is aptly captured in a quote from a Bangladeshi mother in a study by Waqar Ahmad and colleagues (2000: 71) where a Bangladeshi mother says 'I send my child to school and he comes back an Englishman.'

We now know a great deal about what happens in schools, thanks to a wealth of ethnographic studies and interview studies which come from a range of different countries and different age groups (e.g. Connolly, 1998; Hey, 1997; Sewell, 1997). One of the striking features of such ethnographic work is that the everyday cultures of schools continually produce and reproduce differentiated gender relations and gendered cultures. Of course children and young people are positioned differently within their schools and classrooms and, in different ways, they reproduce, resist and are complicit with many facets of their age-structured school cultures. However, research from around the United Kingdom, the USA and Australia identifies common patterns in the reproduction of gender relations within schools (Eder *et al.*, 1995; Gilbert and Gilbert, 1998; Mac an Ghaill, 1994). In recent years, social concern about boys' educational performance in relation to that of girls has meant that particular attention has been paid to the ways in which masculinities are constructed within schools. This interest has been fuelled by concern that that it is boys' 'laddish' behaviour within schools that is responsible for their poor educational performance.

This chapter uses data collected in a study of 11–14 year old London boys from a range of ethnicised and racialised groups to explore the ways in which masculine identities are constituted within everyday school cultures. The first section briefly considers how everyday cultures are produced in everyday interactions and contested in everyday practices. After a description of the study that informs the chapter, the two main sections that follow focus on a discussion of boys' narratives of how masculinities should be lived in everyday cultures ('canonical narratives') and the importance of racialisation to the performance of masculinities in the everyday cultures of London secondary schools.

While, to some extent, each school in the study produced its own local, situated culture, the chapter argues that the attributes identified by the boys as characterising 'popular boys' were common to all schools (state and private; single sex and co-educational). At the same time, boys were positioned in a variety of ways in relation to these constructions of masculinity. Pervasive notions that 'real' masculinity involves toughness, sporting prowess and a casual attitude to schoolwork serve to produce and reproduce school cultures that constrain what boys can do. The chapter demonstrates that boys' everyday cultures are simultaneously gendered and racialised with black boys of African-Caribbean descent being considered the most hegemonically masculine, and boys of Asian descent the least so.

Cultural contestations in practice

Ethnographic and discursive studies of boys' cultural practices mostly agree that some of the theoretical ideas developed by Robert Connell (1987, 1995, 2000) are important to understandings of masculinities (see Pattman *et al.*, 1998 for a review). These ideas suggest that the everyday practices central to constructions of masculinity are the products of interpersonal work and that, far from naturally occurring, they are achieved in social relations through the use of the cultural resources available to particular boys. These resources include the ideologies of masculinity prevalent in their schools and classrooms, the social structures in which they live and their own social positions. Boys' everyday cultures are, therefore, complex, dynamic, actively constructed, relational (and so experienced most clearly at constructed boundaries) and imbued with power relations – and, hence, a site of contestation as well as commonality – (Brah, 1996; Clifford and Marcus, 1986; Hall and du Gay, 1996). Masculinities (and femininities) are necessarily part of everyday cultures since they are produced in social interaction (Connell, 1995, 1996; Wetherell, 1998).

Since culture is multi-layered, young people in British multiethnic schools come into contact with a range of cultures – those seen as national and religious as well as 'youth cultures'. An understanding of their everyday lives thus necessarily involves recognising that ethnicity and 'race' are plural, dynamic and socially constructed concepts, which are frequently used in overlapping ways – an idea conveyed in the terms 'racialisation' and 'ethnicisation' (Anthias and Yuval-Davis, 1992; Omi and Winant, 1986).

The study

Our study[1] was concerned with the ways in which masculine identities are constructed through narratives and we focused particularly on boys' discussions in groups (mixed gender and boys only) and on interviews with individual boys and a few individual girls. The boys were drawn from twelve secondary schools in London (four in the private and eight in the state education sector; four were boys' schools and eight co-educational). We conducted 45 group interviews with groups usually of 4–6 young people (and a range of 4–8). Thirty of these group interviews were with boys in single sex groups and nine were with groups of boys and girls about boys. This involved a sample of 245 boys and 27 girls (see Frosh *et al.*, 2001 for a fuller description of the study).

Seventy-eight volunteers from the boys who had taken part in the group interviews were selected for individual interviews. The design of the study was for a follow-up to the individual interview approximately two weeks after the first interview; 71 boys were given a second interview. In seven cases, boys were either away from school or excluded and hence were not available for second interviews. Of the boys given individual interviews, 12 boys were 'Asian', 16 black, 6 of mixed-parentage and 44 white. More boys were from middle class (45) than working class (26) backgrounds (we could not establish the social class of 7 boys). Most (51) lived with both of their parents.

The theoretical perspective from which this study comes is one in which 'identity' is viewed as multiple and potentially fluid, constructed through experience and linguistically coded into narratives. Identities are achieved relationally through the use of the cultural resources available in the immediate social networks of individuals and in society as a whole. These include prevalent ideologies of masculinity, the social structures in which boys and men live, and their positioning within those structures. As a result, these resources are, generally speaking, strongly gendered, with males and females receiving different messages, being constrained differently, and having access to different codes. Identity and gender consequently stand in a dynamic relationship to one another: 'gender identity' is a central component in identity construction as a whole and, therefore, other identities (e.g. of ethnicity and class) are gendered. For example, the experience of performing the identity of 'black man (or boy)' is likely to be different from that of 'white man (or boy)', but also different from 'black woman (or girl)'. In general, identity theorists agree that identity construction involves the construction of difference (e.g. of gender and racialisation) and so of 'othering'. Inevitably, therefore, identities are imbued with power relations and are sites of contestation and anxiety as well as commonality.

Given this complexity, it is not surprising that the process of identity-construction is one upon which the contradictions in everyday cultures have a powerful impact. People are both positioned in social situations and are active creators of their identities (Wetherell and Edley, 1998). In recognition of this, the study employs a narrative analytic framework as a way of documenting both the conscious positions taken up by boys in their early secondary school careers, and their less clearly articulated wishes and anxieties.

Narrative analysis has proliferated over recent years so that, while it is concerned with investigating and analysing the stories people tell, different analysts do this in a variety of ways. Thus, it is possible to consider the temporal ordering of a plot, to focus on themes, episodes and drama and/or to analyse narrative as an interactional accomplishment (Riessman, 2001). In the research reported in this paper, narrative was conceptualised as a collaborative, relational process in which the researcher and participant co-constructed identity positions in a variety of ways. However, as Bruner (1990) pointed out, narratives cannot be divorced from the social and historical contexts in which they occur and, for that reason, individual stories also speak of the cultures in which they are located. In Bruner's terms, it is possible to see, in individual stories, ideas about how lives ought to be lived within the culture ('canonical narratives'). One reason why stories are told in particular ways is, therefore, to account for how the individual story fits with, or fails to fit, the canon (Riessman,1993). The canon is particularly clearly identifiable when several narratives on the same issue are available. The analyses that follow address the ways in which the narratives of boys in the masculinities study indicated that boys ought to live their everyday lives at school.

Canonical narratives of hegemonic masculinity

One of our central findings has been that 11–14 year old boys (and the girls we interviewed) have sophisticated understandings of the current contradictions associated with the negotiation of masculine identities. For example, many boys recognised that popular masculinity is pervasively constructed as antithetical to being seen to engage with schoolwork. Yet, some were clear that they wished to attain good qualifications without being labelled by other boys in pejorative terms. Many saw masculinity and toughness as inextricably linked but said that they themselves were not tough. This led many boys to give self-justificatory accounts. A common account constructed by the boys related to the racialisation of masculinity, with African-Caribbean boys being seen (as in other studies – e.g. Sewell, 1997) as particularly masculine, but nevertheless often being denigrated. These contradictions were related to what we identified as the major canonical narratives about masculinity current in London schools. The 'canonical narratives' produced by boys in the study reported here can briefly be summarised in three parts:

- Boys must maintain their difference from girls (and so avoid doing anything that is seen as what girls do).

- Popular masculinity involves 'hardness', sporting prowess, 'coolness', casual treatment of schoolwork and being adept at 'cussing'.

- Some boys are more masculine than others. This is racialised and includes class contestation.

These 'canonical narratives' are highly stereotypic constructions of masculinity that constrain everyday cultural practices, even those of boys who resist them' and so help to constitute and constrain what boys see as acceptable masculine identities and performances. Boys frequently illustrated them with examples from their own experiences. However, they more usually produced generalised narratives making claims about what usually happens or how things typically are. Butler (1993) suggests that it is through repetition of gender performances that particular characteristics come to be taken for granted as masculine or feminine identities. For many boys in the study reported here, the accounts to which we refer as canonical narratives appeared 'well-worn' and, through repetition, are likely to be important to the construction of boys' masculine identities.

Of course, boys are not all the same and do take different positions in relation to masculinities. However, while boys' narratives of the self and self-experience ('personal narratives') were more nuanced, canonical narratives were routinely produced and served as a standard against which boys compared themselves.

Constructed gender oppositions in everyday school practices

One of the marked changes in theorisations of gender over the past few years has been the de-essentialising of gender. It is now quite widely accepted that gender is relational (e.g. Connell, 1995) and performative (Butler, 1993, 1997). This fits well with shifts in the theorisation of identities which emphasise the ways in which individuals occupy multiple positions and therefore have a range of fragmented identities, which are relational, become salient in different contexts and are always in the process of being formed, rather than achieved and fixed.

Theorisations such as these have helped to produce complex and convincing research accounts of gender (including masculinities). For example, Hollway and Jefferson (2000) used psychoanalytic notions that people are meaning-making and have defended subjectivities with anxiety-driven investments (from Melanie Klein) to produce a more complex understanding of fear-of-crime than one that simply argues that women are more afraid of potential crime against them than are men. Instead, their analyses demonstrate that it is not helpful to view men and women as opposites in terms of fear of crime. Rather, both men's and women's fears arise from their experiences and unconscious processes. Deborah Cameron (1997) carefully analysed conversations between young men to demonstrate that the work of producing and warranting oneself as masculine does not always entail talking in ways that are antithetical to femininity (as is often assumed). She shows how, in conversation, young men perform themselves in a variety of ways, including showing emotions and using ways of talking generally considered to typify women.

However, although gender is complex, relational and dynamic, the stories that people tell about themselves do not necessarily demonstrate this in a straightforward way. As Stuart Hall argues, we can acquire and maintain a distinctive and continuous sense of self through the construction of a unified autobiographical narrative in which we reconstruct the past in ways that help us to understand the present (Hall, 1992). In a similar way Charlotte Linde (1993) – and other narrative analysts – argues that we all search for coherence in our life narratives.

The canonical narratives of boys in this study constructed masculinities as relational – to girls, other boys and adults. However, they also worked to maintain essentialist notions of masculinity as they negotiated their everyday school cultures. In particular, they constructed boys and girls as opposites and this construction both constrained and enabled boys' everyday cultural practices.

Table 1 Constructed oppositions between boys and girls

Boys	Girls
Sporty/active	Just talk/do nothing
'Hard'	Weak/soft
Jokey	Over-serious
Casual about schoolwork	Conscientious about schoolwork
Immature	Mature
Familiar	Strange

We found that 'having a laugh' was a way of being a boy in relation to adult authority and classroom learning, and was part of an oppositional culture around which high status could be constructed. Conscientiousness and commitment to work were, in contrast, feminised. Boys were derided for being seen to be too conscientious and constructed as unsporty, weak and antisocial. This constructed opposition meant that many boys' accounts indicated that they did not really know girls or what girls do with their time. This was true for boys in mixed sex schools as well as those in single sex schools, perhaps because some mixed schools had few girls in them.

RP: *Do you mix much with girls here?*

Harry: *No.*

RP: *Why's that?*

Harry: *I just don't.*

RP: *Are there many girls in your class?*

Harry: *No. Five.*

RP: *Oh yeah I remember you saying that in the group interview. Do you think girls are quite different than boys?*

Harry: *Yeah.*

RP: *In what way?*

Harry: *'Cos like girls talk about like all things and like they don't really like sport things.*

RP: *Right. What kind of things do they talk about?*

Harry: *I ain't spied on 'em yet! (laughing)*

RP: *You haven't spied on them. Yeah. Like in class do the girls all sit together then?*

Harry: Yeah at the back. And I sit like second row from the front.
                (12 year old white boy)

RP: You said you didn't mix with girls in your class and you said
                at lunch time that girls just walked around talking girlie stuff.
                Um, but you also said that all the girls in your class were
                friends. I was wondering how you got to be friendly with
                them when you didn't really mix very much with them? I
                mean what do you do with them?

Julian: We're just – we're just friends you know, like, it's not that,
                like we all know each other, everyone knows each other in
                the class and – like, I don't, I don't know what the girls do at
                lunch time just like, they're all either – all sittin' down there
                in a crowd talkin' and then they, you look, and then they're
                gone, they're either eatin' or they just (pause) we don't know
                what they do like ... what we're doin' and that sort of thing
                but   –.
                (12 year old white boy)

Lance: You have to be a good listener to be friends with girls – cos
                like girls like to talk a lot.

RP: ... What do girls talk about?

Lance: Nothing really they just talk – they go on about anything as
                long as they are talking.

RP: ... Do you listen to them ...?

Lance: Like parts of it so that if they ask you a question you can
                answer it ... but not like fully paying attention.
                (14 year old black boy)

Jim: When they [girls] call you over you say I've only got a couple
                of mins 'cause I want to get back to football and they're still
                chatting on and it's the end of break'.
                (12 year old white boy)

In constructing these oppositions between boys and girls, the boys quoted above
were constructing identity positions for themselves as entirely different from
girls. This common narrative device fits with theories of identity which all
construct identity as inextricably linked to the construction of difference. Boys'
narratives constructed themes of routine and habitual differences between 'I'
and 'they'. As we shall see below, this was a narrative device they used to
differentiate themselves from boys they considered unpopular as well as from
girls.

Constructed oppositions between popular masculinity and doing schoolwork

It is all too easy for media reports on boys and education either to treat boys as if they are passive recipients of an educational system that is failing them, or as hooligans whose mindless behaviour is responsible for their educational problems. Neither of these positions can be justified if we consider what boys themselves say (Katz and Buchanan, 1999). In our interviews, many boys explained that they faced contradictions in negotiating both masculine identities and schoolwork. The major reason for this was that popular or 'hegemonic' masculinity is pervasively constructed as antithetical to being seen to work hard academically. This posed problems for some of those boys who wished to attain good qualifications without being labelled by other boys in pejorative terms. Far from being mindless, boys had continually, and actively, to negotiate how to position themselves in relation to popular and unpopular masculinities and, hence, to education. It was, thus, far from a simple matter for them to reconcile educational demands with the constraints imposed by canonical narratives of masculinity.

In a study of boys in a Midlands secondary school, Mac an Ghaill (1994) found that the boys he typified as 'academic achievers' (who worked hard because they aspired to professional jobs) were considered effeminate by boys and teachers alike. Similarly, in our study, a pervasive narrative was that being viewed as 'clever' or a 'swot' was not really masculine and was likely to make for unpopularity. Many boys counterposed schoolwork and sport; being good at the former was a marker of unpopularity, whereas sporting prowess often led to high masculine status. The accounts below demonstrate this clearly, and also exemplify a narrative device commonly used by many boys: the creation of a hierarchy of popularity with boys at different points in the hierarchy being reported to play different games and to do different amounts of schoolwork.

> Sadeem: We are a less popular group of people. We're not the least popular group of people.
>
> RP: So the least popular group of people, could you describe them?
>
> Sadeem: Um, (pause) I would say it's people who, who do lots of work and things like that and (pause) um (long pause) um, that's mainly it actually, just people who are sort of boffins ... We just all play basketball together – and most of the ones at the top they play football – and – the bottom ones just [laughter] stay in the classroom and do homework (pause) and play cards or something.
> (12 year old Asian boy)
>
> RP: Define a boy?
>
> Andrew: A young male who likes mainly sport rather than academic work and would prefer to go out instead of going working and stuff, doing homework and stuff. Um always competitive enters competitions and stuff and try and beat each other.

RP: *What sort of competitions?*

Andrew: *In the playground, football and stuff and rugby always try*
               to be the best of each other ... and like at school trying to get
               the best grades.

RP: *But I thought you said that boys weren't that very academic?*

Andrew: *Um they still try like cos it's quite a good school here. They*
               try and get quite good grades to please their parents ...

RP: *So boys are both competitive academically and also in*
               sports?

Andrew: *Yeah. But they're more (inaudible) sports.*

RP: *So that's more important to them than work is it?*

Andrew: *Yeah.*

RP: *Does that apply to all boys?*

Andrew: *Um I dunno cos some boys just like to sit down and read*
               and do stuff.

RP: *Right so they're not really boys then?*

Andrew: *Um well they are but they just like they don't hang around*
               with people I hang out with the sporty types – they just like
               to stay home and play.
               (14 year old white boy, private school)

These accounts, like many others, indicate that what Edley and Wetherell (1997) call 'jockeying for position' in hegemonic masculinity does not remain outside the classroom. Instead, boys' positioning in the hierarchy of popular masculinity created quite specific expectations of how they would behave both in break times and in lessons. In the first extract above, Sadeem constructs a narrative of difference from 'boffins' while 'we ... play basketball' and Andrew, in the second extract, says 'I hang out with the sporty types' in contradistinction from 'they', who like to stay home and play.

The polarisation of popularity and schoolwork had significant consequences. For example, a major obstacle to boys treating school as a place in which to do serious schoolwork is that this could lead to their being bullied.

Thomas: *It's your attitude, but some people are bullied for no reason*
               whatsoever just because other people are jealous of them
               and I find that quite annoying.

RP: *How do they get bullied?*

Thomas: *There's a boy in our year called James and he's really clever*
             and he's basically got no friends and that's really sad because
             he's such a clever boy and he gets top marks in every test
             and everyone hates him. I mean I like him, when I see
             someone bullying him I just tell them to go and get lost, I
             just find that really annoying.

RP: *Is it clever boys that get bullied?*

Thomas: *No not always, it's also because he's really shy. Some people*
             are really clever and they get bullied, it's just he's just bullied,
             I think he's bullied too much and he never answers back so
             they find it easy to bully him.
             (14 year old white boy)

In the extract above, Thomas deals with the dilemma of presenting himself as a boy who is nevertheless sympathetic to school achievement. He disclaims the notion that everyone hates the really clever boy in his class by professing that he (Thomas) likes him and defends him from bullying. He thus distances himself from the potentially troubled position (Wetherell, 1998) of being one of those who bullies a boy just because his academic attainments are better than everybody else's. Instead, Thomas constructs for himself the untroubled position of being kind and morally responsible.

Since boys who attend private schools generally attain better academic results than boys in state schools, it may be considered that constructed oppositions between schoolwork and masculinity would not affect boys attending such schools. However, while their narratives indicated that they knew they had to gain academic qualifications since their parents were paying for this, many also produced narratives that indicated that they disliked being seen as too soft or too academic.

Albert: *We have like a weak school and not a hard school.*

RP: *Meaning?*

Albert: *Um well we got a reputation of being a very good academic*
             school and not having any good – good hard people so um
             it's quite annoying cos it's quite rough actually, we do rough
             sports and we're quite hard.

RP: *Why do you think you got that reputation?*

Albert: *Cos loads of our pupils are really weak, like really*
             academicos. This counts as a really academic school.

RP: *Why are there so many pupils in this school like that?*

Albert: *Don't know.*

RP: *You feel quite annoyed about that?*

Albert: Yeah 'cos loads of us like we don't deserve this reputation.
           (13 year old white private schoolboy)

RP: Do any boys get teased who do very well precisely because
           they work hard ...?

Justin: Um I think it's their attitude really, there are some boys who
           are really intelligent and there's nothing you can do about
           that. So people don't tease them about that but I think what
           they do tease them about is if they walk around and they
           study, study, study and I mean study at school and in
           lunchtime and you'd much rather being playing football or
           something. That's when they start getting teased or in your
           classroom for one and a half hours when no-one else is.
           That's when people start to tease you and to say 'what are
           you up to you nerd' and so on, but most people are, if you're
           intelligent you're intelligent and if your brain works better
           than other people there's nothing else they can do about.
           People tend to leave them very much alone.

RP: So it's okay to work hard at home is it, but not at school?

Justin: It's okay to work hard at home, work hard at school during
           lessons but when it's lunchtime and break you know, take a
           break. There's boys sitting there working away, people really
           hate that.

RP: And there are boys like that are there?

Justin: There are boys like that, um maybe it's just it could be they're
           shy or something, but there are people who just want to
           work – some people don't understand.
           (14 year old black private schoolboy)

The canonical narrative that produced a constructed opposition between doing schoolwork and being properly masculine also had an impact on boys' construction of girls as an opposite category to boys. A recurrent theme in their narratives was that girls are more conscientious about schoolwork than boys and take it all too seriously. Boys on the other hand were approvingly considered to take schoolwork lightly and to be prepared to have a laugh about it.

Chris: Girls are moody ... Because like you just walk past them and
           you tap their work by accident and they shout at you and
           scream at you ... you do that to a boy, you say sorry to them
           and they just carry on with their work.
           (11 year old white boy)

RP: Do girls make people laugh like boys do?

Terry: Girls – I don't – they're not as funny. (pause) You know they
           take things more seriously.

RP: Right – why's that?

Terry: ... They're just – they wanna get on, you know do all their
            work an' get all GCSEs an' everything. But – the boys – they
            – wanna get the GCSEs an' everything alright, but they just
            wanna have a joke as well.
            (14 year old white boy)

It was not, however, that boys joked about everything. In keeping with the importance of football to the construction of hegemonic masculinity, football was pervasively reported to be taken seriously by most boys and featured in all their narratives – including those of boys (mostly from private schools) who also indicated that they played rugby and considered this a tough game.

Scott: Boys don't really like being – you know – shown up like that
            or miscuing a shot or something – I don't think they like,
            you know – looking the idiot while girls don't mind.

RP: Even though boys muck around quite a bit and have a laugh?

Scott: No, it's more football they don't like looking the idiot 'cause
            a lot of the boys think they're really good 'cause they don't
            like looking the idiot if you nutmeg them [putting the ball
            through their legs in football] or something, but like in the
            classroom or something – if you trip over a chair they just
            laugh about it.
            (12 year old white boy)

In summary, boys' canonical narratives counterposed sporting prowess and being seen to be engaged with schoolwork. Such narratives led many boys to construct oppositions between boys and girls as well as between popular boys and boys who work 'too hard'. Almost all the boys in the study were careful to construct their identities as entirely different from girls and from boys who work too hard. This both arose from, and contributed to, a unitary (rather than plural) canonical narrative in which only one version of masculinity was allowed within schools. Canonical narratives arose from their everyday school cultures, but also impacted on those cultures, limiting what boys felt able to do.

Racialisation of popular masculinity

Studies of young men in multiethnic societies make it clear that masculinities are racialised. For example, research with British young people suggests that black young men of African-Caribbean descent are viewed in some ways as 'super-masculine'. They are constructed as possessing the attributes that are considered to be most masculine – toughness and authentically male style in talk and dress. Paradoxically, while they are feared and discriminated against because of those features, they are also respected, admired and gain power through taking on characteristics which militate against good classroom performance (Back, 1996; Mac an Ghaill, 1988).

Tony Sewell (1997) found that many of the 15 year old black boys he studied were both positioned by others, and positioned themselves, as superior to white and Asian students in terms of their sexual attractiveness, style, creativity and 'hardness'. They were, however, contradictorily positioned:

> *Black boys are Angels and Devils in British (and American) schools. They are heroes of a street fashion culture that dominates most of our inner cities. On the other hand they experience a disproportionate amount of punishment in our schools compared to all other groupings ... This experience of being the darling of popular youth sub-culture and the sinner in the classroom has led to the formation of a range of behaviours. How do African-Caribbean boys in particular respond in a school that sees them as sexy and as sexually threatening? These responses are what I call masculinities. They are linked to how the boys perceive themselves as males and how others perceive them.*
> (Sewell, 1997: ix)

In this study, boys' accounts indicated that masculinities were racialised in two ways: through differential treatment from, for example, teachers; and because black, white and Asian boys were considered to be differentially positioned in terms of 'hegemonic' masculinity. The characteristics of hegemonic masculinity ('hardness', sporting prowess – particularly at football – and resistance to teachers) were qualities that were particularly attributed to black boys.

The following example is notable both for the racialisation of black boys as popular and for the differential racialisation of Asian boys as *not* popular. This racialisation is common among the boys in the study. Boys' narratives frequently constructed black boys as hegemonically masculine, Asian boys as both not properly masculine and unpopular and white boys as in between, but closer to black boys than Asian boys. In the extract below, only three of the four boys speak in this part of the discussion and one dominates the discussion. Note that while he makes general claims about black boys' popularity, it does not appear to be comfortable for Des to apply the notion of black boys as popular to his own school year:

Des:	*Don't know it's just – black boys seem to get friends easier – and they're more popular I suppose.*
RP:	*Yeah, – they get friends more easy yeh /.../ But I was just wondering cos you said that black boys tend to be quite popular and I was wondering if it was the same with Asian boys? What about in your class, are Asian boys as popular as black boys?*
Des:	*No I shouldn't think so.*
Jason:	*No.*
RP:	*They're not no.*

Des: No.

RP: Why's that?

Des: Don't really know sigh – black boys um Asian boys just go
            round with – like who they want – but they don't they don't
            go out picking, they wait for them come to them – they've
            only got a few friends /.../

RP: So you tend to go around you're more likely to go around
            with black boys than Asian boys are you?

Graham: Yeah.

RP: Wh – why is that do you think ?

Graham: (long pause) Probably 'cos like – sometimes you think not –
            you ain't you're not really popular an' – you know someone
            who is popular and you go and like try and hang around
            with them?
            (Group interview with four white boys from year 8 (12–13
            year olds))

In the extract above, Des presents one version of why Asian boys are unpopular – that they go around with other Asian boys, rather than having friends from other groups. This version was widely shared among other boys, even as accounts of informal racialised segregation as part of everyday school cultures formed part of many boys' narratives. The point here is that boys constructed racialised hierarchies of masculinities that served to exclude Asian boys while idealising black boys.

While this theme, of black boys being popular, admired and envied (and Asian boys not being so) and so being viewed as hegemonically masculine, was common, white boys did not generally claim that they themselves wanted to 'be black' – at least not all the time. In the quote below, for example, Paul addresses the direct question of whether white boys envy black boys in the affirmative. However, when asked about himself, he immediately asserts that he is happy to be the colour he is – a common discourse in the study since white young men usually assert that it is other white young men who want to be black (or who are racist). Asked directly about themselves, most produce an egalitarian discourse that colour does not matter to them.

RP: D'you think some white boys then envy black boys (pause)
            'cos they think they're stronger?

Paul: Yeah like, they wanna like, some people wanna be black 'cos
            (pause) they might like be more popular. Like, black people
            like, don't like really cool. Black people have like black slang
            don't they an' they call people – bro an' that (hands – not
            clear). Like white people don't call each other – names like
            that an' black people call some people some. And sometimes
            people wanna be black an' that.

RP: *Oh do they, yeah?*

Paul: *Yeah.*

RP: *Yeah, yeah. What about you?*

Paul: *I'm not really bothered what colour I am. [RP Yeah, yeah.] Happy the way (how I'm made). I don't really mind.*
(11 year old white boy)

RP: *Are there any things that you admire about black people ?*

Luke: *Um (very long pause), they seem more confident in a way they're sort of (very long pause), they act sort of bigger and louder and more confident – and I sort of admire that.*

RP: *Do you wish you were more like that then?*

Luke: *Sometimes (pause) but not like (pause) inaudible. It's not like I don't think about it a lot – I don't think, 'Oh I really want to be black' – or, 'I really want to be like that'.*
(14 year old white boy)

The racialisation of black boys' styles, bodies and cultural practices is part of their common construction as 'cool' and sexy (Majors and Billson, 1992; Sewell, 1997). Although this was a pervasive narrative, some boys recognised that black boys are constructed as hegemonically masculine, but gave more nuanced accounts that indicated that this is an 'initial impression' that is dispelled by familiarity.

RP: *You were telling me that one of the things that make boys popular earlier on is being good at sport and being quite strong and quite big. Does that mean that black boys, because they are bigger and stronger, they tend to be more popular?*

Leroy: *Yeah, I think initially when, I think that's the first initial impression, as you're a black person, you're pretty affluent, you're usually happy, someone will think I like him I'll be his friend kind of thing. But after a while the more you get to know them, you become less bothered about how big or strong they are, it's more of can we relate together and talk about the same kind of things, or what do we have in common and that kind of stuff as well um I think that's more important at this age, though obviously little things like that help. He's big and he's strong. (14 year old black boy)*

The racialisation of black boys' style and bodies as indicative of popular masculinity is more complicated than appears at first sight. The following extract from a group interview with six 12–14 year old white boys, demonstrates how whiteness is implicitly racialised as 'normal' and not 'showy' in opposition to blackness. It demonstrates how some white boys contest black boys' cultural dominance. This source of contestation has long been reported in work by Les Back (1996), Roger Hewitt (1986) and Simon Jones (1988). In addition, the quote below, from a group of white 13 year olds, indicates the differential racialisation of black boys of African-Caribbean and African backgrounds.

> George: White people have their own styles so do black people – sometimes Moroccans have theirs – but Somalis just copy.
>
> RP: What's the white style then?
>
> John: Kind of normal in't it (George: tracksuit) – normal clothes – no flashness no nothing.
>
> RP: No flashness.
>
> Adam: Casual clothes.
>
> RP: So black boys are more flash are they than white boys?
>
> Adam: Yeah they like showing off /.../
>
> RP: Why do the Somalis and Moroccans try and copy the black boys and not the white boys? (pause).
>
> George: It's just that – they learn that – the clothes that look – the – top in'it?
>
> Adam: I – I wouldn't wear them.
>
> John: Black people they wear like like design designer wear (pause).
>
> RP: Right.
>
> John: And like they (Adam: more expensive) yeah much more expensive
>
> RP: More expensive yeh?
>
> John: Yeh (inaudible).
>
> George: Doesn't mean they've got more money or nothing it's just that – they like – they like to show what they've got and everything but – (RP: Right) they're just spending their money just on clothes.

Overall then, racialised hierarchies in which black boys were constructed as the most hegemonically masculine and Asian boys the least underpinned boys' canonical narratives of masculinity. The complexity and situatedness of these narratives were demonstrated in boys' nuancing of such accounts and in the construction of blackness as synonymous with being of African-Caribbean origin. As in the example above, the perceived cultural dominance of black boys in relation to masculinity sometimes made the racialisation of masculinity a site of contestation. However, the pervasiveness of racialised constructions of difference indicated its centrality to the production of identity positions.

In conclusion

Constructions of popular/hegemonic masculinity are pervasive in 11–14 year old boys' accounts and serve to constitute masculine identities within everyday school cultures. This version of masculinity is characterised by stereotyped notions of toughness, footballing prowess and resistance to teachers and education. Everyday school cultures are produced and reproduced as boys negotiate – in a variety of ways – the prescriptions associated with these pervasive constructions of popular masculinity. They are also a resource in the construction of masculinities. As Connell (1995) argues, masculinities are produced from the cultural resources available, which include ideologies, social structures, and boys' and men's particular experiences and social positions.

This chapter has focused particularly on the canonical narratives of masculinities pervasively produced in the everyday cultures of secondary schools and how these constrain the repertoires available to boys. The examination of the ways in which popular notions of masculinity help to constitute and constrain what boys see as acceptable gender identities and performances demonstrates the intersection of ideologies, social structures and identity positions. This is because the ideology of what masculinity should be like (and hence how canonical narratives affect boys' notions of how life should be lived within their school cultures) arises within the social structures of particular schools. In addition, it produces and is produced by the identity positions boys take up and defend in relation to masculinity.

The chapter has argued that boys' canonical narratives of masculinity are unitary (rather than including a range of masculinities) and prescribe that boys should not do what girls do (since girls are constructed as boys' opposites). Similarly, almost all boys in the study attempted to differentiate themselves from boys who pay 'too much' attention to their schoolwork. Their narratives also demonstrated that school cultures were simultaneously racialised as well as gendered. Thus, black boys of African-Caribbean descent were constructed as the most hegemonically masculine boys. While some boys produced narratives that eschewed the notion that all black boys were necessarily tough and 'cool', the racialisation of masculinity produced admiration, envy and contestation in some white boys. Everyday masculine school cultures are thus predicated on the maintenance of different axes of difference, including gender, racialisation and attitudes to schoolwork.

Note

1   This study was conducted by Stephen Frosh, Rob Pattman and myself and was funded by the Economic and Social Research Council (ESRC) grant number: L/129/25/1015. For further details see, Frosh et al. (2001) Young Masculinities. London: Palgrave.

References

Ahmad, W., Darr, A. and Jones, L. (2000) ' "I send my child to school and he comes back an Englishman": minority ethnic deaf people, identity politics and services', in W. Ahmad (ed.) *Ethnicity, Disability and Chronic Illness.* Buckingham: Open University Press

Anthias, F. and Yuval-Davis, N. (1992) *Racialised Boundaries: Race, Gender, Colour and Class and the Anti-Racist Struggle.* London: Routledge

Back, L. (1996) *New Ethnicities and Urban Culture.* London: UCL Press

Brah, A. (1996) *Cartographies of Diaspora: Contesting Identities.* London: Routledge

Bruner, J. (1990) *Acts of Meaning.* Cambridge, MA: Harvard University Press

Butler, J. (1993) *Bodies that Matter.* New York: Routledge

Butler, J. (1997) 'Gender as performance: an interview with Judith Butler for Radical Philosophy', by P. Osborne and L. Segal, in K. Woodward (ed.) *Identity and Difference.* Milton Keynes: Open University Press

Cameron, D. (1997) 'Performing gender identity: young men's talk and the construction of heterosexual masculinity', in S. Johnson and U. H. Meinhof (eds) *Language and Masculinity.* Oxford: Blackwell

Clifford, J. and Marcus, G. (eds) (1986) *Writing Culture: The Poetics and Politics of Ethnography.* Cambridge, MA: Harvard University Press

Connell, R. (1987) *Gender and Power.* Cambridge: Polity Press

Connell, R. (1995) *Masculinities.* Cambridge: Polity Press

Connell, R. (1996) 'Teaching the boys: new research on masculinity, and gender strategies for schools', *Teachers College Record*, Vol. 98, pp. 206–35

Connell, R. (2000) *The Men and the Boys.* Berkeley, CA: University of California Press

Connolly, P. (1998) *Racism, Gender Identities and Young Children.* London: Routledge

Eder, D., Evans, C.C. and Parker, S. (1995) *School Talk: Gender and Adolescent Cultures.* New Brunswick: Rutgers University Press

Edley, N. and Wetherell M. (1997) 'Jockeying for position: the construction of masculine identities', *Discourse and Society*, Vol. 8, No. 2, pp. 203–17

Frosh, S., Phoenix, A. and Pattman, R. (2001) *Young Masculinities*, London: Palgrave

Gilbert, R. and Gilbert, P. (1998) *Masculinity Goes to School.* London: Routledge

Hall, S. (1992) 'The questions of cultural identity', in S. Hall, D. Held and T. McGrew (eds) *Modernity and its Futures.* Cambridge: Polity Press

Hall, S. and du Gay, P. (eds) (1996) *Questions of Cultural Identity*. London: Sage

Hewitt, R. (1986) *White Talk Black Talk*. Cambridge: Cambridge University Press

Hey, V. (1997) *The Company She Keeps*. Buckingham: Open University Press

Hollway, W. and Jefferson, T. (2000) *Doing Qualitative Research Differently*. London: Sage

Jones, S. (1988) *Black Culture, White Youth*. London: Macmillan

Katz, A. and Buchanan, A. (1999) *Leading Lads*. London: Topman

Linde, C. (1993) *Life Stories: The Creation of Coherence*. New York: Oxford University Press

Mac an Ghaill, M. (1988) *Young, Gifted and Black: Student Teacher Relations in the Schooling of Black Youth*. Milton Keynes: Open University Press

Mac an Ghaill, M. (1994) *The Making of Men: Masculinities, Sexualities and Schooling*. Buckingham: Open University Press

Majors, R. and Billson, J. (1992) *Cool Pose: The Dilemmas of Black Manhood in America*. New York: Lexington

Omi, M. and Winant, H. (1986) *Racial Formation in the United States: From the 1960s to the 1980s*. New York: Routledge and Kegan Paul

Pattman, R., Frosh, S. and Phoenix, A. (1998) 'Lads, machos and others: developing "boy-centred" research', *Journal of Youth Studies*, Vol. 1, No. 2, pp.125–42

Riessman, C.K. (1993) *Narrative Analysis*. London: Sage

Riessman C.K. (2001) 'Analysis of personal narratives', in J.F. Gubrium and J.A. Holstein (eds) *Handbook of Interviewing*. London: Sage

Sewell, T. (1997) *Black Masculinities and Schooling: How Black Boys Survive Modern Schooling*. Stoke-on-Trent: Trentham

Wetherell, M. (1998) 'Positioning and interpretive repertoires: conversation analysis and post-structuralism in dialogue', *Discourse and Society*, Vol. 9, pp. 387–412

Wetherell, M. and Edley, N. (1998) 'Gender Practices: Steps in the analysis of men and masculinities', in K. Henwood, C. Griffin and A. Phoenix (eds) *Standpoints and Differences: Essays in the practice of feminist psychology*. London: Sage

Wetherell, M. and Edley, N. (1999) 'Negotiating hegemonic masculinity: imaginary positions and psycho-discursive practices', *Feminism and Psychology*, Vol. 9, 335–56

Chapter 9

It's a wonderful life? Cultures of ageing

Andrew Blaikie

Introduction: the ageing of cultures

Ageism is an index of inequality in contemporary society. It is also a reflection of indifference, and nowhere more than in the otherwise enlightened academy. The life course forms a pivot around which all our lives hinge, yet cultural theorists have not embraced age as an organising principle or motif for identification and contestation in the way they have explored 'race', class and gender. Meanwhile, a policy-dominated tradition of political economy has been crucial in highlighting the structured dependency of 'the elderly', but rather less useful in developing a sociologically informed interpretation of the processes of ageing itself. Despite the need to understand the experiences of the increasing numbers of people in retirement, there has been a persistent focus upon conflict theories that are more concerned with gross inter-generational inequalities than with the meanings of micro-social interaction. There are of course exceptions, but generally the sociology of ageing is both structurally overdetermined and culturally impoverished.

This chapter contends that although the uniform marginality imposed upon older people through retirement is itself becoming redundant in a fragmenting late-modern context, macro-level theories continue to interpret ageing as a field of inter-generational conflict. This anachronistic and stereotypical positioning is reflected in the failure of cultural studies to include age within the framework for interpreting social diversity, inequality and exclusion, partly because the youth-fixated researchers of the 1960s and after have themselves been imbued with a generationally-specific disdain. This appears paradoxical, since the theories developed by cultural theorists have focused on the articulation of agency through micro-scale approaches that have by definition rejected overarching categorisation.

In order to position ageing within the disciplinary discourse of cultural studies, or indeed of cultural sociology, the concepts and methods of cultural analysis must be applied to the everyday worlds of older people. This means effectively explaining the connections between subcultural analysis, popular culture and the ordinary practices of later life by investigating the origins of differing world-views as well as their impact on a range of behaviours and lifestyles. Understanding how older people negotiate the tensions between a lifelong work ethic and consumerist imperatives to enjoy leisure, or how ontological security is maintained under conditions of poverty and declining health, requires the ethnographic interrogation of narrative lifeworlds. Nevertheless, the present state of cultural research *vis-à-vis* the life course forces one to conclude that the ageing youth culture of the baby boom generation is continuing to deny its own destiny by distancing itself from self-reflection.

A major demographic and organisational transition has occurred. A century ago only 5 per cent of the British population was over 65 and two-thirds of older men were still economically active. Notwithstanding the disregard for women's domestic labour, it made sense to talk of a 'work society' that marginalised those outside it (Arber and Ginn, 1991). Today, however, with considerably increased life expectancy, most people can expect to spend several decades in a post-work environment (Laslett, 1987). Under modernity western societies were remarkable for the application of age-graded classifications, not least through the invention of retirement. But that era is fast being superseded by late-modern shifts in the balance of production and consumption that find resonance in the fragmentation of chronological categories (Featherstone and Hepworth, 1989). How, then are we to interpret later life?

Conflict theories as generational bias

Until the late 1960s the study of ageing was dominated by a social problems perspective concerned with policy and welfare needs. Since then, interest has grown in the social construction of ageing, in lived experience, and in normal as against pathological ageing. Nevertheless, most researchers have been concerned with social rather than sociological questions. This reflects an adherence to the political economy perspective whereby retirement levels fluctuate because of politically driven labour force requirements. Correspondingly, the structured dependency of older people on the rest of society indicates unequal access to resources, particularly income. The social construction of later life is guided by responses to policy factors, with 'retirement' reified as something 'out there' to which the individual must adjust. Thus, in the refrain 'workers versus pensioners' we can detect a caricature of cohorts competing for scarce resources (Johnson *et al.*, 1989). Meanwhile, from a social exchange perspective, Bryan Turner defines a generation as 'a cohort of persons passing through time who come to share a common habitus and lifestyle' and also 'a strategic temporal location [sic] to a set of resources as a consequence of historical accident and exclusionary practices of social closure' (Turner, 1998: 302). Hence, 'there is a substantial and growing generational conflict [which] does not refer necessarily to parent-child relationships but to non-familial structures of age-related conflict and generational differences in life-style and economic power' (Turner, 1998: 300–1).

These macro-models require no concept of agency, since the subject is produced as an effect: individuals simply internalise or refract collective norms. Likewise with the typologies developed by marketeers in their attempts at lifestyle analysis. The 'psychographic segmentation' of the mature market effectively reduces lifeworlds to reflexes that can be read off from systems of superficially measurable social preferences (Ostroff, 1989). Thus, in a rejoinder to Turner,

Sarah Irwin contends that: 'To see generations as cohesive and distinct entities which are structurally at odds with each other is to neglect the relations through which successive generations are bound in the reproduction of social life' (Irwin, 1998: 307). There is no reason why old age, any more than femaleness, blackness or working-classness, should be made to represent a monolithic social experience. Nevertheless, Turner asserts, 'the older generations attempt to exclude youth by the creation of cultural hurdles such as credentialism, while younger generations accuse their elders of cultural obsolescence' (Turner, 1998: 302). To what extent might cultural analysis bear this out?

The view from cultural studies

Karl Mannheim (1956) avers that common historical experiences form the foundations of each generation's self-image and self-awareness, hence the differing world-views ('time-signatures') of successive cohorts. Arising out of the dissatisfactions of 1968, cultural studies was itself a revolt of the young against the old, be they scholars or Cold War politicians, 'who, as the elderly will, wanted to keep things settled in the old certainties with which they had grown up' (Inglis, 1993: 14). Thus, in celebrating resistance, they followed a sequence common to the making of all new subjects: 'the attack from the new generation upon the old in an effort to superannuate their seniors; the appeal to the true values made stale or rotten by the quiet-voiced elders' (Inglis, 1993: 15). From the outset cultural studies privileged youth over age. Accordingly, analysis of how older people make their own cultures has been absent because youth has occupied centre stage in the generational focus of cultural studies since the 1960s. Moreover, within the media youth subcultures have invited critical interest because they are threatening in ways that older people cannot be: they are perceived as undermining the normative progress of potential – rather than former – workers and parents on whom economic and social stability will depend. And while the refusal to 'mature' or maturing 'too early' have occasioned recurrent moral panics over torn cinema seats, pitched battles between Mods and Rockers, gymslip mums, or children murdering toddlers, archetypal folk devils of the older generation have not loomed large on the political agenda. Instead, taking a cue from the critique of political economy, the growth in numbers of older people has been presented as a fiscal 'burden of dependency'.

This perception is fast becoming anachronistic. In the popular media, the portrayal of older people as a passive problem group has been partially eclipsed by 'positive ageing' messages about the joys of leisured retirement. Rather than being the 'deserving poor', today's ThirdAgers more nearly resemble the adolescents with whom they share a liminal status. In each instance the attendant problems of social adjustment may give rise to personal problems – teenage trauma or midlife crisis – as well as providing the social licence to experiment with norms, values and personal conduct. However, there exist no ethnographic studies of midlife transition, or 'middlescence', to parallel classic studies of youth subcultures as means of managing change, such as Paul Willis's *Learning to Labour* (1977) or Angela McRobbie's (1991) collected work.

Reinventing culture

This lack of concern with ageing in cultural studies is unfortunate since cultural studies perspectives could provide many useful inroads. Among the nostrums which may be deployed are: the force of hegemony (of positive ageing, the baby boom generation, the imperatives of consumer culture; alternatively the negative ideology of 'the welfare generation' and 'burden of dependency'); the need to 'honour the plurality of perspectives'; and a 'recognition of the fragmentation of both world and theory' (Inglis, 1993: 227, 246). Underlying this are some more complex notions, such as the claim that 'identities are constructed through, not outside, difference ... recognition that it is only through the relation to the Other, the relation to what it is not, that the "positive" meaning of any term – and thus its "identity" – can be constructed' (Hall, 1996: 4–5). Equally, if age is not 'other' then some power is retained, hence the concept of 'normal ageing', whereby the very notion of normality has arisen from concern over a pathology, where biomedicine provides the dominant explanatory framework, and bodily decline the bottom line. This raises questions of immanence: the 'crisis of identity' operates 'under erasure ... in the interval between reversal and emergence; an idea which cannot be thought in the old way, but without which certain key questions cannot be thought at all' (Hall, 1996: 2). Such logic chimes in with the theorisation of the flexible life course, with all its implications for the ageless self, as a nascent cultural tendency (Featherstone and Hepworth, 1989).

Cultural studies have focused on the role of everyday understandings of the popular media. For example, the feminist insight that public and private forms of culture are not sealed against one another has informed the ways in which 'a girls' magazine ... picks up and represents some elements of private cultures of femininity by which young girls live their lives' (Johnson, 1983: 23). Such material tends to be instantly evaluated as 'girls' stuff' and trivial. Yet McRobbie (1991) argues that what is occurring is a re-appropriation among the targeted readership of elements first borrowed from their own culture. Popular literature forms a bedrock of their socialisation to modern adolescence. An analysis of older women's periodicals might reveal a similar story. These also publicly provide raw materials – be these fashion features, advice on relationships, escapist fantasies, or ideologies – on which readers reflect in order to construct their private lives. Indeed, the letters page and readers' photos are representations of this process in action.

A broader aestheticisation occurs in the use of photographs as a reflexive resource in everyday life. Snapshots, often collated as family albums, facilitate comparisons between past and present, both across generations (for instance, changing dress styles and pastimes) and within one's own biography ('Was I really that slim?', 'Did I really wear those shoes?'). Meanwhile, magazines of the Third Age, such as *Choice* and *Saga* use photographs to represent idealised models of the ageing body engaged in appropriate lifestyling (Tidmarsh, 2000).

Traditional pastimes such as bowls and bingo would also benefit from the application of cultural theory. Older working-class women enjoy watching all-in wrestling and appear to invest considerable amounts of emotional energy in following each bout. Roland Barthes (1976) once argued that professional wrestling is a spectacle in which justice is played out in the ring: ultimately the good guy wins and the bad guy gets his come-uppance. One might speculate that such theatre appeals particularly to impoverished older women because they have seen little justice in their own lives, and to see the enactment of just deserts provides a catharsis that has otherwise eluded them.

In the 1960s, sociologists seeking to clarify the functions of systematised leisure activities studied such subjects as 'the "retired" stamp collector' and concluded that 'a very large number of avocational pursuits do have the requisite attributes to allow expansion of significant role inter-relationships' (Christ, 1965: 111–12). Then, and subsequently, they analysed the significance of a range of activities, from church participation (Moberg and Taves, 1965) through tea-drinking (Hazan, 1980), to television (Wada, 1988). Although today rather less stereotyped topics like radical grandparenting (Dench, 2000) or communal house-sharing among old friends (Betts et al., 1999) might appear more apt, understanding the appeal of specific modes of living in and spending retirement remains central (Gubrium and Holstein, 2000). Lest this be construed as a plea for some kind of empirically observable populism, I would also advocate the need to account for the role of 'powerful forces beyond the immediate comprehension and control of ordinary people', particularly via consumer culture, in the material construction of emergent trends (McGuigan, 1992: 175). Cultural research into ageing should aim therefore to evaluate the balance between a Habermasian colonisation of everyday life by modernity and attempts by older people to fashion their own identities from the resources available.

Subcultures to lifestyles

Older people are segregated amongst themselves according to income, health status and age-groups, while retirement itself disperses individuals who might formerly have benefited from the collective focus of the workplace. There is thus no one 'culture of ageing' against which to measure their experience. Youth subcultures differentiate themselves by expressions of style, ideology and behaviour, most visibly through dress and musical tastes. And while the expressive forms through which experience is symbolised lend guidance to the researcher, the explanation of why these particular forms arise when they do is analytically crucial (Hebdige, 1979). Within the cultures of the old, as with the young, distinctions of motive are discernible through identifications that may be broadly classified as resistant, incorporationist or consolationist (Blaikie, 2002). However, collective expressions of each within everyday life vary enormously. Since the 'semiotic guerrilla warfare' (Hebdige, 1979: 101) of subversive stylisation is rarely to the fore, older rebels (resistance) are less overtly visible. Similarly, the development of consumer-driven lifestyle enclaves (incorporation) cannot be read as counter-cultural, whilst much of the culture of ageing remains hidden from public view since it involves generally unexpressed world-views privately accessed for purposes of coping with decline (consolation).

In the late 1970s, when unemployment increased and new fears of delinquency arose, 'resistance through rituals' became the clarion cry of the Birmingham School (Hall and Jefferson, 1976). Although later life groups were not considered, resistances were defined here as 'subcultures of parental class cultures'. This emphasis on the need to understand inter-generational relationships as class-based finds resonance in Featherstone and Hepworth's application of Pierre Bourdieu's concept of habitus to the interpretation of 'positive' ageing, their argument being that an expanding new middle class largely composed of baby boomers will dictate a drift towards increased age-denial through the consumption of particular styles and lifestyles (Featherstone and Hepworth, 1986). What is lacking here is an equally class-based interpretation of the antagonisms such a trend might provoke amongst those who do not have the requisite income or cultural capital.

It is difficult to regard older people as 'folk devils' in the sense Stan Cohen meant when he referred to youth gangs (Cohen, 1972). This may be because relatively few ethnographic studies of group behaviour among older people exist, but it does not mean that profound frustrations do not exist. Rather, the apparent quietude of elders marks a difficulty faced by many in effectively communicating their angst. After Robert Merton (1957) and David Matza (1964) it has been argued that unemployed school-leavers turn to crime both as a means of obtaining goods they could not otherwise afford (i.e. they are motivated by blocked access to social rewards) and a way of temporarily relieving boredom (Frith, 1984). Since retirement is frequently also a form of enforced leisure and relative poverty for many, we might expect a similar response. A recent television documentary about people in their seventies and eighties involved in fraud, embezzlement, bank robbery and bootlegging found they resorted to crime partly because of poverty, but also to find 'something to keep me going', to establish new-found identities ('I'd never been in court. I'd never been in prison. I'd never been nothing'), or, in the case of seventeen 'decent old boys who took up tobacco smuggling for fun and a better pension', as a source of sociability and challenge (Channel Four Television, 2001). Nevertheless, as with earlier press stories, it needs to be said that this programme drew public attention precisely because its protagonists contradicted the stereotype of older people as quietly law-abiding (Blaikie, 1999: 187). Indeed, several interviewees wryly commented that they exploited this myth to fool their victims. Against this, most media reportage finds elderly rebellion a source of mirth, and headlines such as 'Oldies' barney at the bingo! OAPs riot as caller flees' (Notarangelo, 1996: 1) are designed to incite laughter rather than fear in the reader. Crimes are generally regarded as individualised acts with any sting of rebellion nullified by press reports trivialising their behaviour by making light of the age element (Hockey and James, 1993). Acts of deviance on the part of older people have not, to date, manifested themselves in collective rituals of gang warfare, sexual promiscuity or drug-based musical gatherings. This does not mean that resistances are lacking, merely that researchers must look elsewhere within the social landscape of middle and later life.

Where old age differs from adulthood in general is in the system of social, physical and mental constraints that gradually enforce conformity. Perhaps, in such a climate, older people prefer alternative modes of expression via the politics of self? For example, being old, visible and on the street usually indicates poverty, depicted as 'silent suffering'. However, often symbolic forms and social actions that are apparently non-political are in fact resistances. One thinks here of the bag lady or of the Skid Row tramp who refuse institutional support by wearing their independence on their sleeve. Minor forms of rebellion have an ostensibly greater impact when indulged by elders. Thus the poem *Warning* (Joseph, 1974) is frequently quoted because the hypothetical woman who decides she will be subversive when she gets old by wearing purple, spending her money on brandy and learning to spit is seen as advocating behaviours that are shocking in an old lady, but would not be so noteworthy in a young woman. Again however, her deviance, for all the effort in achieving it, reads as humorous rather than dangerous.

For many in the Fourth Age, the institution forms the arena of everyday existence. Effecting resistance is all the more difficult, particularly for those who by definition are signified as communicatively incompetent, such as those lost in the fog of dementia, or whose bodies betray them through disability or incontinence. Research here has focused on 'tiny gestures of defiance and small acts of personal insurrection' – pulling faces or sticking out tongues – designed to undermine the authority of carers who, by infantilising their charges, become metaphoric parent figures (Hockey and James, 1993). Resistances are undoubtedly evident, but because they happen in the closed sphere of the home or institution they rarely demand mass public recognition. Such are the hidden injuries of age.

The concept of subcultures presumes that minority groups are oppositional and may be identified by their patterns of resistance. However, there is some debate as to whether, in a consumer society, these movements are counter-cultural or conservative and commercialised. Chris Rojek (1993: 207) argues that 'flexibility has replaced rigidity in the planning and organisation of labour processes, labour markets, products and patterns of consumption', hence the rise *inter alia* of early retirement, both voluntary and enforced. Given the recent and intense sociological focus on cultures of consumption, it is no longer true that cultural studies 'foregrounds the compulsion to work' or that little analysis exists of 'people's experiences of participation in the commercial mode' (Moorhouse, 1989: 26). Nevertheless, although later life is clearly a major leisure phase for growing numbers of people, there remains a popular perception of retirement as materially impoverished (which, of course, it is for many), therefore unconnected with consumer culture.

Amongst the young, Redhead theorises a shift from subculture – rigid 'alternative' groups opposing dominant cultural trends – to club cultures, which are dispersed, loosely defined and consumerist. In this process he discerns a move from moralistic to hedonistic individualism (Redhead, 1997). Only 3 per cent of British pensioners regularly visit night-clubs (Ascherson, 1998). Nevertheless, in terms of their cultural orientation, 'hedonistic individualism' is undoubtedly apparent. The 'teenage consumer' was 'discovered' in the 1950s, when market researchers found an opportunity to exploit fresh disposable income which could be spent on goods – records, clothes, motorcycles – expressing pleasure at 'not being grown up' (Abrams, 1959; Frith, 1984). By the same token, the grey market now encourages expenditure on leisure items, holidays and health – all in the service of not growing old. The vast potential here – 18 million people over 50 account for 70 per cent of the nation's disposable wealth (Baty, 1998: 11) – has not, of course, gone unnoticed among those who are busy tailoring their products to the requirements of the older consumer. They are a particularly large cohort who, since they have a firm cultural orientation towards 'youth', are especially prone to purchasing goods and services designed to 'combat the signs of ageing'. The hegemonic group is not determined by demographics but class habitus. The traditional working class may still be resigned to fatalistic acceptance of such things as 'belief in the naturalness of overweight as one gets older', but the petite-bourgeoisie's social aspirations have accustomed them to personal self-consciousness. This class fraction is particularly attracted to cosmetics, exercises and body-maintenance techniques 'ostensibly designed to deliver the ideal body' and to involvement with 'symbolic goods and services', because it is through such consumption that differentiation may be sustained. And in terms of their cultural effectivity, this group is in the ascendant (Featherstone and Hepworth, 1986: 91–4).

There is irony here in that it is older people themselves who are contributing to the fixation with youth. Pressures to 'age well' have promoted a sharp distinction between the 'heroes of ageing', who paradoxically appear not to have aged, and the villainous persistence of decline. An insidious contemporary morality asserts that old people should be healthy, sexually active, engaged, and self-reliant. Positive ageing has produced its own tyrannical imperative in the form of a reformulated work ethic: unless you work at being 'liberated' from chronological destiny, you are less than normal, indeed stigmatised. All of which puts more and more clear blue water between the Third Age of active leisure and the Fourth Age of incarceration and decrepitude – the great taboo of the new Millennium.

For and against the work ethic

In endeavouring to escape such a fate, many are motivated to maintain old habits. Exceptional elders who pursue their vocation to a great age – Nobel Prize-winning scientist Sir Joseph Rotblat, 92, and Sir Richard Doll, 88, the epidemiologist who established the link between smoking and lung cancer, both still going to the office daily – are vaunted as paragons of virtue (Lawley, 2001). More generally, Ekerdt (1986: 243) speculates that a continuing 'busy ethic' pervades many leisure activities in retirement by 'giv[ing] definition to the retirement role'. Conversely, as consumerist values come to outweigh production-based ideals, leisure becomes a stronger currency, hence the explicit commitment to competitive individualism found in retirement magazines (Featherstone and Hepworth, 1989). Individual lives have become personal 'projects' revolving around lifestyles which can be bought in the market place. At the same time the notion of an integral, coherent self has been fragmented so that identity can change at different stages in the life course. There is thus a tension between the biographical idea of a continuous developing self and the postmodern notion of the multiple, situational self. As Bauman (1996: 23) underlines, 'the foremost strategy of life as pilgrimage, of life as identity-building, was "saving for the future", but saving for the future made sense as a strategy only in so far as one could be sure that the future would reward the savings with interest'. This statement links directly to the fast-eroding value of the state pension. Meanwhile, against the quest for community evident in, say, retiring to the seaside, there exist countervailing desires for more individualistic pursuits: the 'performing self', obsessed with surface appearances (facelifts and makeovers); the flâneur, whose domain is the shopping mall and the internet; the vagabond who decides where to turn when he comes to the crossroads (the three million-plus Americans over age 55 who have taken to the road in their recreational vehicles, known as RVers); and the tourist beloved of the Saga holidays. Bauman (1996: 23) concludes: 'the real problem is not how to build identity, but how to preserve it' in a world where identities can be adopted and discarded, are disposable, instantly obsolete.

If today's elders are bound paradoxically by the work ethic in their embrace of leisure as a mode of keeping busy, the retirees of the next decades may equally be determined to enjoy leisure as a continuance of an anti-establishment conviction rendered temporarily dormant by the need to earn a crust during most of their adult lives. Successive cohorts 'in retirement' may, therefore, be simultaneously engaged in common activities but for quite opposite reasons. Similarly, the pursuit of travel while appearing superficially materialist may equally be bound up with anti-consumerism. Tens of thousands of northern European pensioners ('Old Age Travellers', oATs) have decamped with their motorhomes to the resorts of the south where, aided to a degree by mobile phones and access to the local internet café, they are able to live 'a deliciously stripped-down existence' jettisoning 'anything that doesn't fit in a van' (Shaw, 2001: 30). Like their American counterparts, they reject possessions while celebrating the freedom to roam. Such Zen affluence relies on an informally co-operative flea-market economy that both 'violates the consumer ethic' and ruptures the received image of older people lacking adventure and retiring to their rocking chairs (Counts and Counts, 1998: 61). Unlike the package tourists – Saga louts – who have rendered the former hippie paradise of Goa 'a utopia for silver-haired sunseekers', these travellers are in for the long haul (Coyle, 2001: 14). Aged 66, Francesca Shaw swapped her house in Leeds for a converted delivery van. She has now been on the road, solo, for seven years. The impetus is readily understood: when people suggested Francesca was brave to have upped sticks, she responded: 'I'd have to be a damn sight braver sitting it out in my street in Leeds' (Shaw, 2001: 31). Less nomadic, but similarly re-enchanted are the growing army of permanent migrants to the Costa del Sol, and the 250,000 who currently inhabit trailer-home parks in the UK, many of which in their age-zoning – residents under age 50 are forbidden – and organised clubs ('everything from cribbage to choir practice') resemble the North American sun cities (King et al., 2000; Middleton, 2001: 6).

Narrative lifeworlds

But the opportunity to relocate remains the privilege of a minority. For most pensioners, maintaining a sense of identity as they navigate the doldrums of deep old age is a matter of clinging on to lifelong convictions. In his community-based study of older Scots, Rory Williams (1990) contends that the Protestant work ethic explains working-class beliefs about illness and death. Being ill has connotations of punishment for idleness and sin, whilst staying healthy might indicate a stronger moral fibre. There is thus an obligation to resist the onset of ill health by remaining appropriately active. His research indicated that disengagement was only legitimated following the diagnosis of serious illness (Williams, 1990). Similarly, Jerrome's study of old people's clubs in 'Seatown' [Hove] found that: 'Responses to [old age] are a matter of virtue and moral strength or weakness. To be happy and to make the best of things in spite of pain and hardship is a moral and social obligation attached to the status of the old or handicapped person. Those who fail are blameworthy, and tend to blame themselves' (Jerrome, 1992: 142). Such monitoring stigmatises those who do not resist decline.

These world-views are contextualised within the confines of collective generational understandings. Likewise, Stephen Conway (2000: 231), working in Hull, argues that vulnerable older people who feel socially marginalised try to make sense of the world using notions of imagined community. As the social circle narrows with the death of spouse and friends, some seek solace in identification with the past-situated mores of dead relatives. His interviewees evoke better times when families and neighbours were 'a little world on our own', then project this idealised image onto their values in the present. Such fabricated re-connection with the past creates a mental and moral resource for sustaining biographical continuity whilst helping individuals to cope with a fractured and bewildering present. Nevertheless, since the community is imagined rather than real it only serves as a consolatory backdrop to a bleak reality.

The above examples indicate the utility of narratives as tools 'for uncovering images and the categorical imperatives of groups, societies and cultures, in ways that could complement ethnographic analyses focused on how social practices are constituted' (Ruth and Kenyon, 1996: 653). This said, the recourse to shared values is but part of the fabric, for as Anthony Giddens (1991: 54) remarks, 'a person's identity is not to be found in behaviour, nor – important though it is – in the reactions of others, but in the capacity to keep a particular narrative going. The individual's biography, if she is to maintain regular interaction with others in the day-to-day world, cannot be wholly fictive'.

Norman Denzin (1992) sees the challenge as an interactionist one, asking, after Mills (1959), how the personal troubles of the postmodern individual transform themselves into public issues. The 'inner' aspects of ageing (feelings, values, beliefs) are relatively unexplored compared to outer presentations of self, and life stories are significant because they 'embody negotiations of self-interpretation and self-identity' (Straughn, 1995: 519). As members of particular cohorts, individuals provide insight into the cumulative experience of their age group, and indeed of their class, 'race', gender and place-bound cultures, but they also reflect personal discontinuity and difference. They can thus become their own versions of social theory (Geertz, 1983).

Nevertheless, there is cause for scepticism. In the movie *It's a Wonderful Life* (1946) a guardian angel descends to re-evaluate suicidal George Bailey's existence. Through a series of flashbacks George is forced to realise the positive impact of all the work he's done to make good in his small town and is slowly born again. His absorption in helping others has blinded him to his own strengths and it takes divine intervention to open his eyes. The film's tagline – 'They're making memories tonight!' – enunciates the feelgood potential of such retrospective stock-taking. Applied to the old, however, life-review sees an easy slippage into the 'deculturated' discourse of nostalgia, where 'the supposed cultural legacy that it keeps in store for future generations ... being previously based on a no longer valid oral tradition, is only humoured and dismissed' (Hazan, 1996: 8–9). Demonstrating or explaining experiences is a long way from eradicating the tensions and inequalities they reflect. Marginality only becomes an area of observation because relations of power have created it in the first place (Spivak, 1993). And, as Kobena Mercer (1992: 33–4) remarks: 'There is nothing remotely groovy about difference and diversity as political problems ... The management of diversity and difference through the bureaucratic mantra of race, class and gender encourages the divisive rhetoric of being more marginal, more oppressed.' The same goes for age.

Conclusion: the ageing of youth culture

Changes in age-appropriate behaviours – the styles, lifestyles and hairstyles conventionally felt to match different age groups – mean that 'acceptable' age-norms of dress, sexuality, pastimes and bodily appearance clearly vary according to one's location in historical time. Yet explaining shifts in cultural norms is a matter not only of accounting for changing fashions, but also of values that have imbued attitudes to ageing. Arguably, the dominance of the work ethic, an orientation towards youthfulness and belief in notions of 'progress' can only be detrimental to those who have retired, are no longer young and are thereby 'outdated'. However, these ideals are being eroded as consumerist values come to outweigh production-based ideals, leisure gains the foreground and the modernist, ever novel promise of capitalism gives way to a preference for niche markets. These are the latent tendencies against which to pit discourses of ageism.

Borrowing from Bourdieu's comments on the development of postwar sociology, Stephen Katz (2001) has suggested that social gerontology illustrates 'The Gerschenkron Effect'. An economic historian, Alexander Gerschenkron argued that capitalism was unique in Russia because of its late development. By analogy, latecoming politically-informed theories of ageing have differed from cultural studies in general. As Marxism gave way to postmodernism, 'feminist, discursive and micropolitical concerns' supplanted metatheoretical discourses of formal political economy. In the 1990s, the social construction of retirement gave way to a critical gerontology aimed at a deconstruction via such slippery ideas as the multiple self, body modification and postmodern citizenship (Gilleard and Higgs, 2000). This critique has cleared the way for a re-positioning of cultural studies within the sociology of ageing. Nevertheless, the contingency of structural factors cannot be ignored. Political economists have emphasised constraints and inequalities, whilst cultural theorists celebrate diversity, reflexivity and agency. Both have a point since contemporary ageing means trading the benefits of welfare for the added risks of self-determination, as successful ageing becomes increasingly reliant upon self-help, self-governance and self-actualisation. The successful individualism of the few still jars against the wholesale penury of the majority. Meanwhile, it would probably be fair to say that so far as the academic study of popular culture goes, 'youth as a social category no longer dominates the field, although the mythology of youth and youthfulness is no less central' (Rowe, 1995: 5).

However, times have changed, and it is now commonplace for journalists to observe that 'the very idea that kids could be revolting, that there may in fact be a youthful duty to question and rebel, provokes widespread amusement' (Gill, 1999: 14). Indeed, sitcoms such as *Absolutely Fabulous* make great play on a world turned upside down, where the ageing ravers of the sixties have become problem adolescents set against the sensible worldweariness of their teenage offspring. Given the simultaneous 'youthing' of the life course and de-radicalisation of youth culture, it is remarkable that theorists still talk of ageing as 'a separation over time – from youth and its attributes' (Cristofovici, 1999: 269), as though youth culture was somehow inevitably avant garde.

Consider the commonly held, derogatory view that 'rock should simply not be played by 55 year-old men with triple chins wearing bad wighats, pretending still to be excited about the songs they wrote 30 or 35 years ago' (Strausbaugh, 2001: 5). An Eliasian disgust is immediately invoked by some rock stars, like film stars, failing to disguise their declining bodies by ageing gracefully. Yet something rather contradictory is being claimed here. On the one hand rock is youth music; it is rebellious because being young is by definition and always rebellious. On the other, however, it is historically specific, part of a culture that 'grew old along with those who made it ... along with its biggest market, the baby boomers ... The revolutionaries of 1968 [who] grew up, grew fat, grew complacent' (Strausbaugh, 2001: 6). This apparent paradox reflects a confused elision of diachronic and synchronic readings of generation that has far-reaching implications. If we adopt the synchronic, even essentialist view, then young people will always pit their differences against the system and youth culture will always be the apogee of countercultural resistance. But, if we understand this subcultural pose to be the special province of the Postwar Babyboom generation, then it is they who will carry its political ideology, its musical tastes and its dress styles with them as they age, and it is perhaps they, and they alone (or, at least, in particular), who will be haunted by the fear of becoming outdated.

For reasons already enumerated, there seems little point in pursuing a political economy line in attempting to discover the vocabularies and visions of older people on the ground. However, in the turn to lifestyle politics, there are elements of a quest for civic innovation. Barbara Caine (1995: 106) argues that during the late 1960s the women's movement was divided in that the liberationist desire 'to break with the ideas, values and organisational methods of the past' threatened the position of older women who had previously lent tradition and respectability to campaigns. But as activists from that youthful era have themselves aged attitudes have softened somewhat. Indeed, striking parallels between feminism and anti-ageism are becoming evident, not just amongst ageing scholars – Friedan (1993), Greer (1991) – but also in radical manuals like The Hen Co-Op's *Growing Old Disgracefully* (1993).

In such a development, as in the albeit largely middle-class University of the Third Age, we can discern a strong element of self-awareness. Nevertheless, although one major imprint of postmodernity has been the emphasis on reflexivity, this has yet to diffuse more widely to our recognising old age as the domain of our future selves. Political economists have emphasised constraints, but cultural theorists celebrate diversity and choice; indeed, 'reflexive gerontologists' regard contemporary consumerism as a landscape providing opportunities for personal development (Hepworth, 1996). Insofar as culture provides information about preferences and tastes, it also conveys messages about appropriate behaviour, values and expectations. Social structure, on the other hand, concerns the ways in which power and status are distributed. If we wish to understand the kinds of issues informing personal identity in later life and to develop appropriate cultural – rather than social – policies we must focus on the disjunction between the aspirations instilled in us by our historically specific upbringing and the failures of society to fulfil them (Merton, 1957). Such disharmony reflects the true measure of inequality both within and between generations.

Acknowledgement

Parts of this article have been adapted from A. Blaikie (1999) 'Can there be a cultural sociology of ageing?', *Education and Ageing*, Vol. 14, No. 2, pp. 127–39. The author wishes to thank the editors for permission to use this material.

References

Abrams, M. (1959) *The Teenage Consumer.* London: Routledge and Kegan Paul

Arber, S. and Ginn, J. (1991) 'The invisibility of age: gender and class in later life', *Sociological Review*, Vol. 39, pp. 260–91

Ascherson, N. (1998) 'Keep on runnning ...', *Observer Review,* 15 November, pp. 1–2

Barthes, R. (1976) *Mythologies.* St Albans: Paladin

Baty, P. (1998) 'New tricks for old dogs', *Times Higher Education Supplement*, 18 September, pp. 11–12

Bauman, Z. (1996) 'From pilgrim to tourist – or a short history of identity', in S. Hall and P. du Gay (eds) *Questions of Cultural Identity.* London: Sage

Betts, J., Green, J. and Wilson, G. (1999) *An Experiment in Living: Sharing a House in Later Life.* London: Third Age Press

Blaikie, A. (1999) *Ageing and Popular Culture.* Cambridge: Cambridge University Press

Blaikie, A. (2002) 'The secret world of subcultural ageing: what unites and what divides?', in L. Andersson (ed.) *Cultural Gerontology.* Westport, CT: Greenwood Press

Caine, B. (1995) 'Generational conflict and the question of ageing in nineteenth and twentieth century feminism', *Australian Cultural History*, Vol. 14, pp. 92–108

Channel Four Television (2001) 'Bus Pass Bandits', *Cutting Edge* documentary, 1 May

Christ, E.A. (1965) 'The "retired" stamp collector: economic and other functions of systematized leisure activity', in A.M. Rose and W.A. Peterson (eds) *Older People and their Social World: the Sub-culture of the Aging*. Philadelphia, PA: Davis

Cohen, S. (1972) *Folk Devils and Moral Panics*. London: McGibbon and Kee

Conway, S. (2000) '"I'd be unhealthy if nobody wanted me any more": a sociological analysis of the relationship between ageing and health beliefs', unpublished PhD thesis, University of Hull

Counts, D.A. and Counts, D.R. (1998) *Over the Next Hill: an Ethnography of RVing Seniors in America*. Peterborough, Ontario: Broadview Press

Coyle, J. (2001) 'Go, go, GOA-way, I yelled ...', *Observer*, 11 March, p. 14

Cristofovici, A. (1999) 'Touching surfaces: photography, aging and an aesthetic of change', in K. Woodward (ed.) *Figuring Age*. Bloomington, IN: University of Indiana Press

Dench, G. (ed.) (2000) *Grandmothers of the Revolution*. London: Neanderthal Books

Denzin, N.K. (1992) *Symbolic Interactionism and Cultural Studies: The Politics of Interpretation*. Oxford: Blackwell

Ekerdt, D.J. (1986) 'The busy ethic: moral continuity between work and retirement', *The Gerontologist*, Vol. 26, pp. 239–44

Featherstone, M. and Hepworth, M. (1986) 'New lifestyles in old age?', in C. Phillipson, M. Bernard and P. Strang (eds) *Dependency and Interdependency in Later Life*. Beckenham: Croom Helm

Featherstone, M. and Hepworth, M. (1989) 'Ageing and old age: reflections on the postmodern life course', in B. Bytheway, T. Keil, P. Allatt and A. Bryman (eds) *Becoming and Being Old: Sociological Approaches to Later Life*. London: Sage

Friedan, B. (1993) *The Fountain of Age*. London: Jonathan Cape

Frith, S. (1984) *The Sociology of Youth*. Ormskirk: Causeway Books

Geertz, C. (1993) *Local Knowledge: Further Essays in Interpretive Anthropology*. London: Fontana Press

Giddens, A. (1991) *Modernity and Self-Identity*. Cambridge: Polity Press

Gill, A. (1999) 'Revolting middle age', *The Independent*, 21 May, p. 14

Gilleard, C. and Higgs, P. (2000) *Cultures of Ageing: Self, Citizen and the Body.* London: Prentice Hall

Greer, G. (1991) *The Change: Women, Ageing and the Menopause.* London: Hamish Hamilton

Gubrium, J.F. and Holstein, J.A. (eds) (2000) *Aging and Everyday Life: Classic and Contemporary Readings.* Oxford: Blackwell

Hall, S. (1996) 'Introduction: who needs identity?', in S. Hall and P. du Gay (eds) *Questions of Cultural Identity.* London: Sage

Hall, S. and Jefferson, T. (eds) (1976) *Resistance Through Rituals.* London: Hutchinson

Hazan, H. (1996) *From First Principles: an Experiment in Ageing.* Westport, CT: Bergin and Garvey

Hazan, H. (1980) 'Continuity and change in a tea-cup: on the symbolic nature of tea-related behaviour among the aged', *Sociological Review*, Vol. 28, pp. 497–516

Hebdige, D. (1979) *Subculture: The Meaning of Style.* Routledge: London

Hen Co-op (1993) *Growing Old Disgracefully.* London: Judy Piatkus Publishers

Hepworth, M. (1996) 'Consumer culture and social gerontology', *Education and Ageing*, Vol. 11, pp. 19–30

Hockey, J. and James, A. (1993) *Growing Up and Growing Old.* London: Sage

Inglis, F. (1993) *Cultural Studies.* Oxford: Blackwell

Irwin, S. (1998) 'Age, generation and inequality: a reply to the reply', *British Journal of Sociology*, Vol. 49, No. 2, pp. 305–10

Jerrome, D. (1992) *Good Company: an Anthropological Study of Old People in Groups.* Edinburgh: Edinburgh University Press

Johnson, R. (1983) 'What is Cultural Studies Anyway?', *CCCS Occasional Paper*, No. 74, University of Birmingham

Johnson, P., Conrad, C. and Thomson, D. (eds) (1989) *Workers Versus Pensioners: Intergenerational Justice in an Ageing World.* Manchester: Manchester University Press

Joseph, J. (1974) *Rose in the Afternoon.* London: Dent, 1974

Katz, S. (2001) 'Critical gerontology discourse: nomadic thinking or postmodern sociology', *Discourse of Sociological Practice*, Vol. 3, No. 1, unpaginated, [http://omega.cc.umb.edu/~sociolgy/Journal/socart2.html]

King, R., Warnes, T. and Williams, A. (2000) *Sunset Lives.* Oxford: Berg

Laslett, P. (1987) 'The emergence of the Third Age', *Ageing and Society*, Vol. 7, pp. 113–60

Lawley, S. (2001) 'The end of age', http://www.bbc.co.uk/radio4/reith2001/sue.shtml.

Mannheim, K. (1956) *Essays on the Sociology of Culture*. London: Routledge and Kegan Paul

Matza, D. (1964) *Delinquency and Drift*. New York: Wiley

McGuigan, J. (1992) *Cultural Populism*. London: Routledge

McRobbie, A. (1991) *Feminism and Youth Culture: from Jackie to Just Seventeen*. Basingstoke: Macmillan

Mercer, K. (1992) 'Back to my routes: a postscript to the '80s', *Ten-8*, Vol. 3, pp. 32–9

Merton, R. (1957) *Social Theory and Social Structure*. New York: Free Press

Middleton, C. (2001) 'Hooked on trailers', *Observer Magazine*, 16 September, p. 6

Mills, C.W. (1959) *The Sociological Imagination*. Oxford: Oxford University Press

Moberg, D.O. and Taves, M.J. (1965) 'Church participation and adjustment in old age', in A.M. Rose and W.A. Peterson (eds) *Older People and their Social World: The Sub-culture of the Aging*. Philadelphia, PA: Davis

Moorhouse, H.F. (1989) 'Models of work, models of leisure', in C. Rojek (ed.) *Leisure for Leisure*. London: Macmillan

Notarangelo, R. (1996) 'Oldies' Barney at the Bingo!', *Scottish Daily Mirror*, 18 December, pp. 1,7

Ostroff, J. (1989) *Successful Marketing to the 50+ Consumer: How to Capture One of the Biggest and Fastest Growing Markets in America*. Englewood Cliffs, NJ: Prentice Hall

Phillipson, C. (1982) *Capitalism and the Construction of Old Age*. London: Macmillan

Redhead, S. (1997) *Subculture to Clubcultures*. Blackwell: Oxford

Rojek, C. (1993) *Ways of Escape: Modern Transformations in Leisure and Travel*. Basingstoke: Macmillan

Rowe, D. (1995) *Popular Cultures: Rock Music, Sport and the Politics of Pleasure*. London: Sage

Ruth, J-E. and Kenyon, G. (1996) 'Introduction: special issue on ageing, biography and practice', *Ageing and Society*, Vol. 16, No. 4, pp. 653–7

Shaw, W. (2001) 'Happy campers', *Observer Magazine*, 11 March, pp. 28–31

Spivak, G. C. (1993) *Outside the Teaching Machine*. New York: Routledge

Straughn, J. (1995) 'Review of C. Linde (1993) life stories: the creation of coherence', *American Journal of Sociology*, Vol. 101, No. 2, pp. 518–20

Strausbaugh, J. (2001) 'Unplug the oldies – for good', *Observer Review*, 12 August, pp. 5–6

Tidmarsh, L.M. (2000) 'Choice and Yours: magazine imagery and the social construction of ageing and later life', unpublished PhD thesis, University of Aberdeen

Turner, B.S. (1998) 'Ageing and generational conflicts: a reply to Sarah Irwin', *British Journal of Sociology*, Vol. 49, No. 2, pp. 299–304

Wada, S. (1988) 'Daily life in later life in the changing Japanese context', in K. Altergott (ed.) *Daily Life in Later Life: Comparative Perspectives*. Beverly Hills, CA: Sage

Williams, R. (1990) *A Protestant Legacy: Attitudes to Illness and Death Among Older Aberdonians*. Oxford: Clarendon Press

Willis, P. (1977) *Learning to Labour*. Aldershot: Saxon House

Chapter 10

Place, belonging and identity: globalisation and the 'Northern middle class'

Mike Savage, Gaynor Bagnall and Brian Longhurst

There can be little doubt that attachment to place has been radically transformed by global social and economic change. Thirty years ago, sociologists focused on involvement in face-to-face 'communities' as the foundation for senses of identity and belonging.[1] However, the recognition that social relationships are increasingly stretched over space has encouraged conceptions that emphasise diasporic, networked, relationships to place. Rather than communities being defined as bounded by the parameters of face-to-face interaction, they are now seen as mobile, imagined, virtual and trans-national.[2] There is however a danger that we neglect to show how fixed attachments to places are still produced, even amidst the flux of late modernity. In this chapter, we shall show how globalising processes do not eclipse the salience of localised identities, but re-work them through the consolidation of new forms of regional belonging. Drawing on research in Wilmslow, one of the most prosperous areas of Northwest England, we show how even amongst the affluent middle classes, fully implicated in various globalising practices, we can see the consolidation of a distinctive 'northern English middle-class'. Globalisation, we argue, generates new kinds of regionalised identities.

The first part of the chapter discusses the relationship between place and identity. After brief consideration of competing perspectives, we focus on Bourdieu's account of the relationship between social and physical space in order to show how, even in globalising environments, places remain crucial for class formation. Bourdieu is rarely regarded as relevant to discussions about the social significance of physical space (see for instance, Painter, 2000). Nonetheless, his analysis of the relationship between social and physical space, and his appreciation of the differential spatial embeddedness of various 'fields' provide a valuable way of comprehending the contemporary significance of spatial identities. The second part details our research methodology, explaining why Wilmslow is a pertinent choice of case study. We then turn to explore the nature of people's attachment to Wilmslow. Here we show how those who were long term, local Wilmslovians, as well as those who are cosmopolitans, tend to feel ill at ease in Wilmslow. Those who are most at home in the area are those who form part of a group of affluent, professional and managerial employees, brought up in the North of England, and whose social lives are strongly embedded in the wider region. Finally, our conclusion returns to consider the implications of our findings for broader debates.

Globalisation, belonging, and identity

If 'society' is not composed of bounded, spatial units, then it becomes important to consider how enduring identities are produced through mobility. Although it is commonplace to note the mutual constitution of the global and the local,[3] there is little sustained explanation of how local identities are currently re-produced. For example, consider Giddens's influential arguments regarding the implications of globalisation and time-space distanciation for weakening people's sense of ontological security. Giddens (1990) emphasises that the reflexivity engendered by globalising processes disrupts traditional forms of social solidarity based around attachments to community. Modernity creates challenges to senses of ontological security as face-to-face contact becomes increasingly over-ridden by wider ranging social relationships. For Giddens key features of the cultural life of late modernity, from the search for 'pure relationships' to fundamentalism, can be attributed to the search for security.

For Giddens these general changes (differentially) affect all social groups. However, his arguments are pitched at a level that does not allow ready understanding of why *particular* places become central to cultural mobilisation. His account switches between global social relations, and the individual (see also Savage, 2000). There is little attention to social processes that mediate this relationship, whether this be wider family relationships, broader social networks, institutional involvements (through workplaces, membership of organisations) and so on. It is therefore not clear how social relationships are differentially tied to places.

In this respect the arguments of Castells (1996), who currently offers the most thoughtful reflections on place and class, are pertinent. He argues that the contemporary 'network society' is organised around the 'space of flows' that depend on (a) electronic, digital, communication, (b) nodes and hubs and (c) the spatial organisation of the dominant managerial elites. In Castells's (1996: 415) pithy formulation, 'elites are cosmopolitan, people are local'. While managerial elites depend on global flows, 'the elites do not want and cannot become flows themselves'(Castells, 1996: 416). They therefore form elite groupings, physically segregated from other social groups with whom they are spatially proximate.[4] But at the same time they also help develop a global culture, sharing cosmopolitan practices that bind them to elites elsewhere, 'thus superseding the historical specificity of each locale' (Castells, 1996: 417). For the majority of the population, place, understood as a locale whose 'form, function and meaning are self contained within the boundaries of physical contiguity' (Castells, 1996: 423) remains important, if increasingly divorced from the 'space of flows'. They, therefore, become detached from the logic of international capitalist business, resulting in social marginalisation (an argument rather similar to Lash and Urry, 1994).

Castells usefully draws out the contradictory relationship of global managerial elites to place. This focus on how globalising practices create local power hubs can be enriched through Bourdieu's arguments about fields and habitus. Despite the prominence of Bourdieu's work in recent social theory, relatively little attention has been played to his sociology of space. This is despite the fact that his perspective is strongly spatial (Skeggs, 2000).[5]

> *Just as physical space ... is defined by the reciprocal externality of positions ... the social space is defined by the mutual exclusion, or distinction, of the positions which constitute it ... Social agents, and also things insofar as they are appropriated by them and therefore constituted as properties, are situated in a place in social space, a distinct and distinctive place which can be characterized by the position it occupies relative to other places (...) and the distance (...) that separates it from them.*
> (Bourdieu, 1997: 134)

Numerous differentiated fields co-exist, each of which define hierarchical spaces of positions. These various fields differ in the ways they articulate with spatial location. Bourdieu's recent account of habitus in *Pascalian Meditations* (1999) is particularly useful in teasing out this sedimentary relationship between place and class formation. Bourdieu emphasises the 'practical sense of a habitus', in which

> *the agent engaged in practice knows the world but with knowledge which ... is not set up in the relation of externality of a knowing consciousness. He (sic) knows it, in a sense, too well ... takes it for granted, precisely because he is caught up in it, bound up with it; he inhabits it like a garment or a familiar habitat.*
> (Bourdieu, 1999: 142–3; emphasis ours)

The mechanism which links habitus and field, or 'the feel for the game, and the game itself' (Bourdieu, 1996: 151), is the sense of bodily comfort and ease which people experience in different social situations – *which are also spatial situations*.

> *The dispositions occupied involve an adjustment to the position – what Erving Goffman calls the 'the sense of one's place'. It is this sense of one's place which in a situation of interaction, prompts those whom we call in French les gens humbles, literally, 'humble people' – perhaps 'common folk' in English – to remain humbly in their place, and which prompts others to 'keep their distance' or to 'keep their station in life'.*
> (Bourdieu, 1986: 5)

People are comfortable when there is a correspondence between habitus and field, but otherwise people feel ill at ease and seek to move – socially *and* spatially – so that their discomfort is relieved. For Bourdieu this is crucial to the 'dialectic of positions and dispositions', ensuring the sorting of people, with their specific habitus to particular kinds of social fields. This mechanism intrinsically depends on the significance of physical space, as this kind of sorting process involves moving between different kinds of spatial locations.

This attention to space is therefore highly pertinent to Bourdieu's claims about the significance of distinction (especially Bourdieu, 1986). Much has been written about the extent to which there are clearly different lifestyles and modes of cultural distinction between various class fractions (Butler and Savage, 1995; Savage *et al.*, 1992). A recent theme has been the claim that 'cultural omnivores', who are able to engage with both 'high' and 'low' culture (e.g. Petersen and Kern, 1996), have disrupted clear boundaries between class lifestlyes and consumption habits. This claim can be related to the rise of fields that are relatively spatially independent, through their reliance on the mass media and global communication. However, it follows that those cultural fields that are still dependent on specific locations are likely to remain significant in generating cultural distinction. Housing and residence continue to be essentially tied to a territorial basis: people continue to live in specific locations. However mobile people's cultural practices may appear to be, their residential location continues to be a key social identifier, as is commercially recognised by the use of postcodes to pinpoint distinctive lifestyle groups by various market research agencies. It is also the case that even in those fields that are less spatially fixed, those elements that continue to be connected to specific locations are most likely to be tied up with claims to distinction (consider the 'authenticity' of live performance within the musical field, for instance).

Even in a mobile, global environment, spatial location may be of increasing relative significance in the generation of social distinction. In examining this process, we have argued that people's sense of belonging plays a key role. Following Bourdieu we see belonging neither in existential terms (as primordial attachment to lived community), nor as a set of discursive constructions, but as a socially constructed, embedded process. Residential place continues to matter since people feel some sense of 'being at home' in an increasingly turbulent world.

Northern affluence: Wilmslow

The old market town of Wilmslow is a major node of the north Cheshire suburban crescent that is one of the most affluent areas in England outside the Southeast. Wilmslow lies twelve miles south of Manchester, close to Manchester airport, and along with its elite hinterland including Alderley Edge and Prestbury, and neighbouring suburbs such as Macclesfield (see Girling et al., 1999), forms probably the largest middle-class suburban complex in the North of England.[6] Its central role as an icon of 'Northern affluence', is attested to by a recent series of Radio 4 programmes presented by Miranda Sawyer (1999) which used the town as a frame for reflections on contemporary suburbia. Wilmslow expanded from the mid-Victorian period as a 'gentleman's suburb' of Manchester, and has in the past thirty years benefitted from the economic expansion associated with Manchester airport and the decentralisation of economic activity from Manchester. Even more recently, there has been a rapid expansion of service facilities, notably cafÈs, restaurants and bars, as the town has generated a distinctive appeal to young, affluent consumers.

Our research was part of an ESRC funded project[7] that compared the lifestyles of residents in four areas in and around Manchester, each area chosen to exemplify a particular kind of middle-class habitus. We studied two sub-areas within Wilmslow that we considered exemplars of an affluent middle-class lifestyle. One was close to the centre of Wilmslow, had inter-war detached houses, worth between £200,000 and £300,000 in 1997/98. The other was an exclusive area to the east of the town centre with large post-war detached houses, worth between £500,000 and £750,000. These were amongst the most expensive houses of their type in the North of England.

We sampled one household in three in selected streets, using a semi-structured interview schedule. Forty-five interviews were carried out in Wilmslow, representing a response rate of 41 per cent. Interviews covered the following topics: neighbourhood, leisure interests, household relationships, activity in voluntary associations, work and employment, with some final questions on social and political attitudes. In this paper, we largely draw on questions which asked respondents for their housing histories and views on the local area. Although this number of interviews does not allow us sufficient cases for statistical analysis, we have enough to allow us to construct simple typologies of respondents. We therefore cluster respondents according to their sense of belonging, and their biographical relationship to Wilmslow. As we go on to show, there are some clear patterns and distinctions amongst these residents. In developing our points, we cite respondents who exemplify the core features of a particular cluster, but also develop our case by drawing on the words of those who lie on the boundaries between clusters, and whose testimony can be read, against the grain, to reveal the salience of those boundaries.

The demographic structure of our sample indicates an overwhelmingly white, middle-class, population. Over half the sample had household incomes of over £60,000, and we did not interview a single manual worker. Nearly two-thirds of respondents had service class occupations,[8] and of those who did not, nearly all were women living with men who did.[9] The sample tended also to be female; although our sampling frame was 50 per cent male and female, the greater likelihood of men being unavailable for interview, often because of their long working hours, meant that we ended with more women respondents. The sample also tended to be middle-aged or elderly (73 per cent being over 45). When respondents themselves were asked about the area, they tended to spontaneously mention its 'middle-class' character. Only 17 per cent did not mention that Wilmslow either had 'middle-class', affluent, managers, professionals or business people living in it.

Respondents found it remarkably easy to formulate a response to the question about whether they felt at home in Wilmslow, even when they were ambivalent. We looked carefully at the entire interviews to make sure that their responses to this question were consistent with other views they expressed, but with very few exceptions, such feelings seemed to be both clear and salient to them. Four types of responses can be distinguished. Sixteen were enthusiastic 'belongers', who strongly endorsed their sense of attachment to Wilmslow, with no equivocation. A smaller number, six, did not feel they belonged, and expressed criticisms of it as a place to live. Despite this, many of their responses showed that they were active and involved in local social life. A third category, comprising ten respondents, said that they did not feel they belonged to Wilmslow when they first came, but now they do. These people became attuned to living in Wilmslow over time. Finally, there are eleven ambivalent respondents who were unable to decide whether they belonged or not, for a variety of reasons we explore below.[10] Some of these were unable to decide whether they belonged at all, others state that they did belong but then equivocated and qualified this statement.

It is interesting that although Wilmslow's housing market would appear to define it as a popular place to live, only a third of the respondents felt unequivocally at home there (though this rises to a half when those who 'now' belong are included). There were no simple occupational or gender differences between those who answered this question differently, with the minor exception that those in relatively poorer households were slightly more likely to feel they belonged in the area. However, there are subtle variations in the way this question was answered according to residents' place of upbringing and mobility. Table 1 breaks the sample down into four types, and indicates a group of 'Northern middle-class residents' who feel at home in this area, compared to locals and cosmopolitans.

Perhaps the most interesting findings of Table 1 are that only six (those defined as 'cosmopolitans') had been brought up outside the North of England, mostly in London. Even more surprising is the fact that only three had been brought up in Manchester (six if Stockport and Salford are included). Nine were brought up in and around Wilmslow. The most intriguing finding is that the largest single group, with 24 respondents, over half the sample, was made up of those who came from other parts of the 'North', taking this (polemically, controversially!) to include the North of England, Scotland and Ireland.[11] In the rest of this paper we explore the local dominance of the 'Northern middle class', and the way that other social groups, especially the locals, are made to feel more marginal to them.

Status, biography and belonging

Local middle class

A general finding in traditional community studies research was that those who lived in a place longest were most embedded in it, and could define themselves as insiders compared to the offcomers who had arrived more recently. However, in Wilmslow those brought up in the area, and long-term residents, seemed less likely to feel at home there. This was particularly the case for the standard suburban types – the 'professional' and the 'housewife' – associated with Wilmslow from its Victorian incarnation as a 'gentleman's' suburb of Manchester. As we go on to show, these groups now felt relatively ill at ease in the town.

Four of the local middle-class men, who had careers in the established professions such as medicine or law, exemplified a strong professional identification.[12] For such men, professional involvement was linked to their participation in regional professional bodies, and embeddedness in the Manchester area. Their relationship to Wilmslow can be seen as a variant of the 'professional suburban habitus' that Chorley (1950) dissects with respect to Alderley Edge.[13] Wives were subordinated to their husbands, with little opportunity for 'careers' of their own. Their children were educated almost exclusively at private schools, from whence they progressed to elite universities and tended to move into professional employment themselves. These professional men were critical of recent changes in Wilmslow, emphasising how the area had changed, and their lack of belonging.

Table 1 Wilmslow: attachment to place and biographical types

Type	Number	Number 'belonging'	Where brought up?	Which university?	Gender and occupations
Local middle class	9	4	Wilmslow – 3 Cheshire – 4 Stockport – 2	Manchester Unis – 4 None – 3 Oxford – 1 London – 1	4 m profs 2 m managers 1 f proprietor 1 f housewife 1 f clerk
'Local climbers'	6	4	Manchester – 3 Stockport/Salford/Oldham – 3	Open University – 1 None – 5	2 m senior managers 3 f professionals 1 f clerical
Cosmopolitans	6	0	London – 3 Southwest – 2 Abroad –1	Cambridge – 1 Unknown – 2 None – 3	2 f professionals 1 f manager 1 m prof 1 f clerical 1 f housewife
'Northern middle class'	24	20	Merseyside – 6 Other Northwest – 4 Scot/Ireland – 5 Northeast – 6 Yorkshire – 2 Midlands – 1 None – 12	Manchester Unis – 6 Leeds – 2 Durham – 1 Liverpool – 1 Dublin – 1 Glasgow – 1 None – 12	6 f clerks 6 m profs 4 m managers 3 f profs 2 f managers 2 housewives 1 f proprietor

Notes: Number 'belonging' includes those who said to belong and those who said they now feel they belong but did not initially.
　　　　Last occupation used of those who were retired.

Key:　Unis = universities; f = female; m = male; profs = professional.

To take a representative example, John, a retired consultant, who had spent his early childhood in nearby Stockport, and was for most of his career employed at the Manchester Royal Infirmary, replied to the question asking for his class identity with a blunt, 'Well, I'm a professional man! I must be, mustn't I?'. He did not feel part of the community. Although semi-infirm, he still took an active part in the cultural life of Manchester, including trips to theatre, concert halls, and libraries. Asked his views on Manchester, he affirmed, 'I'm very happy to have been part of Manchester life. It has got a good university, and is an excellent part of the country'. About Wilmslow, however, he was more guarded, pointing out the rise of new leisure activities used by 'people I have nothing in common with'. He had been an active member of the Conservative Party, and also remained a regular churchgoer, but he has grown disillusioned with the Conservatives because of the Hamilton affair.[14] He had a second home in the Lake District, and his children lived locally. The ambivalence that John had for Wilmsow was linked in part to the way that his professional career in Manchester drew him away from the area itself:

> By now you should be getting a good idea that I haven't got a social life ... Looking back the children didn't get their slice of paternal cake because I was so involved. I have had more personal contact and enjoyment with my grandchildren than with my own children, because the grandchildren have come in the twilight of my career and in retirement and I have been able to watch them more dispassionately, when my children were at a certain age ... I missed out on a part of family life. Fortunately I had a very supportive wife.

John's strong attachment to work and to Manchester-based regional professional institutions, drew him away from a close affiliation to Wilmslow itself except as a dormitory base. Part of John's unease with recent trends was due to his awareness that Wilmslow had now developed more of an independent cultural life, and that it was no longer the simple repository of suburban 'repose'. Several other similar kinds of respondents also exemplified this professional habitus. Andrew, for instance, also noted that 'I don't feel as if I belong here'.

It would be wrong to imply that these views were held by all retired men. Indeed, some older professionals did feel more attached to Wilmslow. Stuart, for instance, a retired professional engineer and academic, stated proudly that:

> Fundamentally I am of this area: I wasn't physically born here ... but I have lived here in Wilmslow from the age of 18 months ... but the forebears on my mother's side, they have been in Dean Row for generations.

Stuart emphasised that 'I feel very much at home here and I think I always have done so', but he was also critical of recent changes to Wimslow, pointing out how it had become 'Globesville' as the local high street had lost its independent shops. He denounced the loss of Wilmslow's local council and facilities. Stuart, unlike John and Andrew, was able to deploy resources from being locally brought up.

> *Well you know what it is like if you grow up in an area and you find all its hidey-holes, corners, advantages, disadvantages, you become one with it.*

Stuart shared the concerns of John and Andrew but he was able to personally 'make peace' with Wilmslow because of his own familiarity with it. This took a nostalgic form.

In general, however, this traditional professional habitus was ill at ease with the development of Wilmslow as a consumer centre and a focus for new kinds of service sector employment. This does not mean that all the elderly professional men we interviewed were unhappy. In some cases their own biographical embeddedness in Wilmslow was enough to make them secure. Others, especially those who had not been brought up in the area, and who had seen Wilmslow as a dormitory for their Manchester-based professional lives, were more likely to feel that they no longer fitted.

This point can be taken further by considering the role of the conventional 'housewives' role in present day Wilmslow. In fact, of 28 women interviewed there were only four 'housewives' in our sample, one of whom was then retired. An important theme for most women was their unease with the housewifely role. Joanna, for instance, was the wife of a musician in a local orchestra, who had stayed at home to bring up the children. When asked if she felt she belonged to Wilmslow, she answered enigmatically:

> Joanna: *Oh there's a question. [laughs] Sometimes I do, sometimes I don't.*
>
> Interviewer: *Right*
>
> Joanna: *Sometimes I feel like an imposter. Maybe that's something to do with recent experiences in life though. And sometimes not.*

This hesitation was connected to her ambivalence about being responsible for bringing up the children and leaving her own career prospects unresolved. This led her to cast doubt on whether she liked living in Wilmslow, which she took to be a place defined by social climbing. While Joanna was aware of the practical advantages of bringing up children in Wilmslow, she also related her ambivalence regarding Wilmslow compared to the cultural pursuits possible in Manchester and London, making reference to the extent to which it was easy to travel to these venues.

Such unease with the housewifely habitus was not unusual. Susan also articulated a sense of the limitations of Wilmslow as a communal space. Married to a chief executive, and with three daughters (aged 14, 17 and 20), she had moved five times to different parts of the country, and was struck by the 'unfriendliness' of Wilmslow. When asked if she felt she belonged to the area, the answer was a crisp 'very definitely not'. Although trained as a nurse and having worked as nurse trainer and as consultant, she had abandoned her career and currently worked part time. Whilst supportive of her husband's career, at various points in the interview, resentments about the inequalities between them surfaced.

The decision to move to the town was based on instrumental calculations of schooling quality, and compared to previous residences, she was struck by the lack of feeling and warmth:

> *I had thought originally that Wilmslow was more of an entire town of its own, but in fact it's not. It's consists largely of people who have moved up from the South ... themselves um and those that have lived here for a very very long time ... Also most women of my age are ... [pause] it's not, yeah I think most people go back to work um may be there isn't such things going on.*

Here, what is striking is the halting recognition of the redundancy of the 'classic' housewifely role, with the observation that 'I think most people go back to work'. For this independent-minded woman, whose career aspirations had been subordinated to her children and husband, and whose half-acknowledged resentments manifested themselves in a dislike of Wilmslow, one of Wilmslow's historic 'functions' as a suburban retreat for women to privately manage family life had little appeal. Even though Wilmslow was a place where respondents brought up children (all our respondents except one had brought up children in the area), this did not lead to an endorsement or positive valuation of a housewifely ethos.

Local climbers

There was a second distinctive group of respondents who had moved out to Wilmslow having been brought up in Manchester. They are significant analytically since they were all 'local climbers' – people brought up in working-class areas in and around Manchester who saw their migration to Wilmslow as a form of social advancement. For them, Wilmslow itself was a social marker, and unlike most respondents, it remained important to differentiate Wilmslow from other local areas.

Jane was a head teacher at a local school, who had been brought up in inner Manchester, where most of her extended family continued to live. Her mother had been a machinist and her father a postman, and she saw herself as socially mobile compared to them. When asked why she had moved to Wilmslow she stated:

> *Because I was a deputy (head) at the time and we had been married a number of years we had been married 8 or 9 years I think. I was desperate for a child and I wanted to find a good area, because we lived in north Manchester in Prestwich, which was going down hill quite rapidly I thought. I worked on the other side of Manchester, and my husband at that time was working in Warrington, so it was a matter of finding another good area. Quite snobbish, I know it sounds awful, but a good area, a good school and that was reasonable for travelling to Wilmslow at the time.*

Jane's evaluation of Wilmslow indicates her concern for the social standing of its residents, as if this were crucial for establishing her own place and standing.

> Interviewer: How would you describe the type of people that live there?

> Jane: Some of them are smashing. I hadn't really met any of them
>   until I had my daughter, because I just used to commute in
>   and out. Although we lived there, I worked at one stage in
>   Stalybridge which is a different kettle of fish completely,
>   and then through Ashton[15], which again is not quite
>   salubrious, but it was only when my daughter was born
>   having to use all the services that you really get to know
>   people. They seem to fall into two camps. They seem to be
>   very well educated. That's the overriding impression you
>   get ...

Jane's concern to differentiate Wilmslow from Stalybridge and Ashton, and then to classify Wilmslow residents according to their cultural standing is striking, and rather unusual compared to most of the sample who did not consciously compare Wilmslow to other places in Manchester. Yet her own sense of belonging to Wilmslow was ambivalent. She denied that she belonged to a local community, and stated that

> In order to be part of a community you have to have some shared history,
> some shared feelings, something that binds you together and I haven't
> been there long enough to establish that.

Those who moved to Wilmslow as a mark of social climbing from Manchester were a distinctive group, whose attachment to the area was in large part through its sense as a marker of their social mobility. For this reason, they liked the idea that Wilmslow represented a superior form of life and tended to emphasise their sense of attachment to it. However, most Wilmslovians we interviewed had not been brought up in Manchester, and for them the kind of narrative of social climbing related to moving to the suburb did not apply.

Cosmopolitans

For many respondents, Wilmslow was not attached to Manchester in any deep-rooted way, whether this is Manchester as key node of professional identification or as a marker of working-class origins since left behind. In this respect, Wilmslow is no longer a suburb of Manchester. A striking example is Fred, an air traffic controller at Manchester airport, who had been born in London and had moved regularly in the course of his work. His attitude to Wilmslow was functional and instrumental:

> The area as far as we are concerned has got everything that we need, as
> I say for schools, work, for shops we just enjoy the area. If you want to
> go to Manchester it's not too far but on the other hand it's really well
> situated to travel around the area, you know you've got a vast selection
> of motorways so you get very quickly from A to B.

When asked if he would be sorry to leave the area he replied bluntly that

I'm pretty adaptable really. I've moved around, ever since I started work I've always moved around the country because the job is mobile and therefore if you've got to go you move on. And possibly because we don't get so very closely involved in the local community it makes it that much easier to move on.

In fact, Fred had an active social life, going hiking and paragliding, and regularly going to the pub with his workmates. Fred also had three school age children, his wife worked part time, and both had a busy schedule ferrying their children round different venues in the area. For Fred, it was the need for mobility, which defined his relationship to place, and his ease with Wilmslow was integrally related to his concern with convenience and spatial mobility.

Compared to Susan, John, and Andrew, Stuart's attitudes to place were unemotional and instrumental. Wilmslow is a convenient place for someone with a job and situation like him. He is many respects the archetypal cosmopolitan suburbanite, familiar to community studies over the years (e.g. Bell, 1968). But as Table 1 shows, there were actually few pure cosmopolitans of this type in our sample. Rather, more significant is what we term the 'Northern middle class'.

The Northern middle class

Peter, the Director of Human Resources for one of the area's largest multi-national firms, initially seems rather similar to Stuart, but there are some important differences. Brought up in a working class family from Birmingham, he graduated from Manchester University, from whence he joined his current firm and moved round the country as he climbed the corporate ladder. Peter combined his hectic work life with a very strong commitment to Wilmslow, and he displayed a clear sense of ease and comfort in his residential surroundings.

The nice thing about Wilmslow is that we've got a strong group of friends. We've got a good social circle, which is outside of work, not really anything to do with work, which is good. So that was a very positive point sort of very early to coming up here. Things that we also like about it was that we bought the house very close to the town centre here, that's worked very well for the kids; as they've grown up and become more independent they've been able to walk in. It's a good point of communication sort of by British Rail both for me and my family, so for me for work in terms of travelling either by air or by rail then the facilities are pretty good, BR or whatever it's called now not withstanding. We're also fresh air sort of people, so and my wife is a North Walean, so actually access to the Lake District and the Peak District and North Wales is very important to us.

Pleased that Wilmslow was a convenient place to live, Peter expressed emotional attachments not to Wilmslow itself but to the general area, encompassing Wales and the Lake District. While recognising himself as a transient, he felt entirely at ease with living in the area.

Well, we have no reason to move away whilst I'm working here, like we could move to another part of Cheshire but we don't feel the need to do that, we're very comfortable where we are.

Peter was involved with many aspects of the social and cultural life available in the area. He had been a governor of the local comprehensive school. He ate out regularly with his wife and friends, and visited local pubs on a weekly basis. He joined the local golf club, and had played badminton regularly in the past. He was an active member of the local church.

In some respects Peter appears to be rather like the new kind of middle-class resident that Bellah *et al.* (1985) suggest is becoming dominant in the USA. They argue that American urban life is becoming organised around people who have moved long distances and whose lives are not rooted in traditional bounded communities. This kind of mobility gives rise, in the view of Bellah and his co-authors, to weakened views of community amongst American residents, as people increasingly participate in 'lifestyle enclaves', where they pick select associates with shared interests, rather than get to know genuinely diverse local residents. However, Peter's case can be read in a different way. Whilst in some ways a cosmopolitan, he also had emotional links to the North. These appeared to play a key role in rooting him in Wilmslow. In his case, they were based on attending Manchester University.

Well, when I did my degree in Manchester sort of nearly 30 years ago it was actually a beautiful city and somehow or other in the last 20 years the local planning authority has gone absolutely wild and destroyed a lot of its beauty. A lot of the lovely buildings are still there but not in the sort of number or quality that they were

Peter was not, therefore, a pure cosmopolitan, who circled above and between localities (in the way that Fred does). He had emotional attachments with Manchester itself and other parts of the North of England. He is typical of our sample. Most respondents, when pressed, had salient personal links with the North of England which allowed them to be seen as part of northern middle class. This differs from the local middle class in three main ways. First, their roots and family contacts are outside the Manchester area, most frequently in Merseyside, West Yorkshire, the Northeast, or Scotland and Ireland. Second, they have usually spent some part of their lives outside the North of England (twelve have worked at some point in the South of England). Third, they (or other earners in their household) depend on employment within national and multi-national organisations (rather than regional professional bodies). If they have professional jobs they tend to be in the private sector. The northern middle class combines elements of the cosmopolitan and the local habitus, fusing them into a globalising habitus that is regionally based. As Wilmslow loses its role as a high-class suburb for Manchester, it has become instead a key base for a more broadly defined Northern English corporate middle class. The habitus of this class embraces Wilmslow for its regional convenience, for work, leisure and also for maintaining links with their families.

A crucial element of this articulation of place is the idea of convenience. This came out in Peter's recognition of the convenience of Wilmslow as a place for busy people to live. Because Wilmslow is a place from which mobility is easy, then it becomes an appropriate place for busy corporate elites to base themselves. We have many examples of this refrain. Geoff gave one further example:

> *Sort of certainly from the work aspect it's very convenient for the motorway system and also if you're travelling to other parts in the UK but now I'm a sort of housewife! I mean, it is ... it's nice because you're within the sort of easy travelling distance of the city centre and yet you're still on the border of the country as well so it's ... it's convenient and as I've since found out since having children it's also very convenient because there's a lot of facilities for children.*

This theme embodies a certain kind of relationship to place. Place is important as a site from which various needs can be met easily, through mobility and the existence of relevant retail or service outlets. Place is important not relationally *vis-à-vis* other places (as tended to be the case for the local climbers who were keen to mark out their departure from Manchester), but as evading fixed social referents. In the case of Geoff, one of the attractive features was Wilmslow's transitional status between the city centre and the countryside. Wilmslow as a fixed, bounded place, either a community in its own right, or as a satellite to Manchester, was not an attractive feature.

Table 1 shows that nearly all the Northern middle class felt they belonged to Wilmslow, though many felt they belonged now, but did not belong when they first moved there. Only four of this group felt they did not belong, and closer examination shows that they are interesting, 'limit' cases. One was from Scotland and another from Northern Ireland, both of whom contrasted Wilmslow's unfriendliness with the community life they recalled from their own childhood, which was itself nurtured by a recognition that Scotland and Ireland were different nations from England. Ethel's case is also interesting. She was brought up in the Northeast, and had spent much of her life in the south and had an unusually strong southern consciousness:

> Interviewer: *What do you like about living in Wilmslow?*
>
> Ethel: *To be honest I don't particularly like the people in Wilmslow. We have moved around – we were at the cottage at Cirencester, we had friends there and we've still got friends there. We went to Bristol when we first got married; he had been to university and we've got friends there, we moved to Taplow.*

Despite engaging in practices that one might expect would lead her to put down roots, such as joining the church and having children, Ethel retained a distance, bordering on antipathy, towards Wilmslow. She drew frequent contrasts with other places she had lived in, and it was indeed striking how often she made (unfavourable) comparisons with the South of England

> *I always used to shop in Slough at Sainsbury's, and I used to say if Sainsbury's ever came north I would be happy. Of course they did come north and I will admit I was happier for a while.*

The constant comparison to the South stands out, as a place that holds out a different kind of appeal and hope. Here is someone whose emotional identification with the South, leads her to a very different view to every other northern born member of our sample. She hoped to retire to Worthing.

The only other case of this kind was Jill, who had been brought up in Sheffield, and had been a graduate at Manchester University. This kind of biography is characteristic of the northern middle class, but Jill was unusual in her ambivalence towards Wilmslow. In her case, this seemed to be related to her student attitudes which embraced more cosmopolitan, urban, living:

> *... as a student, being a student at Manchester University and living in student accommodation you had a lot of very preconceived ideas about places. Didsbury was considered posh! And Chorlton.[16] They were all sort of very far out, Wilmslow was probably the furthest you would go for student living, and I have to say when we were looking for places I thought, I cannot live in Wilmslow. In many ways, our preference would have been to go somewhere like Altrincham, but it was just where a house came up at the right price and so I suppose in many ways ... yes, the idea of a Wilmslow set, is not really us I suppose, but I have to say it's been very interesting actually living here, because it's like everywhere else, there's lots of nice people and there's people you don't get on with and there's the Wilmslow set ...*

Jill was emphatic that she did not feel she belonged to Wilmslow, but went on to say that she relished the convenience of Wilmslow:

> *I know that sounds like a contradiction. I think it's just a funny thing. I quite like it in many ways, but I can't imagine spending the rest of my life here even though I've always said I wouldn't move. So yes, I think part of the community in that when you have a young child at a primary school you do get involved, you feel part of that community, not maybe the community at large, not so much so, but particularly with children at primary school, playing football and things like that. So in that way you do. And also it is a place, it's small enough so that you see the same people all the time, in the banks and everything. So I think in that respect you do feel that it's not as impersonal.*

Jill seemed to be one of those respondents who over time might well have become attuned to living in the area after initial ambivalence. In this respect, she was similar to many others of the northern middle class who noted that they now felt at home but previously did not. Her only difference from them was that because we interviewed her only shortly after moving to Wilmslow, her ambivalence was more manifest.

Conclusion

We have focused on people's sense of belonging to place in order to explore the (often implicit) ways that places become habitats for particular kinds of social groups. It is a telling way of teasing out the nature of social distinction and its reliance on place. In pursuing this analysis, we have emphasised a number of points. First, most people do have distinctive attachments to place. They are mostly able straightforwardly to say whether they feel they belong to a place or not, and other parts of their narratives in the interview rarely contradict this. If they do feel they belong, their pleasure at belonging is clear. If they do not feel they belong, they do not evince the same defensiveness or ambivalence which occurs when talking about other aspects of their social identities, for instance their class (Savage et al., 2001). People's sense of belonging is 'felt'.

Second, attachment to Wilmslow cannot usefully be seen as socialisation into a kind of local culture, as might be suggested by evoking Raymond Williams's (1973) arguments about 'structures of feeling' (Longhurst, 1991), for instance as adapted by Taylor et al. (1996) to examine local identities in Manchester and Sheffield. People do not tend to feel 'proud' about living in Wilmslow, or give evidence of being socialised into its distinctive way of life. Indeed, many old Wilmslovians feel relatively ill at ease in the place. In this respect, attachment to contemporary places is not best seen through ideas of immersion in local custom and local everyday life that may have been more significant in the past. In contemporary Wilmslow, a sense of belonging embodies ease at the convenience and accessibility of Wilmslow for those living busy lives. The fact that Wilmslow is detached from Manchester, Cheshire and surrounding areas gives it a certain kind of freedom and abstraction from social determination, and this is valued by most respondents. The relatively few local residents who had lived in Wilmslow all their lives are different in being able to articulate more emotional attachments to the town, but they were more critical of recent changes in Wilmslow.

People's attachment to Wilmslow tended to come from their sense of it as a convenient site for those with broader ties and loyalties to the North of England. Wilmslow serves the region, rather than just Manchester. Those who were most comfortable with living in the area were cosmopolitans to the extent that they tended to be mobile in the course of their careers and work, and frequently had extensive overseas contacts. However, they had clear personal links with the North of England, and their attachment to Wilmslow was rooted in their sense that Wilmslow was an appropriate place for someone like them to be living. It anchored them in their own biography whilst also permitting convenient access to and from a variety of sites that were significant for work, leisure, family contact and consumption. This is a pattern also found in narratives of media consumption in the same sample (see Longhurst et al. 2001). Pure cosmopolitans, who tended to be unhappy in the area, tended to lack these anchors. Very few cosmopolitan respondents had identities that were not linked to some sense of regional or national belonging.

We can conclude by relating our arguments back to those of Castells and Bourdieu with which we began this paper. We agree with Castells that the corporate elite is indeed territorially based, even amidst the 'space of flows'.

Wilmslow has become a distinctive kind of territorial hub in a global setting, albeit of a secondary kind compared to the major global hubs circled around the major world cities (see Sassen, 2001). Wilmslow bears the stamp as the habitus of a new kind of 'northern middle class'. Residents do not draw on the kinds of relational contrasts and distinctions that Bourdieu emphasises: to most of the respondents we spoke to, there was relatively little concern to distinguish upper-class Wilmslow from working-class Manchester, for instance. In this respect, Wilmslow is not a classic place of distinction, based on veneration of a higher class of life. Rather it is a kind of placeless site, in which residents abstract themselves from spatially contiguous areas, whilst also depending on a particular kind of place to allow this. Wilmslow is a place where one might expect a cultural omnivore to be at home. Since there are limits to the ability of even the most mobile omnivore to evade spatial (and hence social) fixing, Wilmslow takes on its current character in part through its role as double-faced home to a simultaneously local yet cosmopolitan elite.

Our Wilmslow case study therefore indicates the continued significance of place. In this respect, we have sympathies with those, such as Crow (2002), who insist on the continued importance of local community studies. However, we will conclude by noting that our findings challenge many of the stereotypes of traditional community studies. In the 1960s Bell (1968) argued that middle class residents living in suburban Cardiff could be divided into members of a local middle class, dependent on local enterprise, and spiralists who worked for large corporations and had only lived in the area a short time. This contrast between locals and cosmopolitans was widely rehearsed during other community studies of this period (see e.g. Frankenberg, 1966). However, this distinction is no longer very helpful. Rather than exhibiting a clear cultural difference between locals and cosmopolitans, Wilmslow is mainly home to a northern middle class that combines particular characteristics of the local and the cosmopolitan. The 'pure' local or cosmopolitan can be found, but is rare and they tend to be aware of their own marginality within the area.

Acknowledgements

We would like to thank Lisa Adkins, Graham Crow, Fiona Devine, Peter Halfpenny, Beverly Skeggs and Dale Southerton, as well as Tony Bennett and Elizabeth Silva, for comments on earlier drafts.

Notes

1   This was a core assumption of the community studies research tradition that flourished in Europe and the USA until the 1960s. See Frankenberg (1966) and Allan and Crow (1994).

2   These last two terms are taken from the titles of recent ESRC research initiatives.

3   The idea that globalisation and localisation are mutually intertwined is very widely accepted. One emphasis is on the way that mobility requires a fixed infrastructure (Harvey,1985). Another example is approaches derived from post-structuralism (e.g. Massey, 1994) which show how stability is produced, albeit contingently, through the flow of signifiers. A further topical way of considering the dialectic of fixity and flux can

be derived from actor network theory's emphasis on the construction of 'mutable mobiles'. In contingent networks of objects, fixity is only contingently established in specific kinds of ways, when mutable mobiles become objects that convey similar meanings in different places within networks and hence serve as stabilising devices (see Thrift, 1999). See more generally on mobility, Urry (2000).

4   'Elites form their own society, and constitute symbolically secluded communities, retrenched behind the very material barrier of real estate pricing. They define their community as a spatially bound, interpersonally networked subculture' (Castells, 1996: 416).

5   See for instance his argument that: 'The task of science, then is to construct the space which allows us to explain and predict the largest possible number of differences observed between individuals ...' (Bourdieu, 1986: 3).

6   Its main 'competitor' is probably the Wirral, on Merseyside, where the boundary between middle-class Wirral and working class Liverpool is particularly marked by the River Mersey. However, in terms of population size it does not compete with the North Cheshire complex.

7   'Lifestyles and Social Integration: a study of middle-class culture in Manchester', ESRC reference number R000 23 6929. The other locations were Ramsbottom, Cheadle and Chorlton. A fuller account of this project is to be found in Savage, Bagnall and Longhurst (forthcoming).

8   In the case of people not currently employed, their previous job was service class.

9   The only exception being a man employed as a supervisor.

10 In two cases, the relevant data are missing.

11 We include the five respondents brought up in Scotland and Ireland, since these do not conform to a cosmopolitan identity, though on a number of counts they differ from those brought up in the North of England. They tended to retain a sense of cultural apartness from England.

12 We are here only discussing a particular type of professional: elderly men brought up locally and who had worked in Manchester. Table 2 shows that many other professionals, both male and female, could be found in other groups, with rather different senses of attachment and identity.

13 Chorley's is an autobiographical account of growing up in Edwardian Alderley Edge, which she defines as the prime suburb of Manchester's Victorian professional classes. It should be noted that she remarks that Wilmslow was regarded as distinctly lower status than Alderley Edge: nonetheless, her account is relevant.

14 The local Member of Parliament, Neil Hamilton, had been caught up in corruption scandals in the mid 1990s which led to him losing his seat in the 1997 General Election.

15 Ashton and Stalybridge are both deprived former textile towns in greater Manchester.

16 Both Didsbury and Chorlton are middle-class areas in South Manchester, accessible to the University.

References

Allan, G. and Crow, G. (1994) *Community Life: An Introduction to Local Social Relations.*Hemel Hempstead: Harvester Wheatsheaf

Bell, C. (1968) *Middle Class Families.* London: Routledge

Bellah, R., *et al.* (1985) *Habits of the Heart: Individualism and Commitment in American Life*. Berkeley, CA: University of California Press

Bourdieu, P. (1986) 'What makes a social class? On the theoretical and practical existence of groups. *Berkeley Journal of Sociology,* No. 32, pp. 1–28.

Bourdieu, P. (1999) *Pascalian Meditations*. Cambridge: Polity.

Bourdieu, P. (1997) 'The forms of capital' in Halsey A.H., Laude, H. Brown, P and Wells, A.S. (eds) *Education: Culture, Economy and Society.* Oxford: Clarendon.

Butler, T. and Savage M. (1995) *Social Change and the Middle Classes*. London: UCL Press

Castells, M. (1996) *The Network Society.* Oxford: Blackwell

Chorley, K. (1950) *Manchester Made Them*. London: Faber

Crow, G. (2002) 'Community Studies: Fifty Years of Theorisation', in P. Black, N. Crossley, C. Fagan, M. Savage and L. Turney (eds) *Community Studies, Social Change, Globalisation, Theorization,* .Sociological Research Online, Vol. 7, No. 3, <http://www.socresonline.org.uk/7/3/crow.html>

Frankenberg, R. (1966) *Communities in Britain*. Harmondsworth: Penguin

Giddens, A. (1990) *The Consequences of Modernity*, Cambridge: Polity Press

Girling, E., Loader, I. and Sparks, R. (1999) *Crime and Social Change in Middle England*. London: Routledge

Harvey, D. (1985) *Consciousness and the Urban Experience*. Oxford: Blackwell

Lash, S. and Urry, J. (1994) *Economies of Signs and Spaces*. London: Sage

Longhurst, B.J. (1991) 'Raymond Williams and local cultures', *Environment and Planning A*, Vol. 23, No. 2, pp. 229–38

Longhurst, B.J., Bagnall, G. and Savage, M. (2001) 'Ordinary consumption and personal identity: radio and the middle classes in the North West of England', in J. Gronow and A. Warde (eds), *Ordinary Consumption*. London: Routledge

Massey, D. (1994) *Space, place and gender*. Cambridge: Polity Press

Painter, J. (2000) 'Pierre Bourdieu', in M. Crang and N. Thrift (eds) *Thinking Space*. London: Routledge

Petersen, R.A., and Kern, R.M. (1996) 'Changing highbrow taste: from snob to omnivore', *American Sociological Review*, No. 61, pp. 900–7

Sassen, S.K. (2001) *The Global City*. Oxford: Blackwell

Savage, M. (2000) *Class Analysis and Social Transformation*. London: Routledge

Savage, M., Bagnall, G. and Longhurst, B.J. (2004) *Globalisation and Elective*. London: Sage.

Savage, M., Barlow, J., Dickens, P. and Fielding, A.J. (1992) *Property, Bureaucracy and Culture: Middle Class Formation in Britain*. London: Routledge

Savage, M., Bagnall, G. and Longhurst B. (2001) 'Ordinary, ambivalent and defensive: class identities in the North West of England', *Sociology*, Vol. 35, No. 4, pp. 875–92

Sawyer, M. (1999) *Park and Ride*. London: Abacus

Skeggs, B. (2000) 'Class and culture', mimeo, University of Manchester

Taylor, I., Evans, K. and Fraser P. (1996) *A Tale of Two Cities: Global Change, Local Feeling and Everyday Life in the North of England: A Study of Manchester and Sheffield*. London: Routledge

Thrift, N. (1996) *Spatial Formations*. London: Sage

Thrift, N. (1999) 'The place of complexity', Theory, Culture and Society, Vol. 16, No. 3, pp. 31–55

Urry, J. (2000) *Sociology Beyond Societies*. London: Routledge

Williams, R. (1973) *Marxism and Literature*. Oxford; Oxford University Press

Chapter 11

'Everyone is creative'; artists as pioneers of the new economy?

Angela McRobbie

In this chapter I attempt to trace some of the contours of the new creative economy in the UK, which is currently concentrated in London. First, I track the emergence of 'cultural individualisation' as a strategy of UK government through a reading of recent policy statements. Second, I examine the adverse consequences for creativity which accrue from such strategies. Next, I outline new inequities which spring into being where a (youth) cultural economy is pursued without due recourse to a social component, and, finally, I map out some possibilities for 're-socialising' individualisation in cultural and creative labour markets.

To begin with I offer a critical commentary on the recent Green Paper (April 2001) titled *Culture and Creativity: The Next Ten Years* and on the *Creative Industries Mapping Document*, published by the Department for Culture, Media and Sport (DCMS, 2001).[1] The attention to these papers is due to the new direction for policy drafted in the Green Paper, the informational material collated in the *Mapping Document* and more generally for the light they throw on the government's role in the process of 'cultural individualisation'. This commentary also allows consideration of the tendency for the arts and culture industries becoming a model for how economic growth is to be pursued and, with this, the patterns of freelance work and self-employment associated with being an artist. This leads to an account of how the intensification of individualisation impacts in this sector, with the question then being raised of what the prospects might be for 'post-individualist' practices in arts and culture as a requirement for democracy. Maybe this is the right moment to take note of a symptomatic shift in the cultural terrain. Although thoroughly implicated historically in strategies of management and regulation, culture has emerged as more than a practice of government; it has also been a terrain marked by the bold presence of creative forms belonging to or emerging from socially subordinate groups (Bennett, 1998; Nixon, 2000). In both 'high' and 'low' versions, culture has been connected in diverse ways to the state. But it is this connection which is now being shaken to its roots. Culture is being encouraged to look after itself, to 'entrepreneurialise' and thus to find its feet in the free market. In the pages that follow I will attempt to chart this process of disentanglement as it takes place in the field of work, now a critical site of the relations between culture and everyday life.

One might have supposed that as culture becomes central to economic growth the various accounts of creative process found in sociological investigations, and also in cultural studies, would have been of interest to policy makers, but this is not so. There is now an even greater cleavage between accounts which demonstrate the collaborative nature of creative endeavour, the 'outgrowth of multiple stimulated situations at points of interaction between many different participants in local economies' and the emphasis by government on simply uncovering 'talent'(Scott, 2001: 12). The writer with the greatest impact on government, who has been consistently dealing with the transition to the 'new economy', is Charles Leadbeater. Leadbeater is a journalist and policy advisor to New Labour and author of *Living on Thin Air: The New Economy*, a book which carried an enthusiastic blurb written by Tony Blair himself (Leadbeater, 1999). Social scientists have tended to ignore the impact of a book like this because of its journalistic and popular tone. This means that the full force of Leadbeater's new right thinking, disguised by a breezy, youthful tone remains largely unacknowledged. This feeds into a tendency, on the part of both old left and mainstream social scientists, to fail to confront the scale of the transition to more individualised cultural work, often of a freelance or self-employed nature, as a critical feature of UK labour markets. Instead, old left critics bemoan a mantra of losses (the decline of trade unionism, the lack of interest in political culture among the young people who flood into these areas of employment, the loss of rights and regulations in employment from the period of the Thatcher government onwards) and fail to actually look at what is happening.

The individualised careers, which are characteristic of work in this sector, also are overlooked by social scientists who traditionally have been interested in the 'mass worker', or whose workplace studies have had the advantage of fixed location, duration of employment and visible hierarchies of power and responsibility. But these fast moving and precarious careers have a great deal to tell us about the changing dynamics of contemporary cultural life. They can also provide a kind of concrete grounding for what social theorists have variously described as the shift from structures to flows, or the transition to 'reflexive modernisation' (Beck *et al.*, 1994). The Beck model also offers a way of conceptualising individualisation without collapsing it (as do left fatalists, including Bourdieu) into neo-liberalisation (Beck and Beck-Gernsheim, 2002; Bourdieu, 1998). The Becks' model is meta-sociological and independent of the particularities of the political constellation of the day. The advantage of this separation is that it encourages us to consider, perhaps as an irreversible social shift, individualisation as lived, and to reflect then on the prospects of opposition to the lived consequences of neo-liberalisation in the broad field of art-work. In short, while it can easily be argued that cultural individualisation is the means by which current government policy moves to a more overtly neo-liberal approach to the arts, it is important – for political as well as sociological reasons – to imagine a space between these two.

Individualisation is a strategy of government, which in the context of the culture industries, breathes fresh life into the modernist conception of individual creativity as an inner force waiting to be unleashed. Thus, sweeping aside writing and scholarship on the social and collective bases of creative production (Becker, 1982; Bourdieu, 1993; Negus, 1992; Wolff, 1981) the current Green Paper seeks instead to resurrect a traditional notion of tapping into talent. The source of such talent is, of course, 'the individual' who, if provided with the right kind of support, can then be best left alone to his or her own devices to explore personal creativity unhindered by bureaucracy and red tape.

In the Green Paper it is children and young people, indeed babies, who are the particular focus of attention.[2] This indicates how the workforce of the future is to be envisaged. The paper opens with the words 'Everyone is creative' and quite quickly the impact of Leadbeater's ideas can be traced across the pages. The thinking expressed in this Paper is to further extend access to the arts and culture for producers and consumers alike, with particular emphasis on those who in the past considered these fields as 'not for them'. Thus, the encouragement to the socially disadvantaged to develop their own creative capacities has a double purpose, to increase the employability of future generations, including those from low income backgrounds, by channelling creative talent in the direction of economic activity and at the same time to effect the transition from the mass-waged-worker to the self-employed individual freelance. Referring, in passing, to the range of new employability schemes from the New Deal to the Sure Start programme for pre-school children, the report sums these policies as being about 'excellence', 'access', 'education' and 'economy'. The rhetoric is libertarian as the mission of government is to 'free the creative potential of individuals'. To achieve this goal of 'freeing excellence' a number of initiatives are proposed, including a Cultural Pledge which will involve finding creative partners for individual children in school by bringing in artists, performers and others to work with children, setting up Culture Online and access the arts website, and also the provision of 'books for babies', a gift from government in the form of library cards, baby books and invitations to free story-telling sessions. Alongside these are plans for Centres of Excellence, Specialist Arts Colleges and University Innovation Centres. Apart from the acknowledged socially valuable role of the arts and culture, it is the possible contribution to economic growth which underpins these proposals for the reason that the culture industries are, the Paper claims, 'expanding at a rate of 16% per annum'.

This Green Paper brings together three elements, the individual, creativity (now extended to mean 'having ideas') and freedom. Bureaucracy and institutions are said to stifle the creative process, so that the funding councils need to be able to make awards direct to individuals rather than to organisations. The universities and art colleges receive little credit for the long tradition of 'excellence' in training artists and cultural producers. Instead, they are berated for often failing to produce the right kind of cultural workforce. Bypassing completely the need for critical studies in media or culture the aim is to bring together individual practitioners with pupils.[3]

While the Green Paper and the *Mapping Document* produced by DCMS, represent a more popular and determinedly accessible kind of cultural policy characterised by the input of 'fresh ideas' much loved by advocates of the 'Third Way', their lively style resists any engagement with possible difficulties in the transition to a creative economy. The Green Paper looks forward to a future generation of socially diverse creative workers who are brimming with ideas and whose skills need not only be channelled into the fields of art and culture but will also be good for business. Most importantly these will be self-standing or self-sufficient individuals whose efforts will not be hindered by the

'Everyone is creative'; artists as pioneers of the new economy?

189

administrations of the state. Many of these strands are now standard features of consultancy reports and commissions undertaken for government. For example, in the book *The Creative City*, Charles Landry emphasises the breadth of the concept of creativity to encompass almost any kind of strategic solution to perceived urban problems. In this case, cultural (or creative) policy with its connotations of image, glamour and success replaces the traditionally social democratic notion of social policy (Landry, 2000).

The focus in the Green Paper echoes all the themes in Leadbeater's *Living on Thin Air*, and indeed, when we turn to the DCMS *Mapping Document*, we find a phrase from the book quoted in the foreword. This is a report on the culture industries in the UK and the tone is vehemently upbeat. The various comments about the importance of the creative industries to the UK economy, and in particular, the potential for growth (reporting 16 per cent growth from 1998/1999), marks a glossing over of less hopeful features. The growth referred to was almost entirely the result of the expansion in software and computer services, which was also the location for the rise of almost 135,000 jobs from 1998. However, the small print reveals this figure to include 'employees, the self-employed unpaid family workers and people on government training schemes' (p.12.04). Looking at the fashion sector, we find that 75 per cent of companies have a turnover of less than one million. (According to my own study, designers themselves are often surviving on less than £20,000 a year (McRobbie, 1998). The 200 or so fashion companies in existence at any one time might well not exist in five years time. Despite this, the headlines to the section on fashion announce that the UK fashion designer sector is the fourth biggest in the world.[4]

Experts in other sectors could likewise go through the figures and the prose and what would emerge, I would argue, is a conclusion that no matter how important the culture industries are for growth, this is a sector with low capital returns and while employment, in particular self-employment, may be buoyant, it is also a low pay sector ('poor in work'). Finally, the culture industries sector is also as volatile and as vulnerable to the moves of multinational capital as many more traditional fields like manufacturing. In fact, what the culture industries in the UK comprise of are personnel. This is not so much the quick thinkers and ideas people celebrated by Leadbeater, but the product of a long historical tradition of training in fields of expertise developed in the public funded UK art schools and colleges, of which there are no equivalents elsewhere in the world. The chief asset of the culture industries is the art school system. But this is under-funded, with crumbling over-crowded buildings which Sir Christopher Frayling, as the Rector of the Royal College of Art in London, recently commented, were more like Social Security offices in appearance. The industries themselves, from film and TV, to design and publishing, are more thoroughly part of the global economy. Those which are UK-owned tend to be small micro-economies of culture, otherwise it is a matter of the UK feeding the bigger companies and corporations with highly trained graduates. This then is a further source of individualisation. The career pathways are unlike those of traditional occupations. Personnel in the culture industries make their own way, they are always on the move, they have to get their names known, they are their own brands, they have to look after their own self-interest, they are 'artistic individuals', and they are frequently working for big companies, but on a freelance basis.

If the stage is set for the neo-liberalisation of the UK cultural economy, the question must be: How can cultural individualisation be deflected as a force for democratising the creative field of work? This is all the more difficult to imagine since it is in the cultural and creative industries that we find the fullest expression of an 'ideal local labour market', from the viewpoint of a New Labour government committed to freeing individuals from dependency on state subsidies, to creating a thriving entrepreneurial culture and to a new work ethic of self-responsibility. This requires not a labour market as such, more a network of creative persons for whom jobs or projects are negotiated like actors going to audition for a 'part'.

Thus, we find a curious scenario of a centre-left government whose priority it is to perform a double act of neo-liberalisation. First, to minimise social welfare support for those unable to earn a living wage (so that earnings now become multi-sourced, with creative personnel holding down two or three jobs at once). Second, to set individuals to their own devices, in terms of job creation, so that the large corporations are less burdened by the responsibilities of a workforce. 'Paid employees', 'welfare recipients', and 'labour market' become what Beck might call 'zombie categories', both dead and alive, and, in this case, this latter is what is least wanted by key players in the new economy (Beck and Beck-Gernsheim, 2002). New Labour's answer to so many problems across a wide spectrum of the population, for example, mothers at home being not quite ready to go back to work full-time, is self-employment. Set up your own business. Be free to do your own thing. Live and work like an artist. And creative work is particularly appealing to youth because of the emphasis on uncovering talent, because of their proximity to the kinds of fields flagged up as already successful, like popular music, film, art, writing, acting, fashion, graphic design, and so on. Sharon Zukin wrote in the 1980s about how the rise of loft living in New York's former manufacturing neighbourhoods came about when artist living-spaces became a model for urban middle-class lifestyle (Zukin, 1988). We can now extend this to suggest that artists' ways of earning a living becomes a model for livelihoods, as well as lifestyle. This is the logic of 'everyone is creative'.

From the viewpoint of government, the culture industries sector have provided Britain with the possibility of re-invigorating a distinctive national economy in the light of global competition by drawing on an indigenous and migrant tradition of popular (working class, and subsequently, youth) culture which emerged more forcefully in the early 1960s.[5] Forty years later, this warrants a celebratory rhetoric along the lines of 'We're good at this sort of thing, the UK record industry accounts for 16 per cent of trade worldwide. Our fashion designers are internationally well known', and 'our young British artists have re-invigorated the art world, and our writers and columnists are providing Hollywood with some of their best scripts'. But, with hundreds of fine art graduates leaving the many art departments up and down the country we might reasonably ask: How many creatives can the economy accommodate? Or, is it that individuals must become their own labour market?

The labour market melts away; in Bauman's (2000) phrase, it liquidifies. In a talent led economy the individual only has him or herself to blame if the

'Everyone is creative'; artists as pioneers of the new economy?

191

next script, film, book or show is not up to scratch. Or, as Giddens (1991) puts it, individuals must now 'be' their own structures. Will network sociality create new lasting social bonds in the light of the decline of 'narrative sociality'? Will reflexivity extend to the social analysis and critique of new work? Or are Frith's comments more appropriate? He points out that most creative sectors have comprised a large component of freelance labour. He also notes the co-existence of multiplicities of working practices in the various culture industries, some traditional, some innovative as a result of technological changes, others entirely related to sudden or unpredictable demand. Generalisations about the culture industries should therefore be treated warily (Frith, 2001). This is echoed by Scott who points to the 'difficulty of mapping the cultural economy' in his recent study of creative sectors in three major cities (Scott, 2001: 209).

The decline of the indies

Bearing in mind Frith's timely warning, I would nonetheless want to argue that there has been an intensification and speeding up or rapid acceleration of culture industry working practices in the UK with the result that the singularity of a career as freelance artist, writer, musician or designer, is now anachronistic. To be sure, it is extremely difficult to chart with certainty these processes, especially without the benefit of a sector-by-sector longitudinal analysis. But that absence does not warrant silence. My current research points to a shift away from first-wave cultural producers for whom, from the mid 1980s to the mid 1990s, the lines of distinction between working autonomously or independently, and working in a more overtly commercial or corporate environment were clear, and who opted for the former, relying on grants, subsidies, and even the dole, to allow them the time to set up in art or design. Of course, over a longer period of time they might well develop partnerships or contracts with large companies but the early period of experimentation and creativity was a hallmark of this first-wave 'indie work'. In contrast, the second wave is comprised of young creatives who no longer have access to this phase. They are instead multi-tasking, de-specialised cultural entrepreneurs (or entrepreneurs of the self) for whom an even more aggressively free market cultural environment now shapes the opportunities and possibilities for how they work in the cultural sector. If the first-wave is embodied in the figure of the artist/designer, the second wave gives rise to the incubator, the visual merchandiser, the cultural strategist. What this means is that the distinct categories outlined by the DCMS, as marks of training or professional identity or industry sector, are now increasingly diffuse, de-differentiated, blurred and merging in and out of each other in a more speeded up, corporatised and globalised market for cultural goods and services. Architects double up as online editors, arts administrators are employed on a freelance basis by government funded bodies on one off-projects, which keep them going for two or three days a week, which means looking round for projects to fill the remainder of the seven day working week, and increasingly the boundary between art work and media work crumbles.[6]

I would suggest that the first-wave lasted from 1985 to 1995, the time of the 'indies'. The second wave has the effect of interrupting careers and imposing multi-skilling on creative individuals. It comprises de-specialisation, adapting to the growth of new media and its opportunities, and it sees the birth of the 'cultural entrepreneur'. In this more aggressive environment cultural workers are expected to invent their own careers and to self-manage on the longer term. Capital, which in the past had been disinclined to interfere in the creative sector at such an elementary or experimental stage, now designates this as the most propitious moment in the search for new talent. But as government moves out and capital moves in, it exerts its own logic, the bitter consequences of which are concealed by the generous budgets for corporate publicity.[7] Let me illustrate with two quite different examples: fashion and contemporary art. In fashion design, the period which saw the emergence of a distinctive sector, which was neither *haute couture* (as in France or Italy) nor corporate (as in the USA), but was 'independent' (art school trained, conceptually-oriented), came into being out of a combination of unemployment (with some benefits in the form of housing subsidies and the self-employment programme titled the Enterprise Allowance Scheme (EAS)) and the 'do it yourself' ethos which was the product of the punk generation (McRobbie, 1998). Fashion designers graduating in the early 1980s, like those who took part in my own study, were specialists in their fields, and they gained their reputations by working in the first few years following graduation as independents, setting up as small scale entrepreneurs, often as stall holders, or as semi-self-employed in the informal economy.[8] They were able to do this with access to cheap spaces in the form of urban street markets or tiny outlets in busy city locations. However, by the late 1990s the big brands from Europe and the USA, including both the high street chains like Gap and Diesal, and the designer labels like DKNY or Prada, moved determinedly into the fashion market. They priced the 'indies' out of the retail property market. Cheap spaces, often in the form of lanes or corridors between buildings disappeared almost overnight.[9]

These companies were then able to pick and choose from the annual crop of graduates no longer able to work independently. A handful were offered short contracts with the consequence that the crucial period just after graduation, which had often allowed the designers to work in partnerships or even collaboratively, providing the space to develop their own ideas, gave way to what has now become the new norm: the privileged few (a tiny number) being whisked off to company headquarters where their skills will be honed to fit with company requirements, while the rest are left to pick up other jobs, often requiring completely different skills. The whole field of UK independent fashion design has virtually disappeared. The range of small scale producers has dried up and those who have survived are reliant on the capriciousness of a band of buyers from less than half a dozen department stores.[10] Fashion designers (of whom there are almost 4,000 graduating each year) have then been forced from first to second wave. They must diversify and dilute their skills, set up in other related activities, work for dot.com companies, downgrade their expectations about seeing their 'own work' in shop windows, relinquish the time for creative thinking and research, move into the mainstream of the high street chains as 'freelance fashion consultant', if lucky, and perhaps return to teach for a couple of days a week. The fashion and style trends magazine *iD* reports on this phenomenon.

Fashion multi-taskers: suddenly they're everywhere. But it's not easy to do two, three or more things at once: there's never enough time, it does not earn them any more money than having one job and they can't always count on being respected for what they do. And it is addictive. Once you have tried doing four jobs you'll never want anything less.'
(Rushton, 2001: 29)

The shift to the second wave sees the dilution of talent, the dispersal of cohorts of designers working alongside each other, sharing premises which I reported on in my study and thus totally disaggregating what we might even call a collectivity or movement, to a rootless collection of individuals unrepresented, unorganised, and highly mobile. The first-wave thus comprised of an innovation *milieu* or hub, that is, an assortment of small shops, retail outlets, market stall spaces, magazines, as well as clubs and pubs, all of which constituted a network for intense interaction. The second wave is less site specific, more mobile, more located in 'non-places' with a faster turnover of jobs, and consequently less visible. London as a fashion design centre, in effect no longer exists. The moment of there being hundreds of small companies is over. The 'first-wave' model of co-operation and creativity can now be found elsewhere, for example in the new area of Berlin Mitte where propitious circumstances are now seeing the fruits in terms of a thriving indie fashion sector.[11] Back in London, there are corporate fashion companies and individuals moving from one project to the next, and being dropped at short notice, for example when young designers fail to restore profits as in Marks and Spencer.

The second wave cultural practitioners also come to fruition in the UK through the 'young British artists'. This now dates back to 1988 when Damien Hirst mounted his first show titled *Freeze*, followed in 1989 by the British Telecom sponsored *New Contemporaries* in 1989. Hirst shamelessly advocated a business approach to being an artist, but in reality, in the early days, he and his fellow artists benefited from the same kind of collaborative and co-operative ventures which I have already described in relation to fashion design. They too signed on the dole, and found cheap spaces to live and work and put on shows. Wu has shown how the seeds for a new relation between the arts and big business were being set during the Thatcher years, as the UK emulated US models of corporate giving. Wu also shows how this kind of generosity came cheap to the big companies, also allowing them the benefits of being seen as 'enlightened' advocates of 'corporate citizenship'(Wu, 1998). But in practice it took some time for British business culture to pick up on the added value of art. The 'young British artists' were able to make the noise they did, and discover the possibilities of living and working in East London because British financial capital was relatively slow to step in. But that all changed from 1997 onwards, as the London property market responded in the same way as its USA counterpart had done years previously in New York. Zukin (1988) has demonstrated with great clarity just how profitable to the property owning elite of Manhattan was the encouragement of an art scene in an otherwise rundown area. The simple fact of having a prestigious arts centre located in an ungentrified area promised to the property owning elite incredible rewards within a few years.

Many of the themes in Zukin's *Loft Living* are now being rehearsed across London but at an even more accelerated pace. Zukin (1988) argues that the economy of art plays a key role in capital's transformation of urban spaces. Therefore, it is no longer a matter of artist-curators like Hirst seeking out cheap spaces to put on a show, Instead, estate agents make approaches directly to artists and students, suggesting they make good use of derelict premises before they are gutted for re-development into luxury apartments. This is how the *Assembly* exhibition (November 2001) took place, in two adjacent school buildings in London's East End. By being able to transfer the symbolic value of the exhibition onto the site, attracting journalists from across London to the show, and providing the artists with enough space for 130 of them to participate, the whole area bathed in the aura of aesthetic association.[12] Rising land values have a deleterious impact on the ability of artists to contribute to a long-term thriving cultural economy in a city like London, because soon the artists who paved the way for the property speculators to move in, can no longer afford to live there. This disperses the critical mass which Scott (2001) argues is important for creative economies to survive. Sassen (2001) in turn, suggests that, as a global city, London needs its art market and will seek to retain it in some form. My own research indicates that as many young artists need to hold down so many jobs to cover rent and living, the time spent in the studio is barely more than a few hours a week.[13] There is increasingly a sense that London is too hard to live in, with well known artists like Tacita Dean, whose work has been shown at Tate Modern and Tate Britain, moving permanently to Berlin.

For those who remain in London there is a drift away from the now unaffordable Tower Hamlets (while also being London's poorest borough) to run-down Lewisham, in Southeast London where rent for living and working accomodation is nominally cheaper. Here the seeds are being sewn for what Zukin (1988) calls the 'process' of artists paving the way for future speculation on property prices. The local authority in this impoverished and markedly ungentrified area (where Goldsmiths College is located; it is also the single biggest employer in the borough) invests a small amount in encouraging artists to work in the area, by creating a cultural regeneration zone, and the landlords need do nothing to improve their own premises in the expectation that five or even ten years down the line the sites will have multiplied in value and can be sold off for re-development as luxury apartments. The artists are joined in Southeast London (New Cross and Deptford) by other young people working to support this initiative as arts administrators or cultural planners. What Zukin (1988) calls the arts proletariat can now more accurately be described as cultural multi-taskers. But this also includes the artists themselves, few of whom can possibly live by art alone. While there are certainly many more venues to show work and many more curators ready to put on a show, and while there is a market for viewing (less so for sales), for the artists themselves the 'process' they are caught up in creates a 'winner takes all' scenario. The result is a miserable hierarchy, which comprises of corporate winners at the top, artist-teachers in the middle, and all the others at the bottom, putting together a patchwork of careers.

'Everyone is creative'; artists as pioneers of the new economy?

195

The inequities of the informal, the cruelties of cool

To work in these sectors requires endurance and stamina. A good deal of energy must be invested in activities for which there is absolutely no reliable return. Fund-raising for sponsorship to buy new equipment, organising meetings to discuss possible partnerships, simply 'keeping in touch' with the network, all require time and money. Often these take place in the guise of something entirely different, attending a launch party or an event at an arts or cultural centre. The salience of personable attributes (who is on the guest list) marks another point at which individualisation is, as Beck and Beck-Gernsheim (2002) argue, an institutional process.[14] The club is the hub, or, in Castell's terms, the 'innovation milieu' (Castells 1996). These forms of job creation mark a rupture with older notions of 'work', 'job', 'career', and also give rise to new inequities. Over the hill in age terms? Too unconfident to manage the presentation of self? Too miserable to party? These discomforts can only be afforded by the already-famous. This field of activity poses real difficulties for sociological research. The speed and the flows defy traditional methodologies. Despite Beck and Beck-Gernsheim's (2002) reminder that individualisation is a process predicated on new modalities of institutionalisation, cultural individualisation finds itself challenged by the reality of non-groups, non labour markets, non-institutions, as well as non-places.

New social inequities emerge within this informal 'youth cultural' economy. As studies carried out in Glasgow have shown, these fields of work and other associated areas, including the new bar and restaurant business, are also fields of 'aesthetic labour', where workers are employed according to the right look, the right body shape, even the right accent (Warhurst et al., 2000). Age constraints are in operation. Class and cultural capital also have an effect. The young single mother, for example, is less likely to be able to invest in her own appearance than her well educated and childless counterpart. The childfree young women will then mop up as many of these new cultural jobs as are going (like the fashion multi-taskers referred to above). This re-configures and accentuates class divisions between young women. And where deep structures give way to fluid boundaries, project work picked up while propping up the bar appears to be simply 'good luck'.[15] In these locations of leisure characterised by a 'scene' or 'atmosphere', the blurring of the interface between work and leisure conceals the material obstacles which limit discovery of 'talent' on the grounds of poor location, poor education, poor access to the social capital of the network, and lack of access to funds to fall back on between jobs, or while working for nothing, in the hope of it being turned into a paid job. Needless to say these are risks which older people cannot afford to take. There is an unthinkable indignity for older people of 'working for nothing' in the hope of it turning into a real job.

What my ongoing research on this sector shows are:

- Totally de-regulated often intersecting spheres of activities and services, which are cultural and informal, where there are no accountability structures, where problems at work are not systemic but merely time to move on, where an incredible amount of time must be invested in social contacts and networking, because to be out of the loop could mean being out of a job.

- The recognised need for new points of support, the time and space of the public sector often providing a two-day a week haven where there are employment laws in operation even for temporary or part-time workers.

- Incredible investment in self and image, endless self-monitoring, the ethos of success creating a mentality of, as Bauman puts it, 'must try harder and harder' (Bauman, 2000: 38).

- Self-reliance but falling back on parental support without which many wouldn't be able to carry on these experimental careers.

- The extent to which creative workers are motivated by the 'chaos of reward', by the hope of making it as the next successful fashion designer like Stella McCartney, or Alexander McQueen. These dreams merge with the new meritocracy of the Blair government which, with the power of the visual media, further bury the prospect of a renewed social democratic vocabulary of workplace protection, job security, sickness pay and so on, even when the cultural sector becomes a major field of economic activity.

These young people are thus being designated as agents of the neo-liberal order, expected to see it through into fruition, relying only on their own talents, lonely, mobile, over-worked individuals for whom socialising and leisure are only more opportunities to do a deal. The Green Paper produces the categories of 'talented' and 'creative' as disciplinary regimes, whose subjects are taught and told (apparently from birth onwards through primary, secondary and tertiary education), to inspect themselves, look deep inside themselves for capacities which will then serve them well in the future. If, as Spivak (1999: 214) suggests, culture is a 'complex strategic situation', then the brilliant additional move in this new discursive formation is that it simultaneously appears to do away with older forms of reliance on labour markets, on the dull compulsion of labour, and on routine activities. There is now scope for 'pleasure in work' and, as Donzelot (1991) argued, appealing to the authentic self, has the incredible advantage of turning the individual into a willing work-horse, self-flagellating when the inspiration does not flow out onto the page. The Green Paper celebrates the importance of creativity and its encouragement in schools, nurseries, at home, and in other cultural institutions. Children and young people will have to do more than routine tasks, they will now be expected to be creative. Even if they do not go on to earn a living in the cultural sector, thinking creatively is now at the heart of the new knowledge economy and a new articulation of the relations between culture, work and the everyday. But most important is the disconnect feature, the aim is to be individually successful. This means being self-reliant, self-employed and successfully independent of state, welfare and subsidy. By these means the future world of work is profoundly transformed. The political order conforms with economic global rationalities to tax the young with being its new subjects. They are being charged with bearing the brunt of unforeseen circumstances. We might call this a new model of 'cultural domination'. If it exacts new modalities of exploitation on the creative workforce, the question is, how can individualisation, as a sociological *fait accompli*, become more associative, how can it be politicised?

'Everyone is creative'; artists as pioneers of the new economy?

197

Post-individualist cultural practice

'Old left' explanations of new cultural work would propose one of two arguments. *Either* these youngsters are a metropolitan elite, highly educated and with sufficient cultural capital to take risks and test the ground of the new cultural economy, with enough material or symbolic resources to fall back on if things go wrong (Garnham, 1987). They are also able to be individualistic by virtue of their assets and are thus 'in waiting' to have rewards come their way while they are preside over, and in effect complicit with, an economy characterised by ever increasing divides between wealth and poverty. They are well placed as agents of the new anti-egalitarian meritocracy. *Or*, these youngsters are part of a new middle-class strata, now expanded to include women and black and Asian people, currently being proletarianised. The degree of enforced entrepreneurialism combined with the traditional middle-class search for status in work, permits extraordinary degrees of self-exploitation in what is a de-regulated unprotected sector. By virtue of being well educated, this strata of young people will bring to bear progressive elements in regard to identity politics into their cultural practice. But hyper-individualisation, the decline of the politics of the workplace (where there is no workplace), and the access to 'private solutions' means that only the try harder-and-harder mentality will prevail. This is what happens, even to the well educated when a strong tradition of workplace politics is eroded.

In contrast to both of these responses, and as a way of imagining the prospects for re-democratising work (in this case, creative work) we might turn to recent writing on re-thinking the political. We need to be alert to the possibilities for critique and change from strange and interstitial spaces, as part of a chain of connection from one nodal point to another, from one city space to another, from the flows of movement of labour. It's not enough however to gesture to the existence of the flattening of hierarchies in the new media economy, the existence of network sociality, or the wilful optimism, which suggests that meritocracy and talent, in the context of non-bureaucratic workplaces, make them 'open minded spaces'.[16] At the same time, the self-flagellating model of Bauman (2000) ('must try harder and harder') can only interpret pleasure at work as ultimately self-delusion. Scott Lash (2002), in contrast, embraces a 'non-linear' model. He extends Beck and co-authors' (1994) account of reflexive individualisation to argue that choice is predicated on the requirement on the part of the denuded individual without the support of visible structures (the dole office or job centre) to investigate the rules of the new social (dis)order for him or herself. ('Thus chaos becomes totally normal' (Lash, 2002: xi).)

I would argue that the new rules in this case are actually quite apparent and written into government policy as the two documents described earlier indicate. With or without rules, the scenario presents a considerable challenge to those interested in how 'creative-work solidarities' might be developed. If the institutions (or non-institutions) of the new culture are as Lash (2002: xii) puts it, 'not recognisable to us as institutions', then it follows that whatever political sociality, which will appear, will take an almost unimaginable shape. This is clear in the limited ability of the new social movements to track the flows of 'labour power' and harness this potential into something more stable and concrete. While the anti-globalisers can describe the miseries of working in the Free Trade Zones for Nike or Gap, they cannot find ways of connecting this workforce with that 'back home', that is, with the subjects of my own inquiries, many of whom are working for these same companies on a hourly rate. There are such connections, but one has to look very hard for them. Yes, such post-individualist solidarities exist but they are embryonic. They consist of scattered and isolated initiatives, they are as Bauman (2000) says, 'non-additive'.[17]

Hardt and Negri propose that we are witnessing, with the rise of the informational economy and its associated categories, a 'a new mode of becoming human' (Hardt and Negri, 2000: 289). Beck et al. (1994) argue that reflexive modernisation gives rise to both self-critique and social critique. The self-monitoring subjects of the second modernity must have access to information and analysis in order to be reflexive. Where are such resources to be found? Are they wholly reliant on the findings of the neo-liberal think tanks? Or are the pathways to the information and communicative technologies not also interspersed with the post-Marxist analyses of political philosophy, cultural studies and sociology? Access to social critique is well within the orbit of the hyper-individualists. We need more ethnographies of such critical reflexivities.[18] Of course, the means by which such persons may, or may not, find their way to such intellectual resources is truly hard to fathom. Maybe this needs another approach. The individual might be or perceive him or herself to be 'singular', but reflexivity requires continual engagement with texts, images, music, communicative networks, books and writing. She/he might be black or Asian, or also connected to a strand of 'life politics' through some biographical feature, like health, family, children or neighbourhood. Bauman (2000) describes such phenomena as 'non-additive' in the sense that they do not add up to anything properly political. But there are possibilities through these connections for 'productive singularities', despite the attempts by power to 'block community and co-operation' (Hardt and Negri, 2000).

As Hardt and Negri (2000) put it, 'exhausting powerlessness' forces us to overlook the 'productivity of being'. Drawing on Deleuze and Guattari they argue that the current de-differenciation of politics, economics, the social (and I would add the cultural), produces unprecedented energy and desire which are generative (as human labour is) and that 'enriched' with the new informational and knowledge structures, pathways or highways, people are able to confront the forces of 'corruption'. Thus, we can propose that individualisation can give way to 'new productive singularities' (Hardt and Negri, 2000: 395). By drawing on Foucault's concept of bio-power (by which means regulation and discipline are inculcated through individual bodies, so that the individual must self-monitor, and self-regulate) and by combining this with Deleuze and Guattari's concept of the desiring machines (as flows of power), the working body becomes a point of critical intersection with other working bodies. Thus if desire is productive of attachments and identifications, why not consider also the existence of desire or 'energy' in work? Work (and here creative work) can become a site for re-socialisation at the heart of everyday life. But how does a political dimension directed towards the re-democratisation of work emerge through such energies and encounters? Let us at the very least, flag the centrality

'Everyone is creative'; artists as pioneers of the new economy?

199

of this issue. The challenge here would arise from inter-generational exchange between the old subjects of cultural Marxism (academics in the Brecht and Benjamin tradition), able to extend the intellectual fruits of the benefits and privileges accrued from the public welfare regime, now extinct, and the new subjects of cultural individualisation who, deprived of these historical richnesses cannot as yet fully imagine the rewards of collaboration in working life in a political frame.

Acknowledgements

Thanks are extended to James Curran, Simon Frith, Raj Thind, Elizabeth Silva and Tony Bennett for helpful comments.

Notes

1   A Green Paper is a UK government publication with proposals as aids for public debate. It will include a deadline for responses from individuals and organisations.

2   Gordon Brown, Chancellor of the Exchequer, made a speech on 18 June 2001, stressing the importance of building a more successful entrepreneurial culture with children and school pupils being more actively encouraged to consider the future in terms of self-employment.

3   The DCMS established the Creative Industries Task Force in 1997. Minutes and papers showed opposition by members to media and cultural studies, on the grounds of their apparent irrelevance to the needs of industry. It is not surprising then that the Green Paper ignores this area in preference for bringing the creative professionals together with the pupils.

4   There is a huge disparity between revenues for fashion in Italy, France and the USA, and those in the UK.

5   The convergence of working-class youth in the UK art schools from the late 1950s onwards, the increasing visibility of 'race' following the riots of 1958 in London's Notting Hill, and indeed the emergence of cultural studies, are strands variously addressed by Frith and Horne (1987), and Stratton and Ang (1996).

6   Some of the research data gathered at the Cultural Entrepreneurs Club held at the Institute of Contemporary Art (ICA) in London 2001 on multi-tasking in the creative sector is reported in McRobbie (2002).

7   Frith makes the point that in recent years the five multi-national music corporations have developed subsidiaries as semi-independent 'indie' labels. These attempt to preserve the small-scale feel of the original 'indies' like Rough Trade, but are in fact wholly owned and overseen by the likes of Bertelsmann, Chrysalis or EMI (Frith, personal communication, 2001).

8   These are the findings of an extensive study of the working practices in the British fashion design sector from 1984 to 1995. Among the designers I interviewed who had set up on market stalls, street lanes or corridors between buildings, were Helen Storey, Darlajane Gilroy, Pam Hogg and the company called English Eccentrics.

9   The best known site which allowed young designers to sell their work alongside each other in a prominent, but subsidised, location was Hyper-Hyper in Kensington High Street. It was shut down in 1996.

10 Regular strolls around the second floor of Selfridges, London, show a high turnover rate for designers brought in by the buyers. The big company names like Max Mara maintain

their concessionary space, while the small labels like Antoni and Allison (retained 2002), Karen Boyd (dropped 2002), Dutch label Bruns Bazaar (dropped 2002) rarely last longer than a year

11   See ongoing research on Berlin Mitte as a new cultural sector (Ewenstein, 2002).

12   The visual arts *Assembly* exhibition was held in November 2001, curated by Royal College of Arts graduate Gordon Cheung.

13   Diaries from artists in current research titled 'The Economy of Artists' show multi-tasking as the norm. For example, several artists report fitting in studio work (3–6 hours a week) alongside up to 20 hours teaching English as a foreign language.

14   The Cultural Entrepreneur Club, set up by the ICA, Channel 4, The Arts Council and Goldsmiths College, London was indeed an example of the institutionalisation of cultural individualisation. It brought together approximately 400 by invitation only (see McRobbie, 2002).

15   Good luck jobs. By this I mean cultural jobs picked up through chance encounters within fields of 'network sociality'.

16   Michael Hardt, talking at Goldsmiths College, London, November 2001 suggested a political sociality among new media workers by virtue of sitting alongside each other in front of computer screens in small dot.com companies in a long-hours culture.

17   Fashion designer, now product manager and consultant, and also lecturer at the London College of Fashion (i.e. fashion multi-tasker), Harriet Posner, has recently set up a company with two others, titled 'ClothesSource', which brings together designers with global sourcing companies. The aim is to improve the industry at every level, including pay and conditions for the workforce in low income countries.

18   See ongoing PhD research at Goldsmiths College titled 'From Resistance to Reflexivity' (Ewenstein, 2002).

References

Auge, M. (1995) *Non Places. Introduction to an Anthropology of Supermodernity*. London: Verso

Bauman, Z. (2000) *Liquid Modernity*. Cambridge: Polity Press

Beck, U. (1997) *Risk Society*. London: Sage

Beck, U. and Beck-Gernsheim, E. (2002) *Individualisation*. London: Sage

Beck, U., Giddens, A. and Lash, S. (1994) *Reflexive Modernisation*. London: Sage

Becker, H. (1982) *Art Worlds*. Berkeley, CA: University of California Press

Bennett, T. (1998) *Culture. A Reformer's Science*. London: Sage

Bourdieu, P. (1993) *The Field of Cultural Production*. Cambridge: Polity Press

Bourdieu, P. (1998) *Acts of Resistance*. Cambridge, Polity Press

Castells, M. (1996) *The Rise of the Network Society*. Oxford: Blackwell

DCMS (2001) *Creative Industries Mapping Document*. London

'Everyone is creative'; artists as pioneers of the new economy?

201

Donzelot, J. (1991) 'Pleasure in work', in G. Burchell, C. Gordon and P. Miller (eds) *The Foucault Effect; Studies in Governmentality*. London: Harvester Wheatsheaf, pp. 251–81

Ewenstein, B. (2002) 'From Resistance to Reflexivity', PhD in progress, Department of Media and Communications, Goldsmiths College, London

Frith, S. and Horne, H. (1987) *Art Into Pop*. London: Methuen

Garnham, N. (1987) 'Concepts of culture public policy and the culture industries', *Cultural Studies*, Vol. 1, No. 1, pp. 23–9

Giddens, A. (1991) *Modernity and Self Identity*. Cambridge: Polity Press

Green Paper (2001) *Culture and Creativity: The Next Ten Years*. London: DCMS

Hardt, M. and Negri, A. (2000) *Empire*. Cambridge, MA and London: Harvard University Press

Landry, C. (2000) *The Creative City*. London: Earthscan Comedia

Lash, S. (2002) 'Introduction' in U. Beck and E. Beck-Gersheim (eds) *Individualisation*. London: Sage

Lash, S. and Urry, J. (1994) *Economy of Signs and Space*. London: Sage

Leadbeater, C. (1999) *Living on Thin Air. The New Economy*. London: Viking

McRobbie, A. (1998) *British Fashion Design: Rag Trade or Image Industry?* London: Routledge

McRobbie, A. (2002) 'Club to company', in *Cultural Studies*, Special Issue on 'Culture Intermediaries' (eds S. Nixon and P. Du Gay) 16(4) pp. 516–531. London: Routledge

Negus, K. (1992) *Performing Pop: Culture and Conflict in the Popular Music Industry*. London: Edward Arnold

Nixon, S. (2000) 'Intervening in popular culture: cultural politics and the art of translation', in P. Gilroy, L. Grossberg and A. McRobbie (eds) *Without Guarantees*, In Honour of Stuart Hall. London: Verso, pp. 254–65

Rushton, R. (2001) 'Me myself and I' *iD magazine*, The Bathroom Issue, London

Sassen, S.(2001) Paper delivered at Fields of Vision Conference, London Guildhall University, Toynbee Hall, London

Scott, A. (2001) *The Cultural Geography of Cities*. London: Sage

Spivak,G.C. (1999) *A Critique of Postcolonial Reason*. Cambridge, MA: Harvard University Press

Stratton, J. and Ang, I. (1996) 'On the impossibility of global cultural studies: "British" cultural studies in an "international" frame', in D. Morley and K.H. Chen (eds) 'Stuart Hall Critical Dialogues' in *Cultural Studies*, pp. 361–92

Warhurst, C., *et al* (2000) *Looking Good, Sounding Right. Style Counselling for the Unemployed.* London: The Industrial Society

Wolff, J. (1981) *The Social Production of Art.* London: Macmillan

Wu, Z. (1998) 'Embracing the enterprise culture: art institutions since the 1980s', *New Left Review*, No. 230, July/August, pp. 28–57

Zukin, S. (1988) *Loft Living Culture and Capital in Urban Change.* London: Hutchinson